Trollope's
Later
Novels

Robert Tracy

University
of California
Press

Berkeley
Los Angeles
London

U C

University of California Press
Berkeley and Los Angeles, California

University of California Press, Ltd.
London, England

Copyright © 1978 by
The Regents of the University of California

ISBN 0-520-03407-4
Library of Congress Catalog Card Number: 76-55572
Printed in the United States of America

1 2 3 4 5 6 7 8 9

For Becky
without whom not

CONTENTS

PREFACE

I have written this book to offer an alternative to the conventional critical opinion about Trollope, which describes his novels as pleasant enough to read, but undistinguished in style, clumsy and rambling in structure, and uncertain in their social and moral attitudes. I am claiming for Trollope considerable technical skill as a novelist and even a serious commitment to the art of the novel, despite his own insistence (in *An Autobiography*) that he is a craftsman and not an artist. I am also suggesting that Trollope has a consistent moral theory about society and its values; and that both the style and the structure of his novels effectively imply that theory. To borrow a phrase from a nineteenth-century writer who was in most respects Trollope's opposite, "the canons of society are, or should be, the same as the canons of art." Wilde's remark (in *Dorian Gray*) has rather different implications as he develops it, but the phrase will serve here to represent that unity of form and function, and that successful use of literary technique to embody social values, which is characteristic of Trollope's best work. That best work is not found in such novels of his apprenticeship as *The Warden* (1855) and *Barchester Towers* (1857), but in the novels he wrote during the 1870s, after he had attained his artistic maturity.

Trollope once declared that "There is nothing like an opus magnum for thorough enjoyment of life." I have enjoyed writing this book, and not least among its pleasures has been that of receiving many helps and kindnesses. My chief debts of gratitude are to colleagues who read earlier versions of the text, and were generous with encouragement and advice: Professors Ulrich Knoepflmacher, Thomas Parkinson,

ix

Norman Rabkin, and John Henry Raleigh of my own de-
partment, and my transpontine colleague, Professor Eric
Solomon of San Francisco State University. My chairman,
Professor Thomas Flanagan, was consistently encouraging.
I also wish to record my gratitude to the Faculty Committee
on Research of the University of California, and to the
Chancellor at Berkeley for a Summer Faculty Fellowship.
The efficiency of Mrs. Beverly Heinrichs produced an accurate typescript with enviable speed. My final debt is to my
wife, to whom this volume is dedicated. She did not type
the manuscript, compile the index, or appear at intervals
with coffee and sandwiches. But she found time in her own
busy life as teacher, administrator, and mother to read
every one of Trollope's novels and to share with me her
acute perceptions about them; and to give this book several
careful readings.

Robert Tracy

Berkeley, California
12 February 1976

NOTE TO THE READER

Page citations are from the generally available "World's
Classics" editions of Trollope's novels (Oxford University
Press), unless another edition is specified. Passages quoted
from "World's Classics" editions have been checked against
first editions whenever possible, and corrected if necessary.

Passages from Trollope's works are cited by volume (if
applicable), chapter, and page. Thus *Prime Minister* 2:60:
194 refers to volume 2, chapter 60, page 194; *Doctor Thorne*
1:1 refers to chapter 1, page 1.

✳ PART ONE ✳

❋ I ❋

THE ROAD OUT OF BARCHESTER

> Our collectors are very fond of Teniers and Dow,
> but surely Hogarth and Wilkie are as artists, at any
> rate, their equal. The Fleming and the Dutchman
> may have understood more thoroughly the
> mechanism of preparing and laying on their col-
> ours, but when do they tell a story as do the En-
> glishman and the Scotchman? Inner design they
> have none.
>
> —Trollope, *The New Zealander* 12

"TO ME Barset has been a real county," Trollope tells the reader, as he seizes him "affectionately by the arm" in the last paragraph of *The Last Chronicle of Barset* (1866), "and its city a real city, and the spires and towers have been before my eyes, and the voices of the people are known to my ears, and the pavements of the city ways are familiar to my footsteps. To them all I now say farewell."

Trollope meant what he said. Although readers continued for years to request another novel about Barset, he refused any return to the "dear county" until 1882, when he wrote *The Two Heroines of Plumplington* a few months before his death. The great majority of readers, however, have preferred the comforting familiarities of Barsetshire, unwilling to enter the social and psychological turbulence he explores in his later, more complex novels. *The Warden* and *Barchester Towers* remain his most popular works, because they portray the unhurried charm of a rural England that was already disappearing in the early days of Queen Victoria's reign. Trollope celebrates its placidity at the beginning of *Doctor Thorne:*

> There is a county in the west of England not so full of life, indeed, nor so widely spoken of as some of its

3

manufacturing leviathan brethren . . . but which is, nevertheless, very dear to those who know it well . . . It is purely agricultural; agricultural in its produce, agricultural in its poor, and agricultural in its pleasures. There are towns in it, of course, depôts from whence are brought seeds and groceries, ribbons and fire-shovels; in which markets are held and county balls are carried on; which return members to parliament, generally—in spite of reform bills, past, present, and coming—in accordance with the dictates of some neighbouring land magnate. . . . But these towns add nothing to the importance of the county . . . the town population of the county reckons for nothing . . . with the exception . . . of the assize-town, which is also a cathedral city. Herein is a clerical aristocracy, which is certainly not without its due weight. . . .[1]

Even Trollope's first readers found in Barsetshire a kind of escape from a world of constant innovation, and when he died some of his obituaries described him as the celebrator of a way of life that had long since disappeared.[2] In *The Warden* and *Barchester Towers*, the gentility and innocence of the little cathedral city are threatened by the aggressively anti-traditional forces of Victorian progress, but in both novels these forces are routed. Mr. Harding's renunciation of his wardenship, for reasons more subtle than the progressive reformer can comprehend, and the energetic Mr. Slope's departure from Barchester in disgrace, represent triumphs for the traditional moral and social order that Barsetshire embodies.

It would be foolish to condemn readers for seeking this reassuring escape, or to criticize the novelist for providing it. Furthermore, escape is not the only reason for the popularity of these two books. The moral dilemma of *The Warden* is genuinely absorbing and Mr. Harding is one of the few

1. *Doctor Thorne* 1:1.
2. See especially the notices in *The Times* (7 December 1882) and the *Spectator* (9 December), reprinted in Donald Smalley, ed., *Trollope: The Critical Heritage* (London: Routledge and Kegan Paul, 1969), pp. 502-505.

good men in fiction who is believably portrayed. Trollope never surpassed the analysis of a struggle for political power which forms the main subject of *Barchester Towers*, and in Mrs. Proudie, Mr. Slope, Bertie Stanhope, and the Signora Neroni we have four genuinely comic creations fit to stand beside those of Dickens. But to judge Trollope solely on these novels is to do his reputation a serious disservice, for they were written at the beginning of his career, long before he had reached artistic maturity. *The Warden* was his fourth book, *Barchester Towers* his fifth. They were composed between 1852 and 1856. When he died, in 1882, he was the author of seventy books. Forty-seven of these were novels, many of them in three or four volumes.

These forty-seven novels were produced in more than thirty years of constant experimentation and evolution. Trollope seems to have been continually challenging himself by abandoning any theme, method, or social subject that he felt he had mastered. He lost interest in the portrayal of clerical politics after he had delineated Barchester life, and he subsequently wrote few comic scenes in the manner of the Ullathorne fête and Mrs. Proudie's reception. We know from the *Autobiography* how annoyed he was when critics suggested that characters recurred in his novels because he lacked invention. Overhearing two clergymen repeating this charge, he told them that he would "go home and kill [Mrs. Proudie] before the week is over."[3] And so he did, at the same time providing a new insight into the Proudie marriage and writing the most moving episode in the whole Barchester series. He was so eager to test himself that he insisted on publishing *Nina Balatka* (1867) and *Linda Tressel* (1868) anonymously, to find out if his style could be recognized, and if his books were popular simply because his

---

3. *An Autobiography*, "The Oxford Trollope" (London: Oxford University Press, 1950) 15:275. Anthony Arthur, in "The Death of Mrs. Proudie: 'Frivolous Slaughter' or Calculated Dispatch?" *Nineteenth-Century Fiction* 26 (1972): 477-484, argues that the death was not an impulse but artistically inevitable.

5

name was well known. Trollope was by nature a competitive man. He competed with his mother, his brother, his post office colleagues, contemporary novelists, accidental companions of the hunting field, and continually and most strenuously with himself.

His compulsion to experiment, and the inevitable increase in technical skill brought about by long practice, explain the shifts in techniques and, to some extent, in subject matter which mark Trollope's later novels. We need not deplore his departure from Barchester, nor need we agree with A. O. J. Cockshut in seeing the later work as a "Progress to Pessimism."[4] Trollope became aware that his range was limited in his Barchester books, and that he was in danger of being classified as a novelist who could write only about members of one profession in one specific place. His deliberate abandonment of Barsetshire was a recognition of his own artistic and psychological growth. He realized that the Barsetshire novels—except for *The Last Chronicle*—were simple in structure, and that their characters had little real darkness in their lives.

Trollope had admitted darker aspects of human behavior into novels he wrote before *The Warden*, and into some of those he wrote between sections of the Barsetshire series. Here are two passages from his first and second novels, *The Macdermots of Ballycloran* (1847) and *The Kellys and the O'Kellys* (1848). In the first, an unpopular landlord has been seized by some of his tenants; in the second, a drunkard bullies his sister:

> a third, whose face had also been blackened, was kneeling on the road beside him with a small axe in his hand. Keegan's courage utterly failed him, when he saw the sharp instrument . . . he began to promise largely if they would let him escape . . . before the first sentence he uttered was well out of his mouth, the instrument fell on

4. A. O. J. Cockshut, *Anthony Trollope: A Critical Study* (1955; rpt. New York: New York University Press, 1968). Cockshut deals with novels written after 1868 in Part Two, subtitled "Progress to Pessimism."

his leg, just above the ankle, with all the man's force; the first blow only cut his trousers and his boot, and bruised him sorely, for his boots protected him; the second cut the flesh, and grated against the bone; in vain he struggled violently, and with all the force of a man struggling for his life; a third, and a fourth, and a fifth descended, crushing the bone, dividing the marrow, and ultimately severing the foot from the leg. When they had done their work, they left him on the road, till some passer-by should have compassion on him. . . . Keegan fainted from loss of blood, but the cold frost soon brought him to his senses; he got up and hobbled to the nearest cabin, dragging after him the mutilated foot, which still attached itself to his body by some cartilages, which had not been severed, and by the fragments of his boot and trousers. . . .[5]

as she saw her brother's scowling face so near her own, and heard him threatening to drag her to a mad-house, she put her hands before her eyes, and made one rush to escape from him—to the door—to the window— anywhere to get out of his reach.

Barry was quite drunk now. Had he not been so, even he would hardly have done what he then did. As she endeavoured to rush by him, he raised his fist, and struck her on the face, with all his force. The blow fell upon her hands, as they were crossed over her face; but the force of the blow knocked her down, and she fell upon the floor, senseless, striking the back of her head against the table.

"Confound her," muttered the brute, between his teeth, as she fell, "for an obstinate, pig-headed fool! What the d_____l shall I do now? . . ."[6]

Alaric Tudor goes to jail for swindling in *The Three Clerks* (1858), Sir Henry Harcourt commits suicide in *The Bertrams* (1859), the Irish Famine is part of *Castle Richmond* (1860), and even Arcadian Barsetshire is darkened by the death of Mrs. Proudie and the sufferings of Mr. Crawley. Trollope had

5. *The Macdermots of Ballycloran* (London: John Lane, 1906) 25:446-447.
6. *The Kellys and the O'Kellys* 5:65.

always been aware of the darker side of life. With the success of *The Warden*, he discovered that many readers preferred that that darker side be concealed. For a time he gave them what they wanted, but he soon began to develop a more complex and realistic kind of novel. To deplore the change in his books is to deplore the inevitable growth of the man himself.

Nostalgia for Barchester is not the only impediment to a more favorable opinion toward Trollope's later work. Among critics there is a tendency to take Trollope at his own rather modest valuation in *An Autobiography*. There the novelist, scorning those who talk of art and inspiration, describes himself as a kind of novel-writing machine, who sat at his desk for a certain number of hours (three) every day, and produced 250 words every quarter of an hour.[7] Approaching the novels themselves with this confession in mind, we find it all too easy to accept the novelist's mechanical habits as the explanation of their length, multiple plots, and swarms of characters, and to convict Trollope of a general lack of form. But to take Trollope too much at his own word is unwise. He did write to a schedule, but this need not be inimical to art. It is equally unwise to consider the length of his novels, their complexity, multiple plots, and discrete groupings of characters, as evidence that he was insensitive to form—a mistake we are likely to make if we approach Trollope's work too narrowly committed to Henry James's theories of the novel as unified, self-consistent, and clearly controlled by a shaping intelligence.

Furthermore, Trollope's *Autobiography*, while not exactly a work of fiction, is a work organized as the success story of a despised outsider who came to be recognized as an English gentleman among English gentlemen. He insists that he has achieved success simply by hard and regular work and refuses to consider himself in any way exceptional. To admit to artistry or genius would be to undermine the position he

---

7. *An Autobiography* 15:271-272.

claims so proudly, that of an ordinary, good-hearted Philistine at home among his peers.

Trollope's recent critics and biographers[8] have challenged this self-evaluation to some extent, but they have been eager to stress his psychological and social insight rather than his able use of structure and pattern in composing his novels. He has been recognized as a great artist for his content, but not for his form.

A critical evaluation which can only justify Trollope because of his value for the social historian, or his abilities to portray and understand believable human beings, is not completely satisfying, and suggests that modern criticism has not understood the principles that determine the construction of his books. It is necessary to redefine our notions of form and structure until we can explain and evaluate Trollope's achievement in terms of his novels themselves, rather than by their failure to conform to Flaubertian or Jamesian ideals. My main purpose in this book is to offer this kind of evaluation, explaining and justifying Trollope as a formal novelist by analyzing his later fiction.

Trollope's later novels fall into two general types, those with single plots and those with double or multiple plots. The first type need not be defended or analyzed to any great extent, since Trollope's novels of single plot or incident do, in fact, possess form in the usual sense of the word. In the more complex novels, those of multiple plot, Trollope is exploiting structural devices he apparently found in the plays of the Elizabethan and Jacobean dramatists, which are often constructed with double or multiple plots, and were well represented in Trollope's library. They were his favorite reading during the seventies, when he left 257 of them

8. A. O. J. Cockshut; Bradford A. Booth, *Anthony Trollope: Aspects of His Life and Art* (Bloomington: Indiana University Press, 1958); Robert M. Polhemus, *The Changing World of Anthony Trollope* (Berkeley and Los Angeles: University of California Press, 1968); James Pope Hennessy, *Anthony Trollope* (London: Jonathan Cape, 1971); Ruth apRoberts, *The Moral Trollope* (Athens, Ohio: Ohio University Press, 1971); C. P. Snow, *Trollope: His Life and Art* (New York: Charles Scribner's Sons, 1975).

carefully annotated.[9] To understand the function of the apparently unrelated characters, episodes, and plots in the novels of this period we must recognize their kinship with these plays. Trollope, like his dramatist predecessors, was not interested in telling a simple story in a direct and linear manner. He preferred the seventeenth-century method, a group of plots that may not be connected explicitly to one another, but whose implicit relationship gives the play its form. The separate plots are related because they provide a commentary upon one another, either through contrast or through analogy. M. C. Bradbrook describes the alternate plot as "contrasted and not interwoven with the main action: it reflected upon it, either as a criticism or a contrast, or a parallel illustration of the same moral worked out in another manner, a kind of echo or metaphor of the tragedy."[10] Trollope uses his multiple plots in the same way, as contrast or as analogies, illuminating his theme from a number of different directions. When this is understood, those of his novels that have been most often condemned as shapeless emerge as conspicuous formal achievements. Their structure is complex but fully controlled, and the interplay of contrasting or analogical plots becomes a cumulative illustration of the central themes.

In Trollope's use of both single plot and multiple analogical plot there is a close relationship between form and function, for both devices are very closely related to his themes. The central moral of his later work is an exaltation of the ideal Victorian gentleman and a denigration of the romantic or Byronic type. He considers that the Victorian gentleman lives up to his calling only when he functions as a part of society, accepting society's values and fulfilling the duties of his position. To understand and accept social responsibility is virtuous. To reject it is to give way to a dangerous and

9. *An Autobiography* 20:366-367. Booth, pp. 151-155. Trollope's annotated collection of Elizabethan and Jacobean plays is now in the Folger Library, in Washington, D.C.

10. M. C. Bradbrook, *Themes and Conventions of Elizabethan Tragedy* (1935; rpt. Cambridge: Cambridge University Press, 1960), p. 46.

selfish individualism, which leads ultimately to isolation. These two aspects of the one doctrine usually determine Trollope's use of the single or multiple plot.

Trollope uses the single plot, which makes it possible to focus on one or two characters, for psychological studies of those whose refusal to accept ordinary life has led them into some form of isolation. Such a story can end happily only when the hero becomes a functioning member of society again. That which singled him out from ordinary men disappears, and with it the need or possibility of focusing upon him alone, in a single plot. A Trollope novel ends when there is no longer anything unique, or even very interesting, about the protagonist.

When Trollope, instead, writes a complex novel of multiple plot, he is celebrating the complex multiplicity of society. The recurrent pattern of characters and events is a reminder that individuals, and even rebellious individualists, are merely society's by-products. The far-reaching fabric of society itself is the hero, and this society is made up of a number of similar individuals or groups, just as the novel is made up of a number of similar or analogous plots. Such a novel, refusing to focus on one hero or one set of events, expresses an implicit preference for the typical— for the ordinary man, who constantly recurs. There is a corresponding distrust of the man who stands out, for any reason at all. The effect is to emphasize society as a vast far-reaching structure which is self-justifying. In the age of Carlyle, Arnold, and Marx, Trollope knew that this proposition was not self-evident, but he treats it as if it were, asserting what he cannot prove. The cumulative effect of exposing the reader to so many people and their interlocking affairs is to minimize the isolated figure who is apart from them, and to make that figure socially irrelevant. The rebel or outsider becomes a temporary inconvenience, often lost sight of in the press of other lives and events, rather than a heroic center of attention. Form and content are in this way closely related.

Trollope's moral system, which exalts the ordinary man and condemns the romantic hero, constitutes one more impediment to his popularity among modern readers. It is easy to ridicule his belief that the Victorian gentleman is the standard of civilization, and to quarrel with his assumption that a gentleman must have an acceptable background and plenty of money. Trollope's disdain for theories of human equality, and his occasional suggestions that foreigners are not as good as Englishmen, are also unattractive.

In judging this aspect of Trollope, it is important to remember that he did not create Victorian England. He recorded it, and he accepted contemporary values—with all the more fervor because he had himself escaped from the isolation and poverty of his childhood. He believes in order and civilization, symbolized and preserved by the social hierarchy. Like Dostoevsky and Faulkner, he values homogeneity as the basis of social order. He fears interlopers because he considers them a threat to any society whose values they do not natively share. He is not anti-American or anti-Semitic so much as he is fervently English. To him, Americans and Jews are objectively outside the English order and so, on occasion, a threat, not because they are evil but because they are different, and because the social order cannot tolerate one who is different, whether foreigner or native rebel.

Some of these attitudes represent a response to the career of Disraeli. Though Trollope found that career disturbing on moral rather than racial grounds, his essentially conservative attitudes were perhaps strengthened by press attacks on Disraeli as a foreigner and a Jew, a savage feature of the 1860s and 1870s. Trollope sometimes attacks his antagonistic characters in similar terms. He is an anti-romantic novelist,[11] and we cannot understand his work by looking at

11. For a well-argued counter-theory, that Trollope was attracted as well as repelled by Byronism, see Donald D. Stone, "Trollope, Byron, and the Conventionalities," in *The Worlds of Victorian Fiction*, Harvard English Studies 6, ed. Jerome H. Buckley (Cambridge: Harvard University Press, 1975), pp. 179-203.

it from a romantic or a democratic bias. The need for social order and individual conformity constitute the twin pillars on which his whole philosophy rests. And, just as the Trollope who was excluded from the society of his school-fellows at Harrow and Winchester came to write novels justifying the social exclusion of the "outsider," so also did the novelist, who saw the old polity breaking up and the traditional social order no longer able to sustain itself, try again and again to assert the strength and value of a system that was disappearing even as he gained his own place within it.

In Part I of this study, I attempt to define Trollope's theory of the novel during his artistic maturity, and to define his social theory as it determines the themes and structures of his novels. Part II analyzes Trollope's later novels in the light of these theories. The novels are considered in the order in which they were written, from *Sir Harry Hotspur of Humblethwaite* (written December 1868 to January 1869, published 1870) to *The Landleaguers* (written June to November 1882, published 1883), which Trollope left unfinished at his death. I have chosen to begin with the first novel Trollope wrote after he had achieved relative leisure, and had no other profession to distract him from writing. In October 1867 he resigned from the Post Office after more than thirty years, intending to devote himself entirely to literature. His leisure did not come immediately, however, and in *An Autobiography* he describes "these two years, 1867 and 1868 . . . as the busiest in my life."[12] He began a new novel, *He Knew He Was Right*, but finished it in Washington, while carrying out one last mission for the Post Office. While negotiating with the American government, he began *The Vicar of Bullhampton*. This novel was interrupted when Trollope stood unsuccessfully as a Liberal candidate for Parliament (November 1868), at Beverley in the East Riding of Yorkshire. The election was succeeded by what was, for Trollope, leisure, and it was then that he began *Sir Harry Hotspur*.

12. *An Autobiography* 17:322.

The year 1867 was one of personal changes for Trollope, and it was also one of significant political change in England. The death of Palmerston in 1865 marked the end of a period of comparative inactivity in political affairs. "Our quiet days are over; no more peace for us," remarked Sir Charles Wood as he walked away from the old Premier's funeral.[13] Palmerston's death indirectly created the chance for Disraeli's "Toryism of imaginative opportunism,"[14] and especially for the political improvising which resulted in the famous "leap in the dark"—the Second Reform Bill (1867), which doubled the electorate by lowering financial and residential qualifications for voting. The new voters were often poor and uneducated, open to bribery or coercion, and demagoguery. Trollope's experiences at Beverley, where his opponents' bribes carried the day, did not persuade him that these new voters would improve political life. Some of his later novels examine the opportunities for adventurers to win elections by pleasing the ignorant crowd, and he sees these opportunities as dangerous to the continuation of the English social order.

This change in the political atmosphere has its effect on the mood of Trollope's novels after 1868. Robert Blake comments that "a sharper personal feeling became apparent" in politics after Palmerston's death,[15] and Trollope's work becomes sharper and more intense at about the same time. His farewell to placid Barsetshire, and England's farewell to Palmerstonian placidity, occurred simultaneously. There were also drastic economic shifts: from 1868 to 1872 "a convulsion of prosperity"—Disraeli's phrase—and then a long depression that outlasted the seventies, particularly hard on those whose wealth was chiefly in land, those country gentlemen who represent social stability in so many

13. Robert Blake, *Disraeli* (New York: St. Martin's Press, 1967), p. 436. Blake deals at some length with the general sense of change after Palmerston's death.

14. Asa Briggs, *Victorian People: A Reassessment of Persons and Themes, 1851-67* (1955; rpt. New York: Harper and Row, 1963), p. 265.

15. Blake, *Disraeli*, p. 436.

of Trollope's novels.[16] The novelist was aware of their decline even as he insisted on their value. His later novels are written with a greater understanding of political, economic, and moral issues than are the Barsetshire novels. Trollope does not change his allegiances, but he widens his range both technically and morally, to deal with the apparently greater complexity of the 1870s.

Trollope's earliest biographer, his friend T. H. S. Escott, suggests that Trollope's resignation from the Civil Service made him freer to present political issues in his fiction,[17] and generally to assume a more critical attitude toward contemporary life. Escott also argues that Trollope's close friendship with George Eliot and George Henry Lewes, which dated from about 1865, made him more ambitious as a writer, ready to evolve from the "idyllic" Barchester series to the more "epic" work of the seventies.[18] The explicit farewell to Barset is one sign of Trollope's own eagerness for change. Another is his decision to establish a second literary "identity" at considerable financial disadvantage to himself by publishing two novels anonymously.[19] "Change of scene, of characters, and of interest, as well as anonymity of authorship, in the year of his departure from the Post Office, 1867," is Escott's summary.[20] Trollope was ready for experiments.

Relieved from the pressure of outside business, he began to think about the structure of his novels in a more ambitious way than in the fifties and sixties, when the fact that he wrote amid other preoccupations may have imposed an episodic structure upon him. Many of the events in *Barchester Towers*, such as the appearances of Signora Neroni and the fête at Ullathorne, are only loosely connected to the

16. Briggs, *Victorian People*, p. 296.
17. T. H. S. Escott, *Anthony Trollope: His Public Services, Private Friends, and Literary Originals* (1913; rpt. Port Washington, N.Y.: Kennikat Press, 1967), p. 256.
18. Escott, pp. 182-186.
19. *An Autobiography* 11:204.
20. Escott, p. 231.

more central concerns of the book, Mr. Slope's invasion of Barchester and the threat he represents to its ancient and gentle ways. Even here, Trollope is working towards an analogous method, though not very consistently: Signora Neroni is in some ways a comic echo of Slope's invasion, and Ullathorne reinforces our sense of Barsetshire's quiet stability. But with fewer distractions, Trollope was able to structure his novels more carefully. He could now plan a greater and more integrated complexity or, in the case of the short novels of single plot, create a tight and formal organization.

His first instinct seems to have been toward the tightly organized novel of single plot. In *Sir Harry Hotspur of Humblethwaite, An Eye for an Eye* (written 1868-69), and *Lady Anna* (written 1871) he quickly solved the problem of constructing a closely organized novel. It is these books that most repay study by those who consider Trollope loose and prolix, for they are direct in plot, simple in structure, and are told as economically as possible.

At the same time—in fact, from the year preceding his resignation—he was at work on a more ambitious project, a long and multi-plotted but carefully structured novel of society. This novel would condemn romantic individualism and exalt both English society and the ideal product and support of that society, the English gentleman. Trollope's greatest achievement is the vast novel that occupied him intermittently between 1863 and 1876. Later generations have only partially grasped the unity of this novel in six parts, by assigning to it such titles as "The Parliamentary Novels," "The Glencora Novels," or "The Palliser Series." While these titles recognize a unity of subject, they do not satisfactorily recognize the work's unity of theme and structure. Its six parts are best considered as a single work. Trollope tells us that two of its parts, *Phineas Finn* (written 1866-67) and *Phineas Redux* (1870-71), "are, in fact, but one novel, though they were brought out at a considerable interval of time and in different forms," and he seems to feel that their unity would have been obvious had they been published together.[21] In *An Autobiography*, he explains that the lives of Plantagenet Palliser and his wife, Lady Glencora, "these characters with their belongings,"[22] should be considered as a unified whole:

> In conducting these characters from one story to another I realized the necessity, not only of consistency,—which, had it been maintained by a hard exactitude, would have been untrue to nature,—but also of those changes which time always produces. . . . To carry out my scheme I have had to spread my picture over so wide a canvas that I cannot expect that any lover of such art should trouble himself to look at it as a whole. Who will read *Can You Forgive Her? Phineas Finn, Phineas Redux*, and *The Prime Minister* consecutively, in order that he may understand the characters of the Duke of Omnium, of Plantagenet Palliser, and Lady Glencora? I look upon this string of characters,—carried sometimes into other novels than those just named,—as the best work of my life.[23]

The total scheme is one of the longest novels in literature. It occupies nine substantial volumes in the "Oxford Trollope," a little over 3,500 pages. The story of the Pallisers is more than twice as long as *War and Peace*, perhaps a third again as long as *A la recherche du temps perdu*. In length it has few serious competitors—*The Forsyte Saga*, C. P. Snow's *Strangers and Brothers*, Anthony Powell's *A Dance to the Music of Time*, Jules Romains' twenty-seven volume *Les Hommes de bonne volonté*, and of course, *La Comédie humaine*. But some of these, like the "Chronicles of Barsetshire," are too loose and episodic to be considered as continuums in precisely the same way. Romains and Balzac make French society in all its various manifestations the hero of their lengthy works,

21. *An Autobiography* 17:320.
22. *An Autobiography* 10:180.
23. *An Autobiography* 10:183-184. Trollope could not make up his mind whether or not *The Eustace Diamonds* was a part of the Palliser cycle, and when he wrote this passage he had not yet written *The Duke's Children*.

and this sometimes makes them collections of scenes and types which are only thematically connected. Trollope has grouped all his episodes around a small number of explicitly connected characters, and this provides a closer organization and focus.

No English novelist has worked on so colossal a scale. Trollope himself, to be sure, approaches its length in "The Chronicles of Barsetshire," but the "Chronicles" are less interesting technically. The structure is episodic and discontinuous, allowing little real connection between, for example, *Barchester Towers* and *Doctor Thorne*. It is only in *The Last Chronicle of Barset* that Trollope makes an attempt to pretend that everything has been drawing toward a final climax, bringing most of his characters together and making them interact. But this effort is not enough to unify the whole cycle. It remains a group of scenes of provincial life which take place in the same locality and involve people of the same class; the characters and episodes are not organically related.

The Palliser cycle is quite a different thing. In five novels (or six, if *The Eustace Diamonds* is included), written over a period of thirteen years, Trollope tells the story of a marriage and creates a hero who is admirable precisely because he is a rather ordinary man. In a series of ordeals, Palliser learns to live with other people. He comes to realize that events will not fall out in just the way he wants, and that sometimes he will have to accept the second best. His growth is more striking because at the beginning of his adventures, he is already a worthy representative of Victorian society, a man of high rank, high ideals, and marked intelligence, hard-working and sincere. Heir to a dukedom, he is devoted to public service and to the maintenance of that society of which he is a product and an ornament.

When the cycle begins, Palliser, apparently the perfect Victorian gentleman although a little remote and colorless, does not seem in need of change or improvement. In *Can You Forgive Her?* he is described as "born in the purple, noble

18

himself, and heir to the highest rank as well as one of the greatest fortunes . . . he devoted himself to work with the grinding energy of a young penniless barrister labouring for a penniless wife, and did so without any motive more selfish than that of being counted in the roll of the public servants of England."[24] Yet this devotion to the public weal, blameless though it seems, contains the seeds of various temptations that confront him later. He becomes ambitious for political power, the control and guidance of society, while he despises political men and the art of making them work together in harmony. "The strong-minded, thick-skinned, useful, ordinary member, either of the Government or of the Opposition, had been very easy to describe," Trollope tells us.

> . . . But I had also conceived the character of a Statesman of a different nature—of a man who should be in something perhaps superior, but in very much inferior, to these men—of one who could not become a pebble, having too strong an identity of his own. . . . The Statesman of whom I was thinking . . . should have rank, and intellect, and parliamentary habits . . . and he should also have unblemished, unextinguishable, inexhaustible love of country . . . as the ruling principle of his life; and it should so rule him that all other things should be made to give way to it. But he should be scrupulous, and, as being scrupulous, weak . . . he should feel with true modesty his own insufficiency; but not the less should the greed of power grow upon him when he had once allowed himself to taste and to enjoy it.[25]

Ambition for power is one flaw in Palliser's perfection. Another flaw, equally a theme in the cycle, is that pride and "strong identity" which makes him intolerant of the ordinary political man, and so of personal contact with society.

24. *Can You Forgive Her?* "The Oxford Trollope" (London: Oxford University Press, 1948) 1:24:246.
25. *An Autobiography* 20:358-360.

He is willing to work to improve life for his countrymen, and to govern them, but he does not actually enjoy being with other people. "He had hardly made for himself a single intimate friend," Trollope tells us in *The Duke's Children*. ". . . He had so habituated himself to devote his mind and his heart to the service of his country, that he had almost risen above or sunk below humanity."[26] In society he is diffident. He lacks the gregarious instinct that Trollope considered essential for a civilized life. But after many difficulties, Palliser gradually lowers some of the barriers that isolate him, and is able to feel some connection with the rest of mankind. He learns to tolerate the imperfections of his wife and children, and eventually to tolerate some of the imperfections of social and political life.

Palliser is introduced as a minor character in *The Small House at Allington* (written 1862-63), where he appears as "a thin-minded, plodding, respectable man, willing to devote all his youth to work."[27] Trollope himself could not decide whether or not *The Small House at Allington* was part of the Barsetshire series,[28] but the story is set in Barset, and seems to link Trollope's two cycles; Palliser flirts awkwardly with Lady Dumbello, who is Archdeacon Grantly's daughter and Mr. Harding's granddaughter. His story really begins with *Can You Forgive Her?* in which he marries the beautiful and impulsive Lady Glencora, and Trollope's comment on the couple indicates the main stresses of their marriage: "I think that Plantagenet Palliser . . . is a perfect gentleman. . . . She is by no means a perfect lady;—but if she be not all over a woman, then am I not able to describe a woman."[29] Lady Glencora seems to be her husband's antithesis. She is gregarious and gossipy where he is close-mouthed and shy; she wants to enjoy life and cannot share

26. *The Duke's Children*, "The Oxford Trollope" (London: Oxford University Press, 1954) 1:3.

27. *The Small House at Allington* 1:23:319.

28. *An Autobiography* 15:277. He listed it here as one of the Barsetshire series, then deleted it.

29. *An Autobiography* 20:361.

his ideal of public service. But in the course of the book they both learn that some harmonious synthesis is necessary. Bored by Palliser, Lady Glencora plans to elope with her ex-suitor, the romantic Burgo Fitzgerald. When her husband prevents the elopement, she asks him for her freedom. Instead he gives up for her that which he wants most, his public career. He has just been offered the Chancellorship of the Exchequer, but he declines the office. Lady Glencora, in turn, abandons her desire for freedom. "She had received a great wrong," Trollope comments in the *Autobiography*, "having been made, when little more than a child, to marry a man for whom she cared nothing;—when, however, though she was little more than a child, her love had been given elsewhere. She had very heavy troubles, but they did not overcome her. . . . Lady Glencora . . . is brought, partly by her own sense of right and wrong, and partly by the genuine nobility of her husband's conduct, to attach herself to him after a certain fashion."[30] As the novel ends they are finally united in mutual acceptance, and their first child is born, the future Lord Silverbridge.

The next volume, *Phineas Finn* (1866-67), concerns a young Irish M.P. who is another antithesis to Palliser; he is poor, he enjoys society, and he is popular. At the same time, the book is an analogue to its predecessor, for Phineas is also tempted by public life, so much so that he seems ready to marry without love and to abandon his political convictions in order to hold office. Like Palliser, who is eventually to become his friend, he finally chooses personal integrity over his career. He returns to Ireland to marry and live in obscurity, apparently a failure.

Trollope does not seem to consider *The Eustace Diamonds* (written 1869-70) an integral part of the Palliser sequence,[31] although this novel describes some of the adventures of Lady Glencora. The heroine, Lizzie Eustace, is "a cunning

30. *An Autobiography* 10:181-183.
31. *An Autobiography* 10:184. See note 23 above.

little woman of pseudo-fashion,"[32] who wishes to be a romantic heroine and to marry a hero like Byron's Corsair. She is attracted to Lord George Carruthers, who seems to be a Corsair, and who resembles Burgo Fitzgerald in many ways. Lizzie Eustace is a commentary on Lady Glencora, just as Phineas Finn is a commentary on Palliser. She admires Glencora for her more dangerous characteristics, considering her "my beau-ideal of what a woman should be— disinterested, full of spirit, affectionate, with a dash of romance about her. . . . And a determination to be something in the world."[33] Just as Phineas Finn is simpler and more thick-skinned than Palliser, Lizzie Eustace is coarser, more foolishly romantic, and more frivolous than Glencora, and her story serves to underline some of the themes of *Can You Forgive Her?* Eventually Lizzie discovers that Lord George is too timid to be a corsair. She frightens him off by her willingness to commit a crime, just as Byron's Gulnare repels the Corsair by her unladylike murder of the Pasha. In Trollope, as in Byron, corsairs prefer submissive wives to romantic heroines. Later, Lizzie marries a dark foreigner, Mr. Emilius, who treats her badly, murders a Member of Parliament, and goes to jail for bigamy. By exaggerating Lady Glencora's traits in Lizzie, Trollope is able to explore the probable result of Glencora's elopement with Fitzgerald, even though that elopement has not taken place. By stressing Phineas Finn's political ambition and Lizzie Eustace's desires for wild romance, he reminds us that Palliser and Lady Glencora are not unique. Their aims and weaknesses exist all through society. These aims and weaknesses are not necessarily evil in themselves, but if they are not controlled they can lead to disaster.

With *Phineas Redux* (written 1870-71), Trollope's focus is on the Pallisers again. Phineas, now a widower, returns to Parliament. He is brought into the Palliser circle when he

32. *An Autobiography* 19:344.
33. *The Eustace Diamonds,* "The Oxford Trollope" (London: Oxford University Press, 1950) 2:62:211.

marries Madame Goesler, Lady Glencora's dearest friend. This time he is able to marry for both love and money. Palliser succeeds as Duke of Omnium, which condemns him to the political impotence of the House of Lords. His accession to the highest social rank—for the Duke of Omnium is "a duke who was acknowledged to stand above other dukes"[34]—seems to doom him politically.

In *The Prime Minister* (written 1874), however, this man who embodies the best of his society's values finds himself at the peak of both the social and the political order. His life as Prime Minister begins the final stages of his education, for he comes to recognize and begins to conquer his ambition. He is attacked through Lady Glencora for her extravagance and imprudence, and his resentment toward her for embarrassing him is accompanied by his anger and fear lest she be insulted. Finally, his coalition government falls. Palliser is embittered, and decides to abandon politics. The temptation of supreme power has apparently been too much for him—once ruler, he finds that he can no longer serve in a lower place.

But at the end of *The Prime Minister*, the Duke finally overcomes pride and the isolation it would impose. He realizes that political ambitions imply political duties, and that it is still his duty to serve. He resolves that ambitious element in his nature by recognizing that his drive has been toward personal power, and that he must now learn to serve his fellows unselfishly.

Even as this difficult lesson is finally learned, Palliser's ultimate ordeal comes upon him. Lady Glencora is dead when the last volume, *The Duke's Children* (written 1876) opens. Her husband finds himself called upon to function not as a public servant, but as a man and father. He must settle the problems of his three children, all of whom have inherited Glencora's dash and imprudence. His heir, Lord Silverbridge, has been expelled from Oxford, is involved

34. *Phineas Finn*, "The Oxford Trollope" (London: Oxford University Press, 1949) 2:61:209.

with an unscrupulous gambler, and wants to marry an American, granddaughter of a laborer. Lady Mary Palliser also plans an unsuitable marriage, while young Lord Gerald is expelled from Cambridge. The Duke becomes involved with these human problems, and this book completes the process begun so many years and so many volumes before. "No one, probably, ever felt himself to be more alone in the world than our old friend, the Duke of Omnium, when the Duchess died," Trollope tells us, as he commences the tale.

> . . . Though he had loved her dearly, . . . he had at times been inclined to think that in the exuberance of her spirits she had been a trouble rather than a support to him. But now it was as though all outside appliances were taken away from him. There was no one of whom he could ask a question . . . she, who had been essentially human, had been a link between him and the world.[35]

Events force him to become involved with his children and their problems, and to allow them to choose their own solutions, even though he only reluctantly accepts these solutions. On the last page, Lady Mary marries the man she has chosen, as her mother had been unable to do, and her father attends the wedding:

> Perhaps the matter most remarkable in the wedding was the hilarity of the Duke. One who did not know him well might have said that he was a man with few cares, and who now took special joy in the happiness of his children,—who was thoroughly contented to see them marry after their own hearts. And yet, as he stood there on the altar-steps giving his daughter to that new son and looking first at his girl, and then at his married son, he was reminding himself of all that he had suffered.[36]

Palliser has not completely changed. He thaws a little, and allows himself a kind of affection and understanding. He

35. *The Duke's Children* 1:1-3.
36. *The Duke's Children* 80:632-633.

learns to tolerate imperfection, and to accept limitations on his own power. At the end of the book, he is once more a member of the government. He is not Prime Minister, and he cannot have the post he prefers, that of Chancellor of the Exchequer. He prefers that post because it allows its holder to work alone, and "can do, or at any rate attempt to do, some special thing. A man there . . . need not be popular. . . ."[37] He agrees instead to be Lord President of the Council. Trollope is being accurate about contemporary political life; certain reasons made it necessary that the Chancellor be a member of the House of Commons, and that the Lord President be a peer. But perhaps it is important that Palliser has accepted a position that is not solitary or executive, and gives him no control over any department of state. The Lord President in theory presides over the Privy Council, which rarely meets. His only real business is to meet and confer with the other members of the Cabinet. Palliser has become part of a political group, as he has become part of his family at last. His pride is tempered by a willingness to subordinate that pride, his austerity is tempered with humanity, his solitude with companionship.

In this brief description, which singles out only the main and continuous plot operating through the entire Palliser saga, I have said nothing of the multiple plots that occur within each of the separate books. Nor have I discussed the sets of analogous characters, episodes, and plots uniting each part into a formal and intelligible structure. Here I have been concerned only with the main plot and theme, and with the way in which these various books are parts of a single vast novel. There are shifts of emphasis, to be sure, for in three parts the main concern is with the Palliser-Glencora plot, with Phineas Finn in the background. *Phineas Finn* and *Phineas Redux* place Finn in the center of the stage, while the Palliser story is less conspicuously placed. *The Eustace Diamonds* is semi-detached from the rest.

37. *The Duke's Children* 77:623.

As a character, Phineas Finn is developed less fully than the Pallisers. He is, in fact, not really a character at all. His function is that of a stranger in the world of the Pallisers, enabling us to see that world as it appears to an absorbed outsider. His inexperience makes it believable that explanations should be made to him about the customs and organization of this world. Through him, we learn objectively about the social level on which the Pallisers live. Trollope uses Phineas much as Scott often uses the naive young man who is visiting Scotland for the first time, who is continually being informed about customs or historical facts. Phineas's role is also comparable to that of Proust's Marcel, who is gradually introduced to the complex organization of the *Faubourg St. Germain*.

This similarity between Phineas Finn's role and that of Marcel is not the only resemblance that can be found between the cyclic novels of Proust and Trollope. In Trollope's work, as in Proust's, time is a character and a force, and the English novelist is very explicit about his concern with portraying time's passage. "As, here in our outer world, we know that men and women change—become worse or better as temptation or conscience may guide them—so should these creations . . . change, and every change should be noted" by the novelist, he tells us. "On the last day of each month recorded, every person in his novel should be a month older than on the first."[38] While writing *Phineas Finn*, he "had constantly before me the necessity of progression in character,—of marking the changes in men and women which would naturally be produced by the lapse of years. . . . I knew not only their present characters, but how those characters were to be affected by years and circumstances."[39] There is even a touch of plaintiveness when he points out a deliberate discrepancy in *The Prime Minister*, designed to show change after a passage of time:

38. *An Autobiography* 12:233.
39. *An Autobiography* 17:318.

In *The Prime Minister*, my Prime Minister will not allow his wife to take office among, or even over, those ladies who are attached by office to the Queen's Court. "I should not choose," he says to her, "that my wife should have any duties unconnected with our joint family and home." Who will remember in reading those words that in a former story, published some years before, he tells his wife, when she has twitted him with his willingness to clean the Premier's shoes, that he would even allow her to clean them if it were for the good of the country? And yet it is by such details as these that I have, for many years past, been manufacturing within my own mind the characters of the man and his wife.[40]

Trollope is not explicitly concerned with philosophic theories of time, as Proust is, nor with theories of memory. He is concerned with the passage of time as a factor in human life and as a technical device which will increase the apparent reality of his novel. He deals with the effects of this passage of time on his characters as it creates maturity and experience, alters personalities and relationships, and brings about new relationships and problems. Finally, in *The Duke's Children*, the whole cycle returns to something like its starting point, to the problems of *Can You Forgive Her?* Lord Silverbridge, whose birth certifies the Pallisers' domestic concord in that book, and the other Palliser children, must now confront some of the problems that had troubled their parents: how to conform to social norms, and how best to marry. As they do so, we look back to the solution of the same problems many years before, and the two books signal to one another like a pair of mirrors. Palliser frequently recalls his wife's long ago infatuation with Fitzgerald, and sees his daughter repeating "that romantic folly by which [Lady Glencora] had so nearly brought herself to shipwreck in her own early life."[41] "The Duke had taught himself to believe that as his wife would have been

40. *An Autobiography* 20:361.
41. *The Duke's Children* 5:41.

thrown away on the world had she been allowed to marry Burgo Fitzgerald, so would his daughter be thrown away were she allowed to marry Mr. Tregear."[42] Palliser refuses to see the differences between Fitzgerald and Tregear, whose only fault is his poverty. In fact, though his objections to Tregear seem to him to have social validity, Trollope subtly indicates that Palliser is really still fighting Fitzgerald for Glencora, and that he has somehow combined his daughter and his dead wife in his mind:

> His own Duchess, she whose loss to him now was as though he had lost half his limbs,—had not she in the same way loved a Tregear, or worse than a Tregear, in her early days? Ah yes! And though his Cora had been so much to him, had he not often felt, had he not been feeling all his days, that Fate had robbed him of the sweetest joy that is given to man, in that she had not come to him loving him with her early spring of love, as she had loved that poor ne'er-do-well? How infinite had been his regrets. How often had he told himself that, with all that Fortune had given him, still Fortune had been unjust to him because he had been robbed of that. Not to save his life could he have whispered a word of this to anyone, but he had felt it. He had felt it for years. Dear as she had been, she had not been quite what she should have been but for that. And now this girl of his, who was so much dearer to him than anything else left to him, was doing exactly as her mother had done. The young man might be stamped out. He might be made to vanish as that other young man had vanished. But the fact that he had been there, cherished in the girl's heart,—that could not be stamped out.[43]

Palliser's difficulties are not merely social; his proud, remote, self-centered personality is beginning to change, and he is able to let his emotions show a little. There are touches that make him very human: though he often recalls Lady

42. *The Duke's Children* 34:271.
43. *The Duke's Children* 7:54-55.

Glencora's earlier infatuation, he seems to have forgotten his own excitement over Lady Dumbello; he very much enjoys being with the American girl whose marriage to his son he opposes. The girl's freshness and unconventionality attract him. These traits make her reminiscent of Glencora[44] (and throw an interesting light on Silverbridge's choice of a wife), but at the same time seem to make her unsuitable to be Duchess of Omnium.

The young Pallisers show certain inherited characteristics. When Lady Mary impulsively and publicly kisses Tregear, we remember her mother's headstrong frankness. And throughout *The Duke's Children*, we realize that these impulsive young people, determined to marry for love, are the results of a marriage of duty—Lady Glencora's "great wrong" which has, after all, come out right.

This gigantic and involved novel-sequence is the major achievement of Trollope's maturity. Its flaws are attributable to the scale on which he was working, for the very size and scope sometimes bring about uncertainties, while Palliser is for a long time too remote and austere for most readers to like. It is only at the end, looking back, that the reader begins to feel the attraction of the figure, as his gradually revealed imperfections allow us to share Trollope's affection.

A further flaw is the uneven structure of the several books. The first two, written during the Post Office years, display a somewhat primitive double or triple plot of contrasts. *The Eustace Diamonds* is more assured. There the contrast/analogy between Lizzie and Lady Glencora is more organic than the rather simple and obvious parallels in

44. Arthur Mizener points this out in his important discussion of the Palliser novels in *The Sense of Life in the Modern Novel* (Boston: Houghton Mifflin, 1964), pp. 25-54; see p. 53. Mizener's essay originally appeared in *From Jane Austen to Joseph Conrad: Essays Collected in Memory of James T. Hillhouse*, ed. Robert C. Rathburn and Martin Steinmann, Jr. (Minneapolis: University of Minnesota Press, 1958). For a general discussion of *The Duke's Children*, see John Hagan, "Trollope's Psychological Masterpiece," *Nineteenth-Century Fiction* 13 (1958): 1-22.

Can You Forgive Her? In the earlier book, Trollope parallels Alice Vavasor (in love with the sinisterly romantic George Vavasor, loved by quiet Mr. Grey) with Mrs. Greenow; Alice makes the right choice and marries Grey; Mrs. Greenow "chooses the most scampish of two selfish suitors because he is the better looking."[45] (She is a comic figure, and so can make the wrong choice.) Both are parallels to Lady Glencora, with her two suitors. The relationship in *The Eustace Diamonds* is more understated. The Lizzie episodes are not used for parrotlike repetitions of Lady Glencora's problems and tendencies, but for an extension of them into a more extreme and dangerous situation, which is extended still further in the character of Lucinda Roanoke; she looks and acts like a romantic "heroine, and would shoot a fellow as soon as look at him,"[46] and finally goes mad. In *The Prime Minister* and *The Duke's Children* Trollope employs the analogical technique in a fuller and more polished form, both internally and in terms of the whole Palliser cycle. The mixture of perfect and imperfect parts flaws the entire work, however, and it is to such novels of the mid-seventies as *The Way We Live Now* and *The American Senator* that we must look for Trollope's most sophisticated employment of the analogical technique.

Trollope did not confine himself to the analogical method in his later novels. He often employed a tighter and briefer form, appropriately used for studies of rather narrow and obsessed people who are trapped in constricted situations. A close structure reinforces theme in such novels as *Cousin*

45. *An Autobiography* 10:180. There are three perceptive studies of the parallel plots in *Can You Forgive Her?*; all three discuss Trollope's analogous or contrasting characters. See David S. Chamberlain, "Unity and Irony in Trollope's *Can You Forgive Her?*" *Studies in English Literature* 8 (1968): 669-680; Juliet McMaster, "The Meaning of Words and the Nature of Things: Trollope's *Can You Forgive Her?*" *Studies in English Literature* 14 (1974): 603-618; and George Levine, "Can You Forgive Him?: Trollope's *Can You Forgive Her?* and the Myth of Realism," *Victorian Studies* 18 (1974): 5-30.

46. *The Eustace Diamonds* 1:36:331.

Henry (1878), *Kept in the Dark* (1880), and *The Fixed Period* (1880-81). [47]

Trollope's later novels, then, contain a variety of deliberate and highly complex structural techniques, and these techniques are closely related to subject matter. It is the business of the next chapter to explore these techniques more fully, and to suggest some of their origins.

47. See John E. Dustin, "Thematic Alternation in Trollope," *PMLA* 77 (1962): 280-288; William Cadbury, "Shape and Theme: Determinants of Trollope's Forms," *PMLA* 78 (1963): 326-332.

✻ II ✻

TROLLOPE AND THE THEORY
OF MULTIPLE STRUCTURE

"People must be bound together.
They must depend on each other."
—*Doctor Thorne*, 11

"The same story is always coming up," he said,
stopping the girl in her reading. "We have it in
various versions, because it is so true to life."
—*The Last Chronicle of Barset*, 62

AT THE TIME of his death, in December 1882, Trollope's "essentially . . . moral, . . . social interest"[1] was already a little out of fashion, and his solidly downright methods and themes appeared to be in opposition to the newer interests of novelists and novel-readers. The publication of his *Autobiography* in 1883 seemed to prove that his work was not worthy of serious critical attention, for there he repeatedly insists that novel-writing is a craft and a business rather than an art. This insistence was in part an attack on romantic theories of the artist's need for inspiration, and in part an aggressive self-defense against the charge that he had written too much too quickly. But, together with Trollope's lack of an adequate critical vocabulary with which he could discuss his own work, his reiterated insistence that he was craftsman rather than artist seemed to justify the critics' refusal to take him seriously.

---

1. Henry James, "Anthony Trollope," reprinted in Smalley, ed., *Trollope: The Critical Heritage*, pp. 525-545. The passage quoted is on p. 531. James's essay originally appeared in *Century Magazine* (New York), n.s. 4 (July 1883), pp. 385-395. It is also available in James's *The Future of the Novel*, ed. Leon Edel (New York: Vintage Books, 1956).

For many years, critics contented themselves with acknowledging Trollope's accurate pictures of Victorian society and its types. They did not suggest that his novels are important *as novels*, that is, as conscious and successful exploitations of the novel form. To Henry James, Trollope's willingness to come forward and admit that his characters and their adventures were fiction marked him as one of those "accomplished novelists [who] have a habit of giving themselves away which must often bring tears to the eyes of people who take their fiction seriously."[2] He convicted Trollope of a "want of discretion" for hinting "that he can give his narrative any turn the reader may like best," for James considered this unwelcome candor to be "a betrayal" of the novelist's "sacred office." He is patronizing about the "sort

2. James, "The Art of Fiction," *The Future of the Novel*, p. 6. See Wayne Booth's defense of Trollope against this charge in his *The Rhetoric of Fiction* (Chicago: University of Chicago Press, 1961), pp. 205-206. Booth argues that when Trollope directly addresses the reader, he is not suggesting that he can change the lives of his characters, only that he can change the way he tells us about them. When the novelist tells us, at the end of Chapter 4 of *Barchester Towers*, that Eleanor Bold will not marry Mr. Slope, he is telling us what really happened to Eleanor, and insisting that there is no good reason to keep us in suspense about her fate. The device seems to me to heighten a sense of reality rather than diminish it. Trollope was not the only nineteenth-century novelist to address the reader directly, and he had many models for his use of this device. Apart from contemporary novelists, he may have also noted the direct address to the audience in the prologues and epilogues of Elizabethan and Jacobean plays. I see some comparison with Brecht's device of deliberately reminding his audience that they are watching a play rather than "reality"—the famous *Verfremdung*, or alienation technique. Brecht uses the technique to force the spectator to make a moral or social judgment about the events on stage while keeping some emotional distance from the personalities involved. The spectator is supposed to perceive that the situation revealed is typical rather than unique. Samuel F. Pickering, Jr., discusses James's comments on Trollope's habit of intruding personal comments into a novel, and defends Trollope's use of this device as moral commentary, in "Trollope's Poetics and Authorial Intrusion in *The Warden* and *Barchester Towers*," *Journal of Narrative Technique* 3 (1973): 131-140. R. Anthony Arthur, in "Authorial Intrusion as Art in *The Last Chronicle of Barset*," *Journal of Narrative Technique* 1 (1971): 200-206, defends Trollope's practice on different grounds, as a way of telling the reader more about a character than can be shown; he finds the device augmenting rather than intrusive.

of underplot to alternate with his main story"[3] which Trollope so often provides, and generally seems to accuse the English novelist of a lack of form. Even Michael Sadleir's *Trollope: A Commentary* (1927), which effectively urged Trollope's claim to be considered a major Victorian novelist, did so on the grounds of Trollope's "power of characterisation and power of dramatisation of the undramatic," describing his formal treatment of his material as "undistinguished." Sadleir suggests that Trollope came "to gradual technical mastery," but he seems to mean a mastery of psychological and moral analysis, and is condescending about Trollope's use of multiple plot.[4] More recently, F. R. Leavis has excluded Trollope from the "great tradition" of the English novel. Leavis does not consider Trollope one of those "major novelists who . . . change the possibilities of the art for practitioners and readers" and "are significant in terms of the human awareness they promote; awareness of the possibilities of life." He ranks him below Thackeray, charging both writers with "nothing to offer the reader whose demand goes beyond the 'creation of characters' and so on."[5]

Since about 1945, however, there has been a serious attempt to reevaluate Trollope's achievement, especially among American critics. *The Trollopian*, a journal devoted to his work, was founded by Bradford A. Booth in 1945, and many important articles have appeared in its pages (the journal is now called *Nineteenth-Century Fiction*). A. O. J. Cockshut's *Anthony Trollope: A Critical Study* (1955), Professor Booth's *Anthony Trollope: Aspects of his Life and Art* (1958), Robert Polhemus's *The Changing World of Anthony Trollope* (1968), and Ruth apRobert's *The Moral Trollope* (1971) have done much to restore Trollope to critical favor; in addition, Arthur Mizener, Gordon Ray, Jerome Thale, and a number

3. James, "Anthony Trollope," in Smalley, p. 545.
4. Michael Sadleir, *Trollope: A Commentary* (1927; rpt. London: Oxford University Press, 1961), pp. 370, 366, 373.
5. F. R. Leavis, *The Great Tradition* (London: Chatto and Windus, 1948), pp. 2, 21.

of other critics have published articles offering shrewd new assessments of his virtues. But these provocative books and articles, while claiming for Trollope new importance as a serious writer, have not adequately dealt with one important aspect of his work, his formal skill as a writer of novels. They agree on his powers as a creator of character, and on his trustworthiness as a recorder of the mid-Victorian scene. Booth discusses Trollope's attitudes toward the political and clerical worlds portrayed in the novels, and relates his fictional techniques to those prevalent among other nineteenth-century novelists. Cockshut's work is marred by his belief that Trollope's later novels represent "the gradual development of his art, and the gradual darkening of his imagination and failure of his hopes,"[6] although this book is illuminating on a number of the novels. Cockshut also evaluates Trollope's attitudes to the social and moral forces of his day, and he is willing to discuss Trollope as a technician of the novel. Polhemus is primarily interested in Trollope's response to social change; apRoberts in arguing that his moral doctrine is relative—that he makes moral judgments in the context of a given situation rather than in absolute terms.

These critics offer an admirable defense of Trollope against the charge that he lacks seriousness, but do not attempt to defend him for his formal achievements. They virtually agree with James and Leavis about the careless structures of his works. Booth is also unimpressed with Trollope's intellectual content: "Normally one approaches the work of a novelist from the point of view of the ideas that are developed or from the point of view of the techniques that are employed. But Trollope's novels do not deal primarily with ideas, and the technique is elementary. . . . His work resists the kind of formal analysis to which we subject our better fiction." He accuses Trollope of "looseness of structure," and charges that "the pervasiveness

6. Cockshut, p. 11.

of his constructive failures shows itself even in his tightest plots."[7] Cockshut is gentler, for he is willing to allow that there is an occasional "even brilliant technical device . . . an artistic potential and a subtlety which contrast strangely with the ordinariness of the author's purely intellectual powers," and he offers a perceptive discussion of the "passive centre" in *Is He Popenjoy?* But even Trollope's finest books, he suggests, contain "a high proportion of irrelevant matter."[8] Cockshut sins by omission; in an entire chapter devoted to technique, he does not say very much about form and structure in Trollope's novels. He presumably feels that no really effective defense of his subject can be made under this heading. Even among Trollope's most recent critics, Ruth apRoberts remarks that "he exhibits little of those technical excellences the formalists admire beyond all else."[9] To George Levine, "It is hard to imagine, even in spite of some recent very interesting and serious attempts at revaluation and reconstruction, that we can ever take Trollope as seriously as an artist as we take some of the other major Victorians."[10] Hugh L. Hennedy's *Unity in Barsetshire* (1971), which argues persuasively for the careful construction of the Barsetshire novels individually and as a cycle, has apparently made few converts.

To both Cockshut and Booth, as to Sadleir, the chief technical flaw in Trollope's work is the introduction into many of his novels of subplots and episodes that seem irrelevant. By the Jamesian laws of form they are irrelevant, but Trollope's theories of the novel were not those of Flaubert and James. He had inherited the tradition of the eighteenth- and nineteenth-century English novel, with its

7. Bradford A. Booth, *Anthony Trollope*, pp. ix; 232; 94.
8. Cockshut, pp. 154-156; 169.
9. apRoberts, *The Moral Trollope*, p. 16.
10. George Levine, "Can You Forgive him?", p. 5. Trollope's art has been briefly defended by Joseph E. Baker in "Trollope's Third Dimension," *College English* 16 (1955): 222-225; 232; and by Elizabeth Bowen in her introduction to *Doctor Thorne* (Boston: Houghton Mifflin, 1959). But even Ms. Bowen describes his artistry as "an artistry which is inadvertent—more than unconscious, all but unwilling" (p. xxv).

abrupt shifts of mood, its explicit moralizing, straggling incident, occasional satire, and broad humor. To Trollope, irregularity had a beauty of its own, and we can take his description of Orley Farm, in the opening chapter of that novel, as an unconscious metaphor for his own artistic methods. Like a Trollope novel, the farmhouse is "commodious, irregular, picturesque, and straggling . . . irregular and straggling, but at the same time roomy and picturesque," and before it stand ancient apple trees, "large, straggling trees, such as do not delight the eyes of modern gardeners; but they produced fruit by the bushel, very sweet to the palate, though probably not so perfectly round, and large, and handsome as those which the horticultural skill of the present day requires."[11] There is a rebuke here for those who demand that their fruit—or their art—come to them in too symmetrical a form, too obviously pruned and ordered. And a few moments later we are told that Orley Farm itself was a triple structure, like many of Trollope's novels, planned and "gradually added to . . . and ornamented" by Sir Joseph Mason. In Orley Farm three structures exist harmoniously, though in picturesque disorder, and are successfully organized into one house. The total concept makes the apparently unrelated parts a harmonious whole. Trollope's novels are constructed on somewhat the same plan, with perhaps greater emphasis on harmony and order and a lesser emphasis on the picturesque. Those with double, triple, and even more multiple plots are not the work of a blunderer with no interest in the novel's form, but an attempt to relate form and function in a meaningful way. The multiple plots themselves, however mutually irrelevant they may seem to a casual reader, are organically interrelated to form a whole.

Such a method constitutes a challenge to James's theory of the novel and its form. "A novel is a living thing, all one and continuous, like any other organism, and in proportion as it lives will it be found, I think, that in each of the parts

11. *Orley Farm*, 1:1:7-8.

there is something of each of the other parts,"[12] James wrote in "The Art of Fiction" (1884). But with a slight shift of emphasis, Trollope seems to agree with him on the need for unity and harmony. Though a story "should be all one, yet it may have many parts," Trollope announces. "Though the plot itself may require but few characters, it may be so enlarged as to find its full development in many. There may be subsidiary plots, which shall all tend to the elucidation of the main story, and which will take their places as part of one and the same work—as there may be many figures on a canvas which shall not to the spectator seem to form themselves into separate pictures." And a little earlier, we find him delivering a strong warning against episodes: "There should be no episodes in a novel. Every sentence, every word, . . . should tend to the telling of the story . . . episodes distract the attention of the reader, and always do so disagreeably. . . . Though the novel which you have to write must be long, let it be all one. . . . Every sentence and every word used should tend to the telling of the story."[13]

It is clear that Trollope and James were to some extent in agreement about the unity and continuity that is the novelist's goal, but perhaps not about the means by which that goal was to be reached. James would have deplored the insistence on "subsidiary plots," but would have endorsed Trollope's remarks about episodes. However, despite this evidence that the two men had some basic agreement about structure, the modern critic would argue that, in practice, Trollope did not always live up to his good resolutions. Such an accusation makes little sense, however. Trollope was not a very good critic of his own work, but he was an almost morbidly severe one. Had he any suspicion that he had sinned in the matter of episodes, he would have discussed it frankly. The fact that he does not indicates his own assumption that his novels were structurally unified. It suggests also that he considered his subsidiary plots, and what modern critics might consider irrelevant episodes, to

12. James, *The Future of the Novel*, p. 15.
13. *An Autobiography* 12:237-239.

be organic parts of the structures of his novels. To read the passage in any other way is to consider Trollope a fool, a hypocrite, or a man who does not understand the meaning of English words. He was none of these things.

I have already indicated in Chapter I how this impasse can be solved when we recognize that, far from being straggling, episodic, and innocent of plan, form, and structure, Trollope's later novels represent an attempt to adapt the multiple plot structure of Elizabethan and Jacobean dramatists to the novel. They constitute a non-Jamesian attempt to achieve the Jamesian end of unity, and this is achieved, as in Elizabethan and Jacobean plays, by several plots that provide a commentary on one another and collectively elucidate a single theme or moral. Trollope may have found the device particularly useful when publishing in serial form. The need to keep the story's theme continually before the reader at monthly intervals, without monotonous reiterations, could be met by repeating or echoing the same moral issues or personality traits from one character to another. James, discussing a different aspect of Trollope's work, remarks that "it adds to the illusion in any given case that certain other cases correspond with it."[14]

The multiple plots of the old dramatists have been subject to the same kind of critical attack as those of Trollope. They have been charged with being episodic, irrelevant, clumsy, unplanned, and without the faintest rudiments of dramatic form. Swinburne, writing in 1886, declared that "the weeds and briars" of the Elizabethan dramatic "underwood are but too likely to embarrass and offend the feet of the rangers and the gardeners who trim the level flower-pots or preserve the domestic game of enclosed and ordered lowlands in the tamer demesnes of literature." Discussing Middleton, he uses such words as "inequality, irregularity, inconstancy of genius and inconsequences of aim,"[15] when he deals with the multiple plots of each of the plays, their apparent lack of

14. James, "Anthony Trollope," in Smalley, p. 544.
15. *Thomas Middleton*, "The Mermaid Series," ed. A. C. Swinburne and H. Ellis (London: T. Fisher Unwin, n.d.) 1:viii, xxv.

order and form. The charge is repeated by many critics, as when F. S. Boas finds in Middleton's *The Changeling* "a farcical underplot which has the loosest relation to the main action."[16]

Samuel Schoenbaum, writing in 1955, calls the underplot "the worst blemish . . . stupid and tedious."[17] But William Empson, Karl Holzknecht, and Christopher Ricks have all argued convincingly for the play's unity. Holzknecht insists that "the authors have produced a play which is structurally sounder than is sometimes supposed . . . main-plot and sub-plot, far from being flimsily held together, are actually parallels of action . . . there develops in the maligned sub-plot which is said to be so loosely connected with the rest of the play a . . . parallel to the central situation in the main plot."[18]

Critics have come to see that in *The Changeling* and other plays of the Elizabethan and Jacobean dramatists, the subplots are not irrelevant, but instead function as echoes, commentaries, or analogues to the main plots. Indeed, the terms main plot and subplot, with their suggestion of superiority and subordination, are perhaps misnomers. Such terms as double plot, triple plot, or multiple plot are more accurate for discussing plays or novels organized in this way.

"Of late years," Trollope tells us, in the penultimate paragraph of *An Autobiography*,

> putting aside the Latin classics, I have found my greatest pleasure in our old English dramatists,—not from any excessive love of their work, which often irritates me by

16. F. S. Boas, *An Introduction to Stuart Drama* (London: Oxford University Press, 1946), p. 2.

17. Samuel Schoenbaum, *Middleton's Tragedies: A Critical Study* (New York: Columbia University Press, 1955), p. 147.

18. K. J. Holzknecht, "The Dramatic Structure of *The Changeling*," *Renaissance Papers, 1954*, ed. A. H. Gilbert (Columbia, S.C.: University of South Carolina), pp. 81-82. See also William Empson, *Some Visions of Pastoral* (1935; rpt. London: Chatto and Windus, 1950), Chapter II, and Christopher Ricks, "The Moral and Poetic Structure of *The Changeling*," *Essays in Criticism* 10 (July 1960): 290-306.

its want of truth to nature, even while it charms me by its language,—but from curiosity in searching their plots and examining their characters. If I live a few years longer, I shall, I think, leave in my copies of these dramatists, down to the close of the time of James I, written criticisms on every play. No one who has not looked closely into it knows how many there are.[19]

Trollope finished his extensive study of these dramatists early in 1877.[20] Although many of his notes are concerned chiefly with the morality or immorality of the plays, he clearly took a particular interest in their techniques of plot and structure. Professor Booth says that

a fair share of his remarks is devoted to an analysis of plot structure. The first virtue of a good plot, one infers, is intelligibility. To be intelligible a plot must be unified. *Richard III* "is intelligible as the plot is one whole and is not frittered into bits, as in *Henry VI*." If there are two plots, there must be no loose ends. *Monsieur D'Olive* is unintelligible because Chapman "has not taken the trouble so to arrange his ideas as to make plain his plots." The strands of the main and subplots must be closely woven. Marlowe fails in *Edward II* . . . because "he has not understood how to throw many pieces into one piece so as not to rob the actions of his personages or an appearance of rational consequence." In order, then, to produce a continuous sense of plot, all the incidents must bear directly on the plot.[21]

Trollope's critics have neglected this clue to the structural methods used in his complex later novels, though we can

19. *An Autobiography* 20:366-367. See also Lance O. Tingay, "Trollope's Library," *Notes and Queries*, 195 (28 October 1950): 476-478: "Easily the most striking class of books is that devoted to drama." Tingay noted editions of Shakespeare, Beaumont and Fletcher, Jonson, Chapman, Marlowe, Dekker, Cartwright, Congreve, D'Avenant, Crowne, Dryden, Rowe, Shadwell, Farquhar, Cumberland, Shirley, Sheridan, and Wycherley, along with collections of plays edited by Mrs. Inchbald, Hawkin, Baldwyn, Dodsley, and Dike.

20. *The Letters of Anthony Trollope*, ed. Bradford Allen Booth (London: Oxford University Press, 1951), p. 360.

21. Booth, *Anthony Trollope*, pp. 151-152.

perhaps understand this neglect when we remember that it is only recently that the real function of the multiple plot in Renaissance drama has been understood. Some specific links between Trollope's novels and the old dramas have been noted. Gamaliel Bradford pointed out that the source of Trollope's *The Fixed Period* can be found in *The Old Law* by Massinger, Middleton, and Rowley.[22] Professor Booth notes that the leading character in Trollope's *Mr. Scarborough's Family* resembles many of the obsessed and scheming old men of Jacobean drama,[23] and proves that one of Lady Mason's guilty reveries in *Orley Farm* is a careful adaptation of a speech in Marlowe's *Doctor Faustus*.[24] But these are mere external resemblances, although they prove that Trollope could adapt material from his reading. Much more important is the way in which he apparently went to school to the Renaissance dramatists to acquire the method of composing some of his most important books.

Cockshut does seem to approach a realization of Trollope's multiple plots in his discussion of *Mr. Scarborough's Family*. He notes the presence of "relevant and irrelevant sub-plots," rejecting the Brussels episodes involving Florence Mountjoy, but seeing in the story of Mr. Prosper's efforts to disinherit his nephew "a series of ironic contrasts with that of the Scarborough inheritance" which are used "to neutralize the irony" of the Scarborough story.[25] But Cockshut seems to consider this relationship as a happy accident, unusual in a Trollope novel. He does not realize that he has perceived one of Trollope's most important structural techniques.

22. *The Nation* 80 (8 June 1905): 458. Cited by Booth, p. 129. Trollope read the play on 8 July 1876.
23. Booth, pp. 130-131.
24. Bradford A. Booth, "Trollope's Orley Farm: Artistry *Manqué*," *Victorian Literature: Modern Essays in Criticism*, ed. Austin Wright (New York: Oxford University Press, 1961), pp. 365-367. The essay originally appeared in *From Jane Austen to Joseph Conrad*, ed. Robert C. Rathburn and Martin Steinmann, Jr. (Minneapolis: University of Minnesota Press, 1958), pp. 146-159.
25. Cockshut, pp. 150-151.

Like Cockshut, other critics, in discussing individual novels, have perceived that parallels or contrasts between the various plots operate to create a formal unity, but have not realized that Trollope frequently makes use of this device. In 1958, Arthur Mizener cited the way in which the major characters in the apparently discrete plots of *The Prime Minister* are contrasted or paralleled, and Jerome Thale made a similar point about *The Last Chronicle of Barset* two years later. More recently, Helmut Klingler has reexamined *The Prime Minister* and agreed with Mizener in seeing "correspondences between the plots in actions and attitudes which significantly evaluate each other"—but then suggests that Trollope must be taking unusual care with this particular novel. Juliet McMaster has discussed the common trait of perversity that makes several of the women in *The Small House at Allington* analogues for one another, and the parallel vacillations that perform a similar function in *Can You Forgive Her?*[26] George Levine, discussing the same novel, sees it as unusual in its unity and coherence:

> . . . *Can You Forgive Her?* . . . has a loose structure, which I take to be generally characteristic, but it has a stronger than normal thematic coherence among the various plots. It has, moreover, one of those rare, essentially symbolic moments, the presence of which might help define its absence in other works, and its essential irrelevance to Trollope's mode. . . . Trollope seems to have felt obliged to do something about connecting the two plots, and so we have quite conscious and repeated parallels between the problems of the two women. The nature of the parallels is complicated and very rich—

26. Mizener, *The Sense of Life in the Modern Novel*, pp. 25-54, especially pp. 33-34; Jerome Thale, "The Problem of Structure in Trollope," *Nineteenth-Century Fiction* 15 (1960): pp. 147-157; Helmut Klingler, "Varieties of Failure: The Significance of Trollope's *The Prime Minister*," *English Miscellany* 23 (1972): 167-183; Juliet McMaster, " 'The Unfortunate Moth': Unifying Theme in *The Small House at Allington*," *Nineteenth-Century Fiction* 26 (1971): 127-144; Juliet McMaster, "The Meaning of Words and the Nature of Things: Trollope's *Can You Forgive Her?*" *Studies in English Literature* 14 (1974): 603-618.

almost altogether unusual for a Trollope novel. Trollope's narrative mode does not usually entail that the relationships among subplots be tight.[27]

When we understand Trollope's debt to the Elizabethan and Jacobean dramatists, we no longer need to speak of his novels as confused and rambling. Their complexity and their deliberately unconnected but parallel plots are not a failure of form, but rather a form developed in an attempt to render the complexity of social life realistically, and the accidental juxtapositions the observer can find in that complexity. Like the vast projected structure of the *Comédie humaine*, and Faulkner's Yoknapatawpha saga, Trollope attempted, in Balzac's phrase, to carry "une société entière dans ma tête." This aim helped to determine his method or, more accurately, helped him to realize that the analogical method of the Elizabethan and Jacobean playwrights could provide the kind of multiple and multilinear plot development that would enable him to work out his portrait of society in all its complexity, and would enable him to emphasize the implications of one set of characters and events by presenting the reader with an analogical or contrasting set. I do not suggest that Trollope was acting as a conscious theoretician of the novel when he did this. But he was acting as a conscious—and conscientious—writer of novels.

In an illuminating passage in his *Principles of Art History*, Heinrich Wölfflin argues that the art of the Renaissance achieves a multiple unity when in a painting there are parts that seem independent but are held together by a theme which those parts reiterate.[28] Such paintings as Breughel's "Kermesse" or "The Fall of Icarus" give visual proof of this

27. George Levine, "Can You Forgive Him?" p. 8. See also, for an extended defence of the Barsetshire novels as unified by parallel plots, Hugh L. Hennedy, *Unity in Barsetshire* (The Hague: Mouton, 1971).

28. Heinrich Wölfflin, *The Principles of Art History*, trans. M. D. Hottinger (New York: Dover Publications, n.d.), Chapter IV, esp. p. 159. For this reference, and for the development of the argument about dramatic "multiple unity" that follows, I am indebted to Madeleine Doran, *Endeavors of Art: A Study of Form in Elizabethan Drama* (Madison: University of Wisconsin Press, 1954).

theory, but for literary purposes, it is more useful to consider its relevance to the drama of Renaissance England.

This drama grew out of medieval miracle plays, which were constructed as a series of formally unrelated episodes brought together to reiterate some unifying theme, such as God's mercy or the Virgin's power and benevolence. The Renaissance drama's use of the multiple plot developed out of these episodes, as did its device of reiterating a theme in a number of characters. Hamlet, Laertes, Ophelia, and Fortinbras all reiterate the theme of filial piety in different ways. The emotional response to a father's murder is distributed among several different people, and then developed and explored, for Ophelia's madness, Laertes's fury, Fortinbras's search for a way of asserting honor, and Hamlet's careful investigation are all responses to a father's murder. In each character, one of these responses predominates, although each character also participates in most of the other responses to some degree. Hamlet expresses the responses of fury and a need for honor even as he is carefully investigating Claudius's guilt. Laertes's fury and Ophelia's madness suggest the possibilities of these responses in Hamlet, and they develop and explore these responses for him. The spectator senses that the intensity of their responses can also be applied to Hamlet's suffering, so that the response of each of the characters to a father's murder is emotionally—but not logically—transferred to the other characters. Hamlet does not go mad, but he is included in our emotional response to Ophelia's madness.

Elsewhere, Lear's fate at the hands of his children is reiterated in the episodes involving Gloucester; in *The Changeling*, those who pretend that they have changed to madmen to gain access to Isabella, the action of the second plot, are contrasted with the real change to lust and a kind of obsessive madness that takes place in Beatrice, and the play explores real and feigned madness. In such plays, the causal and formal links between events or plots are loose, and the real links are thematic ones.

Trollope adapted this method to the novel to create a

portrait of a multifarious and varied society. The effect is to make society the center of interest by reducing somewhat the importance of the individual, and reminding us that no individual's traits are unique.

Trollope's commitment to society and social order caused him to adopt one other device from Renaissance drama, that of introducing a figure of high rank who presides at the end of the play to reassert order. Fortinbras, Albany, Octavius Caesar, Malcolm, Prince Escalus of Verona, Alsemero in *The Changeling*, the Magistrates in *Volpone*, Giovanni in *The White Devil*, Theodosius in Massinger's *The Emperor of the East*, and Duke Evander in *The Old Law* all perform this function, and in many of Trollope's novels we find a similar spokesman for the social order appearing to end the action. The Duke of Omnium accepts the advice of Mr. Monk, one of the leaders of his party, at the end of *The Prime Minister*, and the advice restores Palliser's awareness of his proper place in the social and political order. In *Lady Anna*, the Solicitor-General approves the heroine's final actions, as does Lord Lovel, the head of her family. The Duke of Mayfair approves the marriage of Arabella Trefoil at the end of *The American Senator* in an explicit demonstration of familial and social approbation. *Dr. Wortle's School* ends with the proper remarriage of the Peacockes, and Mr. Puddicombe, who speaks for social order and who has criticized Mr. Peacocke's individualism, volunteers to attend because perhaps "Mr. Peacocke will like to find that the clergymen from his neighbourhood are standing with him."[29] Roger Carbury attends a whole series of weddings at the end of *The Way We Live Now*, all of them reaffirmations of the values of that social tradition which he represents. In this way, the solutions arrived at are certified by a high-ranking representative of society.

Trollope's celebration of social order, and his use of the Elizabethan and Jacobean multiple plot to portray social complexity, can be understood by an examination of one of

29. *Dr. Wortle's School*, Conclusion, 11:259.

his most effective novels, *The Prime Minister*. I have already discussed the place of this book in the Palliser cycle. In it, Plantagenet Palliser becomes Prime Minister. When his government falls, he realizes his own appetite for power. At the end, he learns that it is his duty to work for society's benefit by serving in the government rather than by working for his own political eminence.

Palliser is only partially successful as Prime Minister, because he cannot subordinate his own personality to his political—and social—role. Trollope explores the ways in which too many scruples, too fine a sense of personal dignity and honor, can isolate and so make a man unfit for political business. Palliser is too proud and remote to control the complex political and social worlds successfully. He disdains not only intrigue, but any political manipulation, and even refuses to practice diplomacy. He is set against the villain of the book, Ferdinand Lopez, who shares his desire for power, but who is entirely without scruples. If Palliser is too open and honest for political life, Lopez is too devious for it. He is so wedded to intrigue and scheming that he employs them even when they are not necessary, and his over-elaborate plotting brings him to disgrace and death. Except for his failure at the end, he is a Disraeli hero: "An audacious conjurer . . . some youth who, by wonderful cleverness, can obtain success by every intrigue that comes to his hand."[30]

Palliser and Lopez are simultaneously similar and different. In the book they represent the extremes of social good

---

30. *An Autobiography* 13:259. Trollope is discussing Disraeli's fictional heroes, but he felt the same way about Disraeli himself. See *The Way We Live Now*, ed. Robert Tracy (Indianapolis: The Bobbs-Merrill Company, 1974) 69:552, 554. Lopez's character and career resemble Disraeli's in many ways, and the prejudice against him as a Jew suggests the tone of contemporary attacks made on Disraeli as a Jew and a "foreigner." See Robert Blake, *Disraeli* (New York: St. Martin's Press, 1967) especially pp. 406 ("a Jew Adventurer"), 427, and 605. Carlyle called him "a cursed old Jew" (Blake, p. 552), and Trollope's friend, the historian Edward Freeman, described one of Disraeli's speeches in print as "the Jew in his drunken insolence" (Blake, p. 607).

and evil, but because they are both extremes they are alike in their inability to function successfully with society. Trollope poses a series of implicit questions: What kind of a man is liked and trusted by Englishmen? What arouses their distrust and dislike? If to govern them harmoniously, to live among them harmoniously, and to be accepted by them require more or less the same traits and dispositions, what then are these traits and dispositions? The events of the book are an attempt to answer this question, and Trollope's premise—ignoring the rich tradition of English eccentricity—is that English society abhors the man who stands out, who is too markedly different from the norm. Excessive vice, excessive talent, an excess of mystery about his activities or origins, excessive scruples—all these can render a man unfit for ordinary life. To Trollope, the acceptance of Disraeli was a sign of the degeneracy of the age.

Society's instinctive dislike of the unusual destroys Lopez. Although he is in fact unscrupulous, those who dislike him do so instinctively and are open to the charge of unreasoning prejudice. To the modern reader, Trollope appears to be saying that Lopez is contemptible because he is poor, and of obscure Portuguese-Jewish parentage, but in fact Trollope never does say that Lopez is a Jew. His origin remains a mystery. What Trollope does tell us is that a man who looks like a Jew, and whose origins are unusual or obscure, is often instinctively disliked by those who have an unquestioned pedigree and an unquestioned position in society. The outsider who provokes this dislike is isolated, and can expect no courtesy, no friendship, and no mercy. If he cannot make friends within the charmed circle he cannot enter it, and without friends he cannot survive. The social mechanism inexorably forces him into unscrupulous ways by its pressures after he has been tentatively admitted through someone's mistaken tolerance. Then the mechanism rejects him, and finally it destroys him. Trollope does not criticize society for doing this, nor does he defend it. He seems to think that the process is virtually inevitable, once that mistaken tolerance has been shown,

and therefore it had better not be shown. He accepts society's collective and instinctive judgment as right because it is
society's judgment rather than the judgment of an individual. At the same time—and here we are very close to the
friendless Harrow schoolboy of the *Autobiography*—
Trollope is understanding about Lopez's ineffective attempts to find a place for himself and gain acceptance.

Palliser is the social opposite of Lopez. He is of the highest lineage, noble, rich, and conscientious, a Duke and the
Prime Minister of England. But he too is not popular with
ordinary men. He cannot be one of them, any more than
Lopez can. Although they are widely separated socially and
morally, the two men make the ordinary English gentleman
uncomfortable in their presence.

Without the power of making friends it is impossible for
Palliser to achieve sustained political success, and it is impossible for Lopez to get the help he needs for success in the
social world that controls both politics and business. A
political leader can only succeed if he has the ability to make
and retain friends:

> If one were asked in these days what gift should a
> Prime Minister ask first from the fairies, one would name
> the power of attracting personal friends. . . . A Jove-
> born intellect is hardly wanted, and clashes with the in-
> feriorities. Industry is exacting. Honesty is unpractical.
> Truth is easily offended. Dignity will not bend. But the
> man who can be all things to all men, who can forgive all
> sins, who is ever prepared for friend or foe but never very
> bitter to the latter, who forgets not men's names, and is
> always ready with little words,—he is the man who will
> be supported at a crisis. . . . It is for him that men will
> struggle, and talk, and, if needs be, fight as though the
> very existence of the country depended on his political
> security. The present man [Palliser] would receive no
> such defence.[31]

31. *The Prime Minister*, "The Oxford Trollope" (London: Oxford University Press, 1952) 2:73:314-315. Arthur Mizener briefly suggests parallels
between Abel Wharton and the Duke; between Emily and the Duchess;

To be ordinary, not outstanding, and to be able to make and retain friends—these are the requisites for political and social success in Trollope's world. His brief biography of Lord Palmerston (written 1867, published 1882) makes much of Palmerston's extraordinary popularity, and praises his ability to seem typical.

Lopez's father-in-law, Abel Wharton, shares the English disdain for erudition. He is not pleased when Lopez seems to boast of his education, when his son Everett praises Lopez as "thorough linguist,"[32] and when his daughter Emily declares that her future husband is "well-educated;—oh, so much better than most men that one meets. And he is clever."[33] Wharton instinctively dislikes him, but he can only formulate his dislike into the vague accusation that Lopez is not an Englishman, and is not the kind of man whose society is pleasant to an Englishman. And, though Lopez insists that he is "utterly indifferent to the opinion of the world at large,"[34] he is finally destroyed, in part because, as one of the characters remarks, "He isn't of our sort. He's too clever, too cosmopolitan,—a sort of man . . . who . . . never had an association in his life."[35]

There is therefore an analogy as well as an opposition between the Prime Minister/Duke and Lopez. Both are socially isolated men. The Duke is self-conscious and almost morbidly troubled by criticism; Lopez is "essentially one of those men who are always, in the inner workings of their minds, defending themselves and attacking others."[36] Both are cut off from almost everyone, even their wives. Palliser

Lopez and the Duchess; Emily and the Duke. See his *The Sense of Life in the Modern Novel*, p. 34. Helmut Klingler, in "Varieties of Failure," adds to these parallels between the Duke and Lopez, and between Emily and Lopez. Polhemus notes the parallels between Lopez and the Duchess in *The Changing World of Anthony Trollope*, p. 209.

32. *The Prime Minister* 1:4:34.
33. 1:5:43.   34. 1:2:18.   35. 1:16:152.
36. 1:1:5. The Duke, watching preparations for an entertainment at Gatherum Castle, broods: "Suppose the papers were to say of him that he built a new conservatory and made an archery ground for the sake of

cannot open his mind to the Duchess, nor Lopez to Emily. It is only in an emergency that the barriers between these two men and their wives come down for a moment. The Duchess is amazed to hear an avowal of love from her husband at the moment when she has brought possible disgrace upon him by involving him in Lopez's affairs, and Lopez is closest to his wife on the morning of his suicide.

These resemblances between the Duke and Lopez are reinforced by the plot, for the two men are linked by the Duchess. She promises to support Lopez's candidacy when he stands for the Duke's family borough, although the Duke has forbidden his household to meddle in the election. Her interest in this dark, handsome, and romantic man is related to her desire for power, but it is also one of those touches that Trollope introduces to suggest the past adventures of his people. Lopez resembles Burgo Fitzgerald, who tempted a younger Lady Glencora in *Can You Forgive Her?* Lopez is defeated, and because Glencora encouraged his candidacy, he demands that the ducal pair repay his expenses. "Though this man lived nearly all his life in England, he had not quite acquired that knowledge of the way in which things are done which is so general among men of a certain class,"[37] Trollope comments. The Duke pays because he is over-scrupulous and eager to protect the Duchess,[38] and the result is a press campaign against them both. The affairs of the base Lopez are publicly involved with the affairs of the proudest Duke in England.

---

maintaining the Coalition!" (1:19:176). Lady Glencora has persuaded him to entertain some of his political supporters, much against his own inclinations (the chapter is entitled "Vulgarity"). Disraeli, like Lady Glencora, was a strong believer in such entertainments. He complained bitterly because the head of his party, Lord Derby (Prime Minister 1852, 1858-59, 1866-68), was reluctant to entertain supporters. See Blake, *Disraeli*, pp. 359-360.

37. 2:53:24.

38. This repeats an episode in *Can You Forgive Her?* John Grey, who parallels Palliser in that novel, pays the election expenses of his rival in love, George Vavasor (Fitzgerald's parallel), to protect Alice Vavasor

It may be objected that it is only the plot that links Lopez with the Duke, or that the whole Lopez episode is introduced solely to deepen our impression of the Duchess's frivolity and irresponsibility.[39] If this were so, the objection would still serve to absolve Trollope of irrelevant plotting by admitting the relationship of the Lopez episode to the Pallisers. But the personality traits which the two men share indicate that the relationship is not merely one of plot. Lopez is introduced as an analogue to the Duke to deepen our understanding of Palliser's nature, of that vulnerability which isolates him from other men. Through Lopez, Trollope is able to explore some of the horror of that isolation. We are reminded of what it is like to be physically and emotionally alone, suspicious of every man's intentions, able to communicate with no one. It would be unrealistic to show a Prime Minister in such a state, and therefore Trollope develops Palliser's potential for isolation through his analogue. We realize that a similar solitude might become Palliser's fate, and his possible fall becomes a matter of concern to the reader. When the final horror of Lopez's despairing suicide comes, and he is "knocked into bloody atoms"[40] by a speeding train, we are ready to understand the psychological implications of Palliser's state of mind, and to appreciate the strength he finally summons to overcome his own desperation and emerge from isolation. His rise out of despair is more meaningful in the light of Lopez's surrender to despair. Lopez's death shows us the possible fate of a Palliser-type who is not sustained by society, and dramatizes the possible fate of Palliser himself, were the Duke a weaker man.

But this analogy between the Duke and Lopez is only a part of the complex analogical structure of *The Prime Minis-*

(Glencora's parallel). Later Grey stands successfully for Parliament in his rival's stead, as Arthur Fletcher does in *The Prime Minister*.

39. Trollope implies this in a letter to Mary Holmes (15 June 1876): "The Lopez part of the book has only been to me a shoe-horn for the other"— that is, the story of the Duke and Duchess. *Letters*, p. 355.

40. 2:60:194.

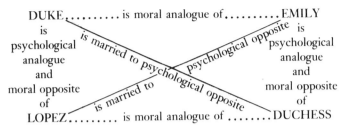

THE PRIME MINISTER

ter. While these two men are simultaneously moral opposites and psychological analogues, Trollope has enriched his book by another pair of characters in whom this formula is reversed. Lopez, the unscrupulous schemer, is a much exaggerated moral analogue for the scheming Duchess, as well as a psychological analogue for the Duke. Emily (Wharton) Lopez, his proud and innocent wife, is morally an analogue for the proud and innocent Duke. And, to complete the quadrille, Emily shares some psychological traits with the Duchess, for both women are imprudent and headstrong, and both are attracted to dark, romantic, rather dangerous men.

Both the Duke and Emily are victims of those who are less honest and open than themselves. The Duchess's schemes expose Palliser to criticism; Emily is used by her ambitious husband. When she finally becomes aware of his actions she responds with exaggerated shame and humility, just as the Duke is humiliated by his wife's petty transgressions. After Lopez dies, Emily considers herself tainted. She refuses to believe that her association with Lopez can be forgiven, and that she can go on to ordinary happiness as the wife of her cousin, Arthur Fletcher. Her self-reproach, like her marriage to Lopez, has its origin in pride and self-will. In this she resembles the Duke, for he blames himself for the fall of his government. He persists in speaking of himself as "beaten,"[41] refusing to heed his colleagues when they assure him that he is not at fault. In the same way, Emily

41. 2:78:361.

refuses the comfort offered by her family and friends. She cannot imagine another marriage, the Duke cannot imagine any return to political life. Both are blind because they assign to their own actions a guilt and a shameful importance they do not have. At the last, however, each realizes the danger of wilfully refusing what life offers. Each learns that a refusal to share in life comes not from humility but from pride, and to realize this is to be recalled to life. Both come back into the world, Emily to marry Arthur Fletcher, the Duke to promise that "I will endeavour to look forward to a time when I may again perhaps be of some humble use."[42]

Trollope uses Emily's irritating combination of purity, probity, and pride to stress for us some of the dangers inherent in such a combination so that, appreciating them in her, we can better understand the Duke. To remind us continually of these qualities in Palliser would be to weary us with the character, and eventually to make him seem ridiculously good. Instead, Trollope presents us with a parallel character, the kind of innocent young girl from whom we expect purity. He heightens her probity almost to exaggeration, and endows her with dangerous pride and stubbornness. Our emotions are engaged with her moral dilemma when she discovers that she has been victimized by Lopez, and with the course her pride leads her to take. Our engagement makes us better able to sympathize with the more remote Duke; Emily prepares us emotionally for his character, and deepens our understanding of him, just as Lopez prepares us emotionally to understand the Duke's isolation and its dangers. For the reader, the result is a heightened sense of involvement with the apparently forbidding Prime Minister.

A further set of analogues appears when we compare Lopez with the Duchess. Both are ambitious, self-assertive, and fond of intrigue. If the analogue between the Duke and Lopez is designed to heighten the dark and tragic impact of the book by emphasizing the evils of isolation, that between

42. 2:80:386.

the Duchess and Lopez is designed to remind us of the world of political manipulation against which the double drama of loneliness is played out. The Duchess schemes to further her husband's political power. She also schemes to further the Lopez–Emily Wharton marriage, and later Emily's second marriage. She prefers intrigue to any other political method.

Lopez's name suggests Dr. Roderigo Lopez, the Portuguese Jew who was executed for conspiring to poison Queen Elizabeth I[43] (Trollope's Lopez is of Portuguese ancestry), and who may have been a prototype for Shylock. The Latin name and origin also recall Spanish or Italian villains in Renaissance tragedies or in Gothic novels, who involve pure and highly born ladies in their intrigues, then drag them down to disgrace and death. A comment made by Arthur Fletcher about Emily is equally true of the Duchess: "Girls . . . I think they like dark, greasy men with slippery voices, who are up to dodges and full of secrets."[44]

Fletcher's comment also reminds us of the psychological resemblances between Emily and the Duchess. The accents of Elizabethan drama are invoked when Emily's father describes her preference for Lopez over Fletcher as "Hyperion to a Satyr,"[45] and John Fletcher advises his brother not to act like the rejected lover in a Renaissance drama: "What you have read, in the old plays, for instance, must have taught you that when a man is cut up about a woman . . . he never does get over it. He never gets all right after a time,—does he? Such a one had better go and turn monk at once, as the world is over for him altogether;—isn't it? Men don't recover after a month or two, and go on just the

---

43. J. E. Neale, *Queen Elizabeth I* (New York: Anchor Books, 1957 [1934]), pp. 348–349.

44. 1:15:138-139.

45. 1:13:124. See also p. 117: "He thought as did Brabantio, that it could not be that without magic his daughter who had shunned—

    'The wealthy curled darlings of our nation,
    Would ever have, to incur a general mock,
    Run from her gaurdage to the sooty bosom
    Of such a thing as'—[*Othello* 1:2:68-71]

this distasteful Portuguese."

same."[46] These echoes indicate that some seventeenth-century dramatic conventions were present in Trollope's mind as he composed his story, and can perhaps be considered as additional evidence of the source of his analogical method.

The efficiency with which the book's four major characters, and its two major plots, function analogically, provides the theme and structure which gives the novel form, and disposes of the criticism that the story of Emily and Lopez is "only very slenderly and artificially linked with the main narrative."[47] Perhaps the nature of Trollope's structural achievement in this novel, and the artistic maturity to which it testifies, can best be realized by comparing *The Prime Minister* with a novel that seems to resemble it, and may have been a kind of source, Trollope's own *Barchester Towers*. With the change of one letter, the interloping clergyman, Mr. Slope, becomes the interloping foreigner, Mr. Lopez. Bishop Proudie holds but rarely exercises power, and is isolated in his diocese; he is replaced by the isolated and inactive Duke. In his search for power Mr. Slope intrigues with Mrs. Proudie, who believes that she is helping her husband to rule successfully. The intrigues of Lopez and the Duchess echo this situation, while the general feeling against Mr. Slope among the Barchester clergy recurs in the instinctive dislike that gentlemen feel for Lopez. Eleanor Bold is condemned by her friends for an alleged plan to marry Slope, as Emily Wharton's friends mourn her marriage with Lopez. Eleanor actually marries Mr. Arabin, and Arabin becomes Dean of Barchester instead of Slope; Emily later marries Arthur Fletcher after he has defeated Lopez in the Silverbridge election. The episodic structure of the earlier novel is replaced by the firmly controlled complexity of *The Prime Minister*. The earlier comic mood is replaced with a careful analysis of isolation, pride, and the drive for power and acceptance. To compare the two novels is to realize the development of Trollope's art.

46. 1:16:148.
47. L. S. Amery, Preface to *The Prime Minister* 1:vi.

In this complex and panoramic novel, and in others like it, Trollope celebrates society and its values.[48] Its complexity duplicates the complexity of the society he is celebrating. The book's structure implicitly rejects the excessively individualistic man in favor of the familiar, the common, the typical, while the plot makes this rejection explicit. Lopez can only disrupt the social order temporarily. He cannot become a part of it, and the vast machinery of finance and politics, organized socially as an alliance of like-minded men, cannot be affected for very long by his intrigues. As in so many Elizabethan and Jacobean plays, a restoration of moral and social order creates the happy ending.

Novels and plays that celebrate order must themselves be ordered if they are to be successful, although to the careless observer their complexity might seem chaotic. Trollope seldom writes metaphorically, but near the end of *The Prime Minister* a passage graphically sums up his double commitment to order as a social ideal and as a literary necessity. He is describing the railway-junction at Tenway, near London, the scene of Ferdinand Lopez's suicide:

> It is a marvellous place, quite unintelligible to the uninitiated, and yet daily used by thousands who only know that when they get there, they are to do what someone tells them. The space occupied by the convergent rails seems to be sufficient for a large farm. And these rails always run one into another with sloping points, and

48. Both Jerome Thale, in "The Problem of Structure in Trollope," and William Cadbury, "Shape and Theme: Determinants of Trollope's Forms," use the term *panoramic* in discussions of Trollope's novels. George Levine, in "Can You Forgive Him?" argues that "the myth of realism" implies a novel defending conformity to social norms: "The techniques of realism in English fiction tend to release energies to which the techniques themselves are unequal. For Trollope, these techniques are expressions of that myth of the real which is more pervasive in his fiction than in the work of any other English realist. This is the myth that wisdom resides in learning the rules of society and acquiescing in them . . . realism tends to treat feelings and ideas which cannot accommodate themselves to 'reality'—that is, to surfaces and social conventions—as aberrations . . . realism in English has almost always invited an anti-romantic, anti-ideal compromise . . ." (pp. 6-7).

cross passages, and mysterious meandering sidings, till it seems to the thoughtful stranger to be impossible that the best trained engine should know its own line. Here and there and around there is ever a wilderness of waggons, some loaded, some empty, some smoking with close-packed oxen, and others furlongs in length black with coals, which look as though they had been stranded there by chance, and were never destined to get again into the right path of traffic. Not a minute passes without a train going here or there, some rushing by without noticing Tenway in the least, crashing through like flashes of substantial lightning, and others stopping, disgorging and taking up passengers by the hundreds. Men and women,—especially the men, for the women knowing their ignorance are generally willing to trust to the pundits of the place,—look doubtful, uneasy, and bewildered. But they all do get properly placed and unplaced, so that the spectator at last acknowledges that over all this apparent chaos there is presiding a great genius of order.[49]

This passage is an implicit metaphor for the apparently unrelated plots and characters of *The Prime Minister* and other novels by Trollope. The plots and characters, like the tracks, parallel each other but do not meet in direct confrontation. Like the trains, the plots must exist together in harmony, so that neither the junction nor the novel will fall into chaos. But the junction is a metaphor that does more than sum up Trollope's structural technique. It is also an image of order in society. Each train follows its own appointed way, its path marked out for it and its time of arrival and departure decided by the "great genius of order." Like the junction, society operates smoothly so long as no unexpected arrival and no sudden change from one track to another disturbs this order.

In the novel, the junction symbolizes the social order, which Lopez has violated by attempting to force himself

49. 2:60:191-192. See Polhemus's discussion of this passage as a metaphor for the modern world, pp. 205-207.

into it. "Quite unintelligible to the uninitiated," the social order has destroyed this interloper who "had not quite acquired that knowledge of the way in which things are done which is so general among men of a certain class." When he throws himself into the order of Tenway junction and is "knocked into bloody atoms," the gruesome accident is a symbolic working out of what has already been his fate, that of failing because he has invaded an order where he does not belong. The Duchess makes this explicit, when she tells Mrs. Finn, "I have a sort of feeling, you know, that among us we made the train run over him."[50] So closely do the parallels run that Lopez is instantly recognized as an outsider on the platform by one of the servants of the "great genius of order," who "are very clever, and have much experience in men and women."[51] This one recognizes Lopez as one who has no legitimate business on the platform, just as most of his acquaintances have instinctively felt that he has no legitimate place in their society. Lopez is challenged and ordered to leave, but he evades the guard and commits suicide instead.

Lopez, the romantic invader, departs simultaneously from the junction, from society, and from the novel itself. Because he does not belong, he "is bound by none of the ordinary rules of mankind,"[52] and this makes him intolerable to society. His dangerous individualism is defeated by society, and is diminished in the novel. Trollope's multiple plot makes it impossible for Lopez to occupy the center of the book to achieve implicitly the importance that the events of the plot deny him. The use of other characters as his moral or psychological analogues reminds us that all the traits which seem most striking and personal, and which seem to make him a romantic hero, are traits shared in some degree by others. Their combination in Lopez makes it impossible for him to fit into society, even though other characters, who possess some of these traits, can be accepted. The character, and his fate, is typical of Trollope's

50. 2:76:348.   51. 2:60:192.   52. 2:60:184.

panoramic novels, which celebrate the man who can live as a part of the social order by juxtaposing a group of analogous plots that themselves constitute a kind of society.

The close relationship between the structure of Trollope's novels and his themes reveals the control he was able to exert over his work. The presence of these themes, which express a consistent social doctrine, and the use of a seventeenth-century dramatic structure to embody them, absolve Trollope from F. R. Leavis's charge that he does not "change the possibilities of the [novelist's] art" and does not promote "awareness of the possibilities of life."[53]

Trollope's social doctrine, with its broad and generally consistent underlying theory, and its allowances for exceptions in practice, has some bearing on the related question of his moral attitudes. Communal standards usually define good or bad behavior; he has little interest in the more metaphysical aspects of a moral issue, or in the objective legal issues sometimes raised by his characters' behavior—despite his ability to present a dramatic courtroom scene. Melmotte's financial chicanery, for example, is presented as abhorrent, but the real issue is society's willingness to accept him, and the way in which this acceptance indicates a general breakdown of values. Trollope presents moral issues in terms of their social implications and consequences, and so refuses to judge them on abstract grounds. They are always complex because they involve real people. Trollope's attitude has created something of a controversy among some of his critics in recent years. He has been portrayed both as a moral relativist and as one who accepts at least some moral imperatives.[54] In fact, he is always prepared to present as

53. F. R. Leavis, *The Great Tradition*, p. 2.

54. The relativist position is most effectively stated by Ruth apRoberts in *The Moral Trollope*; her book includes several articles published earlier: "Trollope Empiricus," *Victorian Newsletter* 34 (1968): 1-7; "*Cousin Henry*: Trollope's Note from Antiquity," *Nineteenth-Century Fiction* 24 (1969): 93-98; "Trollope's Moral Casuistry," *Novel* 3 (1969): 17-27. Certain aspects of the relativist position are explored or defended by Jerome Thale, in "The Problem of Structure in Trollope," who stresses the complexity of honest behavior in Trollope; by Sheila M. Smith, in "Anthony Trollope: The

favorably as possible a character who has done something wrong out of some good motive, while admitting that the act itself is ultimately wrong; and he even offers some extenuation when a character's motives in acting badly are selfish or crass. He is able to keep in mind simultaneously the social and individual aspects of an immoral act— society's disdain for someone who has acted badly and the complex social and psychological factors which can drive a man or woman to behavior that will bring that disdain upon them. Few of his characters are wholly good or wholly bad. Their motives, their actions, and the consequences of those actions are his concern, rather than the allotment of praise or blame in terms of a systematic moral code.

I shall discuss Trollope's social doctrines more fully in the next chapter, and shall concern myself here with their relationship to those technical innovations which do, in fact, seem to "change the possibilities" of art for the novelist. Unlike many of his predecessors and contemporaries, Trollope did not usually connect his multiple plots in explicit— as opposed to analogous—ways. He used the multiple plot, with its possibilities of keeping characters and groups of characters apart from one another for long periods, to create a picture of a complex and traditional society which demands conformity and which has no room for exaggerated heroics or grandly romantic love. His protagonists succeed only when they accept the ordinary complex reality of the world around them. They fail when they deny that reality, when they do not understand it, or when they resort to histrionics. That reality is most convincingly portrayed by the analogical method, which reproduces the complex and apparently accidental relationships that bind a society together.

Novelist as Moralist," *Renaissance and Modern Essays presented to Vivian de Sola Pinto in celebration of his Seventieth Birthday*, ed. G. R. Hibbard (New York: Barnes and Noble, 1966), pp. 129-136, also arguing that Trollope does not present moral issues in terms of black and white. Roger L. Slakey forcibly states "Trollope's Case for Moral Imperative" in *Nineteenth-Century Fiction* 28 (1973): 305-320. See also Sadleir, *Trollope: A Commentary*, pp. 342-344.

It appears that this kind of method often attracts the novelist of conservative tendencies, who wishes to celebrate a traditional and homogeneous society and to attack interlopers who would change it. There is no direct evidence that Trollope read Balzac, or that Faulkner read much Trollope (the American novelist admitted reading "some of Balzac almost every year"),[55] but there are striking technical similarities between these three men whose social attitudes were similar. Balzac attacks the speculators and men of no tradition who came to power under the corrupt regime of Louis Philippe. Traditional royalism and traditional Catholicism provide an alternative to this regime: "I write in the light of two eternal verities, religion and monarchy." Jean Cassou points out that Balzac "identified the social order with the natural order. If society was an organic whole, the family was a molecular cell, and the transgressing individual was unnatural as well as antisocial."[56] Balzac diagnoses the sickness of the social organism, and prescribes a return to an older and simpler way of life. Faulkner's themes are roughly the same. He too prescribes a return to an older and simpler way of life, one lived in a harmony with nature that will bring about social harmony. His good men, such characters as Gavin Stevens, V. K. Ratliff, and Ike McCaslin, are defenders of the best in their social tradition, and typical good products of that tradition. His best

55. *Faulkner in the University*, ed. Frederick L. Gwynn and Joseph L. Blotner (Charlottesville: University of Virginia Press, 1959), p. 50. Faulkner owned a copy of *Barchester Towers*, inherited from his grandfather, Colonel J.W.T. Falkner. The novelist signed his name in the volume in 1933, an indication, according to his bibliographer, that this was a book he "cared about." See Joseph Blotner, *William Faulkner's Library: A Catalogue* (Charlottesville: University Press of Virginia, 1964), pp. 7, 75. Slope, Snopes (and Lopez) are suggestively homophonous. Faulkner owned a thirty-volume set of *La Comédie humaine* (in English). Most of these were signed, and he publicly admitted his debt to the French novelist (Blotner, pp. 7, 90-92). Stephen Wall, in "Trollope, Balzac, and the Reappearing Character," *Essays in Criticism* 25 (1975): 123-144, argues that Trollope and Balzac use the reappearing character in different ways.

56. Cited and summarized in Harry Levin, *Towards Balzac, Direction Three* (1947), p. 33.

known interlopers, the Snopeses, are rootless but clever financial speculators like the bankers and financiers of Balzac and Trollope. The invasion of the Snopeses, together with the decay of the old families who should guard the traditional way of life, constitute the sickness of a society.

A novelist who is exalting society must write many novels to reveal his vast subject and justify it. Balzac, Trollope, and Faulkner all produced novel cycles. In these cycles, certain moral or psychological personalities typical of their societies recur, or else specific individuals appear in more than one novel. This proliferation creates in the reader the sense of a society large and complex enough to contain many variations on its basic types, a society powerful enough to resist or destroy the nonconformist because it assumes a general social decorum which cannot be violated.

The employment of recurrent character types or recurrent characters is the chief method these novelists employ to build up a picture of a vast and far-reaching society. In Trollope's Palliser cycle, as we have seen, Lady Glencora's preference for the romantic Burgo Fitzgerald over the worthy Mr. Palliser recurs in Lizzie Eustace's desire for a "Corsair," and in Emily Wharton's marriage with Ferdinand Lopez. There is also a recurrence of types between novels that are not in cycles. Mr. Harding's rigid sense of honor recurs in Palliser. Archdeacon Grantly combines his clerical profession with a worldliness that seeks social rank and wealth for his family, a typical combination which recurs in the Dean of Brotherton in *Is He Popenjoy?* Mrs. Hurtle in *The Way We Live Now*, and Lucinda Roanoke in *The Eustace Diamonds*, are both violent American "heroines." Lucinda seems like a woman who "would shoot a fellow as soon as look at him,"[57] and Mrs. Hurtle has actually done so. The insane jealousy of Robert Kennedy (*Phineas Finn* and *Phineas Redux*) recurs in Louis Trevelyan (*He Knew He*

57. *The Eustace Diamonds* 1:36:331. John E. Dustin, in "Thematic Alternation in Trollope," suggests that the repeated use of these character types is a partial explanation of Trollope's prolificacy.

Was Right) and later in George Western (*Kept in the Dark*). The recurrence of types, and Trollope's judgment on these types, sets up analogies between his books. They show us what kinds of personalities society creates or rejects, and so establish norms of behavior, unifying the various novels into a cumulative portrait of society, and a commentary on society.

Trollope achieves this effect in an even more striking way when he carries specific individuals from novel to novel, "a practice which he may be said to have inherited from Thackeray," Henry James tells us, "as Thackeray may be said to have borrowed it from Balzac."[58] Balzac explains the device in his preface to *Une Fille d'Ève* (1839):

> . . . il en est ainsi dans le monde social. Vous rencontrez au milieu d'un salon un homme que vous avez perdu du vue depuis dix ans; il est premier ministre et capitaliste; vous l'avez connu sans redingote. . . . Il n'y a rien qui soit d'un seul bloc dans ce monde; tout y est mosaïque.[59]

To James, it is a device that would "naturally occur to a writer proposing to himself to make a general portrait of a society. He has to construct that society. . . ."[60] These recurrences create for the reader a complex and actual-seeming world in which one vista or series of events leads on to another. In reading each book we bring to bear information and attitudes not explicitly presented in that book, and a sense of Trollope's world as a continuum creates itself in a reader's consciousness, episode by episode, character by character, novel by novel. We apply information as we do in life, and we understand events by bringing past experience to bear upon them as we do in life. Our knowledge carries over from one book to another. A minor character in one novel may have been a major character in another; when he or she appears, we know a good deal and our information

58. Henry James, "Anthony Trollope," in Smalley, p. 544.
59. Balzac, *L'Oeuvre de Balzac* (Paris: Formes et Reflets, 1953), 15:306.
60. James, "Anthony Trollope," in Smalley, p. 544.

gives significance to even very trivial incidents. In *The Duke's Children*, there is a luncheon attended by the American minister to the Court of St. James, Mr. Gotobed:

> Sir Timothy and the minister kept up the conversation very much between them, Sir Timothy flattering everything that was American, and the minister finding fault with very many things that were English. Now and then Mr. Boncassen would put in a word to soften the severe honesty of his countryman, or to correct the euphemistic falsehoods of Sir Timothy . . . they moved about . . . Mr. Boncassen being rather anxious to stop the flood of American eloquence which came from his friend Mr. Gotobed. British viands had become subject to his criticism, and Mr. Gotobed had declared . . . that he didn't believe that London could produce a dish of squash or tomatoes. He was quite sure you couldn't have sweet corn.[61]

We have already seen Mr. Gotobed in action, studying and strongly criticizing almost every aspect of English life, as the titular hero of *The American Senator*. The stupid and lethargic Dolly Longestaffe, who has lounged through *The Way We Live Now* and thought vaguely of marrying Marie Melmotte, suddenly falls in love with Isabel Boncassen in *The Duke's Children*; if we remember his earlier torpidity, we relaize how very deeply he is stirred by the American girl.

The result cannot quite be called realism. It is rather an attempt to make the reader understand certain things that are happening without explicitly informing him, as we often understand in real life. Trollope wanted the reader to remember characters and events from his novels, as he remembered them himself. "Of course I forget every word of [*Barchester Towers*]!" he wrote in 1881. "But I dont. [sic] There is not a passage in it I do not remember. I always have to pretend to forget when people talk to me about my

---

61. *The Duke's Children* 70:551-552. "I have . . . heard Hawthorne discuss, almost with violence, the superiority of American vegetables." Trollope, "The Genius of Nathaniel Hawthorne," *North American Review*, 274 (September 1879), p. 207.

own old books. It looks modest;—and to do the other things looks the reverse. But the writer never forgets."[62]

This is perhaps the ultimate realistic device. It breaks down the barriers which mark the limits of a particular book so that its characters and incidents can possess an independent existence in the reader's consciousness. As a result, the reader's sense of reality is heightened because he participates in each book by bringing to it a body of information the author has not immediately and specifically given him. A kind of intercourse is set up between the book and the real world when the reader is actively involved in this way.

Trollope's assertion of general social truths or attitudes by showing a number of analogous situations has established his authority as a recorder of his age. Through his novels the social historian can begin to understand the typical and the common in Victorian life. "His great, his inestimable merit was a complete appreciation of the usual," wrote James,[63] and perhaps Trollope's most striking characteristic is his ability to realize actuality, to create in his novels a strong illusion of substance. "We are, most of us, apt to love Raphael's madonnas better than Rembrandt's matrons," he reminds us at the end of *The Last Chronicle of Barset*. "But, though we do so, we know that Rembrandt's matrons existed; but we have a strong belief that no such woman as Raphael painted ever did exist."[64]

In the *Autobiography*, Trollope defines himself as a realist and contrasts himself with the "sensational" Wilkie Collins. "The readers who prefer the one are supposed to take delight in the elucidation of character. They who hold by the other are charmed by the construction and gradual development of a plot."[65] Trollope argues that a plot is often unrealistic because it is too obviously an assertion of the

---

62. *Letters* (Trollope to Arthur Tilley, 5 December 1881), p. 465.
63. James, "Anthony Trollope," in Smalley, p. 527.
64. *The Last Chronicle of Barset* 2:84:451.
65. *An Autobiography* 12:227.

novelist's control over his story and characters.[66] He declares that "a good plot . . . is the most insignificant part of a tale,"[67] and relies instead upon "a most distinct conception of some character or characters" even if at first nothing is "settled . . . as to the final development of events."[68] A novelist "has other aims than the elucidation of his plot," he tells us. "He desires to make his readers so intimately acquainted with his characters that the creations of his brain should be to them speaking, moving, living, human creatures."[69] The title question of *Is He Popenjoy?* is never answered, and the book gives us instead the pattern of behavior caused by the existence of the question. In *Cousin Henry* we are told the whereabouts of a missing will almost immediately, then invited to watch the effect that Henry's knowledge of its whereabouts has upon him. Instead of characters who control events, we are given the reactions of believable characters to events over which they have little control, and the pattern of these reactions constitutes the novel. Since to Trollope a "plot" is usually the response of a character or a group of characters to an issue, it may be useful to think of a plot as a "movement," in the sense that the term is used in music: a fully developed structural division of an extended work. In *The Way We Live Now*, for example, we have the Melmotte movement, the Sir Felix movement, the Roger Carbury movement, the Paul Montague movement, the Mrs. Hurtle movement.

The pattern is the unity imposed upon these several movements. Two or more parallel movements are made to develop in more or less the same way. They may differ

66. *An Autobiography* 13:251, p. 257. "The construction is most minute and most wonderful. But I can never lose the taste of the construction. . . . Such work gives me no pleasure."

67. *An Autobiography* 7:126.

68. *An Autobiography* 10:175.

69. *An Autobiography* 12:232. Compare James: "What is character but the determination of incident? What is incident but the illustration of character? What is either a picture or a novel that is *not* of character?" Henry James, "The Art of Fiction," *The Future of the Novel*, pp. 15-16.

externally, but internally they are alike. In this way, movements that are physically distinct can be seen as organically similar. When confronted with one another they emerge as a unity because their internal similarities impose a pattern upon the whole work, while their superficial differences maintain the richness of real life in the novel.

It is presumably this patterned variety, and the air of realism it creates, that was recognized by George Eliot and Nathaniel Hawthorne, two of Trollope's most enthusiastic and perceptive readers in his own lifetime (Tolstoy was a third). "I am not at all sure," George Eliot told Mrs. Linton, "that, but for Anthony Trollope, I should ever have planned my studies on so extensive a scale for *Middlemarch*, or that I should, through all its episodes, have persevered with it to the close."[70] *Middlemarch*, too, uses analogy, separate but parallel lives that give the illusion of reality and its random juxtapositions. Hawthorne, in a passage to which

70. Escott, pp. 184-185. "Trollope captivates me with his mastery," Tolstoy wrote in his diary (2 October 1865) while he was reading *The Bertrams*. "I console myself that he has his [mastery] and I have mine. To know one's self, or rather, that which is *not one's own self*, that is the greatest skill. As for me, I must work like a pianist" (that is, practice). A few days earlier, Tolstoy's comment (29 September) was "Read Trollope. If only there was not *diffusness*. Excellent." *Diffusness* (diffuseness) is in English in the original. See L. N. Tolstoy, *Polnoe sobranie sochinenii* (Moscow: Gosudarstvennoe izdatel'stvo khudozhestvennoi literatury, 1952), 48/9, pp. 63-64. In a letter (10 January 1877) to his son Sergei, Tolstoy says "*Prime Minister* excellent" (*Prime Minister* in English in original). See *Polnoe sobranie sochinenii* (Moscow, 1953) 62:302. On 25 October 1891, Tolstoy sent M. M. Lederle a list of books that had greatly influenced him at various periods of his life, and graded their impact. Between his thirty-fifth and fiftieth year (c. 1863-78) this list is as follows:

Odyssey and *Iliad* (in Greek)	enormous
Byliny	enormous
Xenophon's *Anabasis*	very great
Victor Hugo—*Misérables*	great
Mrs. Wood—Novels	great
George Elliot (sic)—Novels	great
Trollope—Novels	great

[*Byliny* are heroic songs from ancient Russia. Mrs. Wood (1814-87) wrote *East Lynne* (1861) and other novels.] See *Polnoe sobranie sochinenii* (Moscow, 1953) 66:68. There were eleven novels by Trollope, in Tauchnitz editions, in Tolstoy's library at Yásnaya Polyána (p. 71).

Trollope gave a kind of *imprimatur* by including it in his *Autobiography*, described Trollope's novels as "solid and substantial, . . . just as real as if some giant had hewn a great lump out of the earth and put it under a glass case, with all its inhabitants going about their daily business, and not suspecting that they were being made a show of."[71] Hawthorne does not have the feeling that the novelist is imposing form upon his characters and events, and this gives him a sense that he is observing real life.

Trollope's method achieves organic unity in a novel without that unity seeming to have been rigidly imposed. The pattern emerges from the juxtaposition of the several distinct movements, and the novel expands into formal unity. Trollope's novels are not compressed or pruned into shape. Their ample fruit and spreading leaves may "not delight the eyes of modern gardeners" who look at them with a rigid notion of form, but when they are properly surveyed, the observer will see that they possess even that elusive virtue.

71. *An Autobiography* 8:144.

✳ III ✳

IMAGES OF ORDER:
TROLLOPE'S SOCIAL DOCTRINE

> "He is a gentleman, papa."
>
> "So is my private secretary. There is not a clerk
> in one of our public offices who does not consider
> himself to be a gentleman. The curate of the parish
> is a gentleman, and the medical man who comes
> here from Bradstock. The word is too vague to
> carry with it any meaning that ought to be service-
> able to you. . . ."
>
> "I do not know any other way of dividing
> people," said she. . . .
>
> —*The Duke's Children* 8

IN *An Autobiography*, Trollope defends his profession by
claiming for the novel the moral and educative value of a
sermon:

> In these times, when the desire to be honest is pressed
> so hard, is so violently assaulted, by the ambition to be
> great; in which riches are the easiest road to greatness;
> when the temptations to which men are subjected dull
> their eyes to the perfected iniquities of others; when it is
> so hard for a man to decide vigorously that the pitch,
> which so many are handling, will defile him if it be
> touched; men's conduct will be actuated much by that
> which is from day to day depicted to them as leading to
> glorious or inglorious results . . . the novelist . . . must
> preach his sermons with the same purpose as the clergy-
> man, and must have his own system of ethics.[1]

Like Matthew Arnold, Trollope considered that the professional writer had an important moral and social function.
Trollope believed that function to be teaching men how to

---

1. *An Autobiography* 12:220-222.

act well in the world. In a sense, he was writing a Victorian version of *The Courtier*; or, like Spenser, he could claim that "the general end" of all his books "is to fashion a gentleman or noble person in virtuous and gentle discipline." The Palliser cycle is an epic that defines and celebrates the English gentleman, the essential guarantor of social and moral values, and the other novels consistently explore this theme.

M. C. Bradbrook describes the typical villain of Renaissance drama as embittered by some defect that separates him from other people.[2] The word *villain* is usually too strong for one of Trollope's excluded characters, but they also suffer some defect. It may not always embitter them, but it does isolate them from society. This defect can take two basic forms. In the first, the excluded character is socially isolated. He lacks money, friends, or a defined social position. The general judgment of society excludes him. In the second category is the character who is self-excluded because he is wicked, refuses to obey society's laws, or has some morbid quality that makes him unable to get along easily with others. Trollope sometimes presents a protagonist who is excluded or threatened with exclusion, and must prove his or her right to social admission by bringing society to recognize merit, or by suppressing morbidly self-isolating tendencies. By showing us that exclusion and isolation can be either social or psychological, and can threaten protagonists as well as characters who invite our disapproval, he makes it difficult for the reader to see isolation as romantic and Byronic.

Trollope described civilization as "produced in the world by the congregated intelligences of many persons."[3] A man must recognize and perform his social role; evil is defined as social and/or moral isolation. We need not look far to understand why the fear of isolation is so obsessive in Trollope's work. In *An Autobiography* he depicts his own father's morbid isolation, first as a failing barrister in "dingy, almost

2. M. C. Bradbrook, *Themes and Conventions of Elizabethan Tragedy*, (1935; rpt. Cambridge: Cambridge University Press, 1960) p. 57.
3. *South Africa* (London: Chapman and Hall, 1878) 2:1:10.

suicidal chambers . . . plagued with so bad a temper, that he drove the attorneys from him. . . . My father's clients deserted him." After his law practice and his attempts at farming had both failed, Mr. Trollope toiled over a vast and useless *Encyclopedia Ecclesiastica* in "a parlour . . . shut up among big books."[4] The future novelist was left behind in England when the rest of the family went to the United States. He describes his loneliness and particularly emphasizes the ways in which his schoolfellows at Harrow and Winchester excluded him because of his shabbiness and poverty. "I became a Pariah," he tells us.

> I had no friend to whom I could pour out my sorrows. . . . I considered whether I should always be alone; whether I could not find my way up to the top of that college tower, and from thence put an end to everything?[5]

Trollope's successful overcoming of this social exclusion is the theme of his *Autobiography*. "I acknowledge the weakness of a great desire to be loved," he remarks, "—of a strong wish to be popular with my associates."[6] As a boy, he recalled, he had been afraid

> that the mud and solitude and poverty of the time would insure me mud and solitude and poverty through my life. Those lads about me would go into Parliament, or become rectors and deans, or squires of parishes, or advocates thundering at the Bar. They would not live with me now,—but neither should I be able to live with them in after years.[7]

And there is real triumph in the next sentence: "Nevertheless I have lived with them."

4. *An Autobiography* 1:2-3, 12.

5. *An Autobiography* 1:9. Many years later, his Harrow contemporary and later friend, Sir William Gregory, recalled that "poor Trollope was tabooed, and had not, so far as I am aware, a single friend. . . . There was a story afloat . . . that his father had been outlawed. . . ." See Sir William Gregory, *An Autobiography*, ed. Lady Gregory (London: J. Murray, 1894), p. 35.

6. *An Autobiography* 4:60.

7. *An Autobiography* 9:168-169.

Trollope's fear of exclusion and isolation is a constant element in his novels. Isolation tempts or threatens his characters. The isolated man receives his scorn or pity, while his heroes resist isolation. His typical protagonist has a generally recognized place in the social order, and accepts that place; or else the social order concedes a newcomer such a recognized place. Social integration depends on money, birth, an instinctive recognition of social laws, and an awareness of social tradition; it is synonymous with moral integration. Trollope's heroes do not criticize the social order, either explicitly or implicitly. They accept it and are accepted by it. They do not aspire to be anything but ordinary gentlemen; if they have other aspirations, they eventually abandon them. Ordinary decency is the heart of this moral and social doctrine, and in fact Trollope's moral and social doctrine are one. Morality consists in knowing one's proper place in the social order, and in conforming to society's demands. Acts that invoke exclusion or isolation are evil. The ordinary gentleman is the product and the mainstay of the social order. His virtues are essentially secular; he has high moral standards, but, unlike Thomas Arnold's "Christian gentleman," his role does not seem to have any explicit religious dimension.

In Trollope's pages, this status of being a gentleman—or a lady—is simultaneously a moral, a traditional, and an economic position. Moral excellence cannot confer a position in society, while a high social position does not automatically guarantee virtue. Gentle birth is useful, but it is not socially viable without a fortune to support it: when Lady Mary Palliser tells her father that her lover, a poor man from an ancient family, is a gentleman, the Duke dismisses the term as meaningless under the circumstances and forbids the match.[8] He finds the suitor objectionable because he "has nothing; not even a profession . . . neither rank, nor means, nor profession, nor name."[9] Mr. Crawley realizes that even a clergyman must be rich if his moral teaching is

8. *The Duke's Children* 8:67.
9. *The Duke's Children* 11:88.

73

to affect his hearers: ". . . there was nothing so bitter to the man as the derogation from the spiritual grandeur of his position as priest among men, which came as one necessary result from his poverty . . . if only the faithful would have believed in him, poor as he was, as they would have believed in him had he been rich!"[10] Earl Lovel, in *Lady Anna*, "with a thousand a year, and that probably already embarrassed, would be a poor, wretched creature, a mock lord, an earl without the very essence of an earldom. But Earl Lovel with fifteen or twenty thousand a year would be as good as most other earls."[11] Trollope is recording his society's general attitudes, which had been held for a long time. "All's gone!" says Witgood in *A Trick to Catch the Old One*, "still thou'rt a gentleman, that's all; but a poor one, that's nothing."[12]

Although money is necessary to a gentleman, Trollope feels that too direct an involvement in getting it can be a social and moral disqualification. The man whose primary interest is in gaining a fortune risks corruption; the man whose primary interest lies in some occupation or profession that may bring him a fortune is comparatively safe. Describing different kinds of London tradesmen in a series of newspaper sketches, Trollope quibbles about the chemist's status, and argues that he should probably be considered a gentleman because "It is not in fact the goods he sells, but the goods so arranged as to preserve instead of injuring life."[13] His preoccupations are scientific rather than commercial. A man can be an attorney and at the same time a gentleman, so long as his attention is fixed on the law itself rather than on his fees. He may think of his clients' money without harm, but is in danger if he gives much thought to his own. In *Mr. Scarborough's Family* there are two attorneys, sharp Mr. Barry and gentlemanly Mr. Grey. Barry falls from grace:

10. *The Last Chronicle of Barset* 1:12:118.
11. *Lady Anna* 5:46-47.
12. Thomas Middleton, *A Trick to Catch the Old One*, 1:1.
13. *London Tradesmen* (London: Elkin Matthews and Marrot, 1927), p. 21.

Mr. Barry was beginning to love his clients,—not with a proper attorney's affection, as his children, but as sheep to be shorn. With Mr. Grey the bills had gone out and had been paid no doubt, and the money had in some shape found its way into Mr. Grey's pockets. But he had never looked at the two things together. Mr. Barry seemed to be thinking of the wool as every client came, or was dismissed.[14]

The landowner should be concerned directly with wisely managing his estate, and only indirectly with the profits that may then result.

Trollope's own attitude toward the money he earned by writing novels seems a little at odds with this. In *An Autobiography*, he lists for us the sum made by each book, and gives us the total: £ 68,959 17s 5d.[15] He criticizes those who preach against the love of money "by customary but unintelligent piety," and insists that

All material progress has come from man's desire to do the best he can for himself and those about him, and civilisation and Christianity itself have been made possible by such progress . . . the more a man earns the more useful he is to his fellow-men. . . . As far as we know, Shakespeare worked always for money . . . it is a mistake to suppose that a man is a better man because he despises money. Few do so, and those few in doing so suffer a defect.

There is some inner conflict here. Trollope's boyhood poverty and the financial ruin of his family had made him aware of the importance of money, and he knew that by his writing he had created his own "comfortable but not splendid"[16] fortune and made a social position for himself. In *An Autobiography* he emphasizes his dedication to his craft, his hard work and serious purpose. Like Mr. Grey, he placed the intelligent pursuit of his profession first and the profits second. But in *The Duke's Children*, the novel he began two

14. *Mr. Scarborough's Family* 58:559.
15. *An Autobiography* 20:363-364.
16. *An Autobiography* 6:105-107.

days after he had added up the "something near £70,000"[17] earned by his books, there is a curious detail: young Lord Silverbridge loses £70,000 on the St. Leger because his horse has been tampered with. The Duke pays the money, and though he describes it as "an enormous sum," treats the actual amount as comparatively unimportant:

> . . . if you are cured of this evil, the money is nothing. What is it all for but for you and your brother and sister? It was a large sum, but that shall not grieve me. The thing itself is so dangerous that, if with that much of loss we can escape, I will think that we have made not a bad market. . . .[18]

The essence of Mr. Harding's gentility is that he is not capable of thinking about his income at all until events force him to do so, nor of connecting it in any way with duties he actually performs. In the Palliser novels, Madame Max Goesler earns Trollope's approval (and social acceptance, even though she is Jewish and a foreigner) because she does not value money for its own sake: ". . . though she prized wealth, and knew that her money was her only rock of strength, she could be lavish with it, as though it were dirt."[19]

The demoralizing effects of being directly concerned with getting money are frequently portrayed in the novels, especially in the figures of Lopez and Melmotte. Trollope's ideas on the subject are explicit when he describes the Kimberley diamond-hunters in his *South Africa* (1877):

> It is not only the thing procured but the manner of procuring it that makes or mars the nobility of the work. If there be an employment in which the labourer has actually to grovel in the earth it is this search for diamonds. . . . Let the man rise as high as he may in the

17. *An Autobiography* 20:365.
18. *The Duke's Children* 45:363-364.
19. *Phineas Finn*, "The Oxford Trollope" (London: Oxford University Press, 1949) 2:57:170. "I, personally, regard saving as a mistake, thinking that the improvement of the world generally is best furthered by a free use of the good things which are earned . . ." (*South Africa* 2:13).

calling, . . . still he stands by and sees the grit turned, — still he picks out the diamonds from the other dirt with his own fingers, and carries his produce about with him in his own pocket. If a man be working a coal mine, though he be himself the hardest worked as well as the head workman in the business, he is removed from actual contact with the coal. . . . But here . . . the feeling engendered . . . is carried so far that the mind never rests from business . . . ladies, and children, do turn dirt instead of making pretty needle-work or wholesome mud pies. . . . How shall a child shake off a stain which has been so early incurred?[20]

"A real gentleman . . . ," Lady Mabel Grex declares, "should never think of money at all."[21] The usual corollary of this for Trollope is the exclusion of the self-made man from the ranks of gentlemen. Such a man has been forced to think almost exclusively of making money over a long period, and this obsession, like any other obsession, isolates him from ordinary gentlemen. Already excluded by birth, he is further barred because he cannot understand or share values and attitudes created over many generations of freedom from the need to compete. Since the gentleman has not had to struggle, he has not needed to assert himself, and so has not become too individual or too obsessed with his own advancement to be accepted. A man or woman too determinedly seeking money or social recognition becomes discordant; like morbid jealousy, guilt, an unwholesome addiction to romance, or any of the other excluding states of mind that Trollope explores in his novels, this obsession militates against social harmony.

Trollope considered egalitarianism to be impracticable. Despite his personal disapproval of Disraeli—who was too flamboyantly an outsider—Disraeli's principles would serve equally well to summarize Trollope's:

. . . Like Gladstone he was "an out-and-out inequalitarian." He believed in a hierarchical ladder which

20. *South Africa* 2:202-203.
21. *The Duke's Children* 20:159.

certainly should not be inaccessible to men of talent . . . but which should on no account be laid flat or broken or removed. He thought that under such a dispensation people of all classes would enjoy greater freedom and happiness than they would get under the dead hand of a centralizing Benthamite bureaucracy, however "democratic."[22]

Trollope rejected the word *equality* as a description of his own political goals, "for the word is offensive, and presents to the imaginations of men ideas of communism, of ruin, and insane democracy." He defined himself as "an advanced conservative Liberal." He agreed with Conservatives that class distinctions were "of divine origin," and that sudden social changes were not desirable. But Conservatives, he argued, are opposed to any dimunition of inequality, while the Liberal "is alive to the fact that these distances are day by day becoming less, and he regards this continual dimunition as a series of steps towards that human millennium of which he dreams." Trollope approved not of equality but of "a tendency towards equality," and that tendency should always be braked "by the repressive action of a Conservative opponent."[23] "The theory of equality is very grand," Trollope makes his Solicitor-General say in *Lady Anna*,

22. Blake, *Disraeli*, p. 762. "I am for an aristocracy," Mr. Millbank tells Coningsby, "but a real one; a natural one . . . men whom a nation recognizes as the most eminent for virtue, talents and property, and, if you please, birth and standing in the land. They guide opinion; and, therefore, they govern. I am no leveller; I look upon an artificial equality as equally pernicious with a factitious aristocracy; both depressing the energies and checking the enterprise of a nation" (Benjamin Disraeli, *Coningsby, or, The New Generation* [New York: P. F. Collier and Son, n.d.] 4:4:155-157).

23. *An Autobiography* 16:293-294. See *The Duke's Children* 55:438-439: Frank Tregear is explaining political parties to Lord Silverbridge. Tregear is a Conservative, and so he is Palliser's, and Trollope's, opponent, but all three are in agreement about the value of a Conservative "brake" to slow down progress:

". . . . If the party that calls itself Liberal were to have all its own way who is there that doesn't believe that the church would go at once, then all distinction between boroughs, the House of Lords immediately afterwards, and after that the Crown?"

"Those are not my governor's [Palliser's] ideas."

". . . one to which all legislative and all human efforts should and must tend." But even if absolute equality were established,

> the inequality of men's minds and character would re-establish an aristocracy within twenty years. The energetic, the talented, the honest, and the unselfish will always be moving towards an aristocratic side of society, because their virtues will beget esteem, and esteem will beget wealth,—and wealth gives power for good offices. . . . At present . . . the sense of the country is in favour of an aristocracy of birth.[24]

The last phrase is an echo of Gladstone's claim during the Crimean War, that if England was "more aristocratic . . . than it ought to be, it is not owing to any legal privileges possessed by the aristocracy . . . it is owing partly perhaps to the strong prejudices in favour of the aristocracy which pervade all ranks and classes of the community."[25]

Trollope is aware that he is open to the charge of snobbery. He tries to explain himself in *An Autobiography* with perhaps more honesty than precision:

> There are places in life which can hardly be well filled except by "Gentlemen." The word is one the use of which almost subjects one to ignominy. If I say that a judge should be a gentleman, or a bishop, I am met with scornful allusion to "Nature's Gentlemen." Were I to make such an assertion with reference to the House of

---

"Your governor couldn't help himself. A Liberal party, with plenipotentiary power, must go on right away to the logical conclusion of its arguments. It is only the conservative feeling of the country which saves such men as your father from being carried headlong to ruin by their own machinery. . . ."

24. *Lady Anna* 47:500-501. "Make all men equal to-day, and God has so created them that they shall be all unequal to-morrow" (*Autobiography* 16:292). Frances Trollope said that "if some fine morning all classes were leveled, by night half the people would be making beds for the other half." See Lucy Poate Stebbins and Richard Poate Stebbins, *The Trollopes: The Chronicle of a Writing Family* (New York: Columbia University Press, 1945), p. 258.

25. Quoted in Briggs, *Victorian People*, p. 92.

Commons, nothing that I ever said again would receive the slightest attention. A man in public life could not do himself a greater injury than by saying in public that commissions in the army or navy, or berths in the Civil Service, should be given exclusively to gentlemen. He would be defied to define the term,—and would fail should he attempt to do so. But he would know what he meant, and so very probably would they who defied him. It may be that the son of the butcher in the village shall become as well fitted for employments requiring gentle culture as the son of the parson. Such is often the case. When such is the case, no one has been more prone to give the butcher's son all the welcome he has merited than I myself; but the chances are greatly in favour of the parson's son. The gates of the one class should be open to the other; but neither to one class or to the other can good be done by declaring that there are no gates, no barrier, no difference.[26]

John Hagan charges that Trollope had a "divided mind" on social questions, and complains that his "treatment of the whole question of individual social advancement answers fewer problems than it raises, and is not to be reduced to any coherent philosophy at all."[27] Trollope's theory is not precise because he distrusted precise definitions and simplifications. He was dealing with a civilization in flux, and attempting to define a moral and social standard that men could recognize. This standard was the gentleman. For Trollope, the gentleman has a greater stake in the preservation of civilization than anyone else, and is better equipped

26. *An Autobiography* 3:39-40.
27. John Hagan, "The Divided Mind of Anthony Trollope," *Nineteenth-Century Fiction* 14 (1959): 1-26. The passage quoted is on p. 4. Hagan attacks Trollope for failing to "separate principles from personalities" in *The American Senator*. But Trollope's novels are often about the impossibility of making such a separation. An abstract moral or rational principle is portrayed as inadequate or inappropriate in the context of a real situation. Sadleir describes Trollope as "the supreme novelist of acquiescence" (*Trollope: A Commentary*, p. 367). George Levine, in "Can You Forgive Him?" argues that Trollope's "techniques are expressions of that myth of the real which is more pervasive in his fiction than in the work of any other English realist. This is the myth that wisdom resides in learning the rules of society and acquiescing in them" (p. 6).

to work for that preservation. Furthermore, the gentleman is more likely to be a good man because his early training and easy circumstances can make virtue easier for him, while the man who must struggle with life can easily be corrupted by his struggles. Like Walter Bagehot, whose *The English Constitution* appeared in that year of conscious change, 1867, Trollope preferred that government be handled by "a select few," men who had "a life of leisure, a long culture, a varied experience, an existence by which the judgment is incessantly exercized and by which it may be incessantly improved."[28]

It is this doctrine of the gentleman and his role as preserver and embodiment of order that Trollope means when he speaks of the novelist's task of inculcating morality. No attempt to understand his novels and their methods can succeed without striving to understand his doctrine, which is intimately related to his use of theme, plot, and structure. To the modern reader, Trollope's ideal social order may seem reactionary, but we cannot condemn him because he does not share the democratic ideas of another time and place.

Trollope's social ideas really do function within the novels, and the novels, in fact, depend upon those ideas. They may never have been realistic in terms of the real world, but in the imaginary world of the novels they are consistent. Since Trollope's created social world is governed by his social theories, his ideal gentleman is artistically valid.

Trollope is well aware that the word *gentleman*—like the words *lady* and *nobleman*—is both an abstract and specific noun. The difference between the two offers him continual opportunity for irony. Generally speaking, he does not separate the moral meaning of the word from its social meaning, and the term is not fully operative unless both are present. It is possible to condemn a man whose social rank is

28. Bagehot, *The English Constitution*, quoted in Briggs, *Victorian People*, p. 93. Briggs devotes his Chapter 4 to comparing the doctrines of Trollope and Bagehot. I am also indebted to Briggs's discussion of Disraeli in Chapter 10.

high when he lacks the gentle or noble virtues, but such a man is not easily condemned. Even Plantagenet Palliser, great Liberal though he is, finds it difficult. He knows that Lord Grex is "a wretched unprincipled old man, bad all round; . . . But the blue blood and the rank were there."[29] And society continues to receive Lord Brotherton despite his wickedness.

Trollope manoeuvres in the uncertain moral, social, and linguistic area created by the word's dual implications. He would basically accept William Harrison's social definition, made in 1577: a gentleman is one who "can live without manuell labour."[30] The novels examine and attempt to refine this definition. Plantagenet Palliser, Duke of Omnium, is clearly a gentleman; Dan Goarly, a rascally and unsuccessful farmer in *The American Senator*, clearly is not. Larry Twentyman is a more prosperous farmer in the same novel, and a much more attractive person, even though "It was the foible of his life to be esteemed a gentleman, and his poor ambition to be allowed to live among men of higher social standing than himself";[31] when Lord Rufford invites him to dinner and is kind to him, he becomes more highly considered socially, and some of the local squires begin to entertain him occasionally, though he is still not fully recognized. Mr. Neefit, the wealthy breeches-maker (in *Ralph the Heir*) tries desperately to gain a gentleman for a son-in-law; he is not a gentleman himself, both because he is in trade and because he does not really understand a gentleman's values; a tailor, Trollope says in *London Tradesmen*, is often "gentleman-like," but "were you to examine him closely, you would find in his features some trace of the

---

29. *The Duke's Children* 48:391.
30. William Harrison, *Description of England . . . The Second and Third Books*, ed. Frederick J. Furnivall (London: New Shakespeare Society, 1877), Series 6, no. 1, Book 2, chap. 5, p. 128. Harrison admits lawyers, university students, physicians, and "captains," as well as all noblemen, clergymen, and knights. "Gentlemen be those whome their race and bloud [or at the leaft their vertues] doo make noble and knowne. . . ."
31. *The American Senator* 48:328.

retail tradesman. There would be to be discerned there those lines of little but still anxious thought which comes from the daily making of money in small parcels."[32] The Marquis of Brotherton (*Is He Popenjoy?*) does not qualify; his high rank and wealth are negated by vicious habits. The American Senator is a good man of high position, "but . . . not looking quite like an English gentleman."[33] In England he is an oddity; he misunderstands and is misunderstood. Trollope writes a short story about Miss Ophelia Gledd, from Boston's Beacon Hill, to ask his "readers to answer this question—was Ophelia Gledd a lady?"[34] Father Barham, in *The Way We Live Now*, is a gentleman by birth and education, but he has isolated himself by becoming a Catholic, and he is so obsessed with this choice that he cannot live in harmony with ordinary Englishmen.

These cases all make it easier to decide who is not a gentleman than to arrive at any accurate definition, but they help us to recognize some of Trollope's requirements. The gentleman must have fine feelings, a good education, and social position. None of these qualities should be over-developed, for a man whose feelings are too fine becomes thin-skinned and useless. Palliser's sensitivity prevents that easy intercourse with his fellows which Cardinal Newman considered to be necessary if a group of men were to work together effectively.[35]

32. *London Tradesmen*, pp. 3-4. Compare *Miss Mackenzie* 1:2-3: "Sir John Ball was the first baronet, and . . . had simply been . . . a political Lord Mayor in the leather business; but, then, his business had been undoubtedly wholesale; and a man who gets himself to be made a baronet cleanses himself from the stains of trade, even though he have traded in leather."

33. *The American Senator* 16:105. The Oxford text incorrectly reads "not yet looking quite. . . ." The Random House edition (New York, 1940) is correct (p. 107).

34. *Lotta Schmidt, and Other Stories* (London: Alexander Strahan, 1867), "Miss Ophelia Gledd," p. 321. Trollope's story, querying a non-Englishwoman's right to be considered an English lady, was his slightly odd contribution to *A Welcome*, a volume of poetry and prose published to welcome the Danish Princess Alexandra when she arrived in England to marry the Prince of Wales.

35. "A far more essential unity was that of antecedents.—a common

A man who is too proud of his own social position, or too learned, can also be socially isolated; learning can be a particularly serious impediment. In his *Life of Cicero* (written after 1877; published 1880), Trollope sees the Roman orator as a man in equilibrium with his society, and praises him for that easy intercourse with his fellows which the novelist valued so highly. "What a man he would have been for London life!" Trollope exclaims. "How he would have enjoyed his club. . . . How popular he would have been at the Carlton." Trollope admires Cicero because, like Palmerston, he could get along with his peers and so could practice politics successfully. He insists that all Cicero's learning "was with him a game of play," that "Cicero of the world, Cicero the polished gentleman"[36] never took his studies so seriously as to let them interfere with the business of life.

Trollope defined the gentleman, then, not only as a virtuous individual, but also as participating actively in social and political life. Like Carlyle in *Sartor Resartus*, Trollope urges a move away from excessive self-consciousness—which leads to isolation—and toward integrating and working with society. The gentleman must accept social responsibilities. Sir William Patterson defends aristocracy to the radical tailor in *Lady Anna* by reminding him that it is wrong to think "that there is not hard work done at the one pole [of

---

history, common memories, and intercourse of mind with mind in the past, and a progress and increase of that intercourse in the present. . . . Mr. Palmer had many conditions of authority and influence . . . [but no] insight into the force of personal influence and congeniality of thought in carrying out a religious theory. . . . Dr. Pusey . . . was to the Movement all that Mr. Rose might have been, with that indispensable addition, which was wanting to Mr. Rose, the intimate friendship and the familiar daily society of the persons who had commenced it" (John Henry Cardinal Newman, *Apologia Pro Vita Sua*, ed. Martin J. Svaglic [Oxford: Clarendon Press, 1967], Ch. 2. "History of My Religious Opinions from 1833 to 1839," pp. 47, 65). Compare Terence Kenny's description of Newman's basic political attitude in *The Political Thought of John Henry Newman* (London: Longmans, Green, 1957): "The state was a unity of mind for him . . ." (p. 164).

36. *The Life of Cicero* (London: Chapman and Hall, 1880) 1:1:37-38; 2:12:339-340. See apRoberts, *The Moral Trollope*, pp. 62-63; 67-68.

society] as well as the other."[37] Plantagenet Palliser and Roger Carbury are two examples of the dutiful and responsible gentleman, accepting the obligations of his rank. Palliser devotes himself unstintingly to the government of his country, believing that "the British House of Commons is everything. . . . That and the Constitution are everything."[38] Carbury performs the no less important task of governing his estate wisely and well, and is aware of its needs and the needs of its people. Like Disraeli's Coningsby, they understand that the "essence of all tenure is the performance of duty."[39] Both men are immune from the aristocratic vice of idleness, a vice Sir William Patterson defines as the necessary waste that must inevitably occur whenever something is well done.[40]

For Trollope, *political* and *social* are almost interchangeable terms. Cousin Henry's brief and wretched reign as Squire of Llanfeare is a political as well as a social outrage because he lacks the social talents to rule as well as the right to rule. In the Palliser cycle, political power is closely involved with social relationships. Trollope was in agreement with Walter Bagehot, who planned a book that would study the family connections between political leaders and the effect of those connections on Victorian political history. The anatomy of a small town like Dillsborough in *The American Senator*, and the analysis of the Scarborough family tree, reveal the intense politics of these miniature societies, the complicated stress and balance systems through which they exist.

The gentleman must serve society in order to justify his social privileges, for only by doing so can he prove his possession of the moral traits that should accompany his rank. His service will be political in character, whether he enters the Church, Parliament, or one of the other larger

---

37. *Lady Anna* 47:499.
38. *Can You Forgive Her?* 2:80:417.
39. Disraeli, *Coningsby* 8:3:374.
40. *Lady Anna* 47:501.

political complexes, or whether he remains in the country to govern his own little estate or parish. In either case, he must take care of his inferiors and live in harmony with his peers. Trollope seems to prefer the career of the country gentle-man who dwells upon his own acres among his own tenants, perhaps because a parliamentary career can engender ambi-tion for power. This is Palliser's temptation; and his public career, useful and well-intentioned though it is, does not fully satisfy him. Furthermore, a parliamentary career, noble in theory, is in practice open to men who are not gentlemen in any sense of the word, and the presence of such men in Parliament can render the good man ineffectual at times. The squire does not suffer from such limitations. He is bounded only by good sense, tradition, and the wel-fare of his people. If he is really one with his estate—as Roger Carbury is "Carbury of Carbury"—he will be aware of tradition and respect it. He will seek the consent of his people and recognize their welfare.

Trollope often draws for us a picture of his ideal country gentleman and squire. Here is Sir Harry Hotspur of Humblethwaite:

> Sir Harry Hotspur of Humblethwaite was a mighty person in Cumberland, and one who well understood of what nature were the duties, and of what sort the mag-nificence, which his position as a great English com-moner required of him. He had twenty thousand a year derived from land. His forefathers had owned the same property in Cumberland for nearly four centuries. . . . He . . . had always lived among men and women not only of high rank, but also of high character. He had kept race-horses when he was young . . . with no view to profit, calculating fairly their cost as a part of his annual outlay, and thinking that it was the proper thing to do for the improvement of horses and for the amusement of the people. He had been in Parliament, but had made no figure there, and had given it up . . . the life that he led was led at Humblethwaite, and there he was a great man, with a great domain around him,—with many tenants, with a world of dependants among whom he spent his

wealth freely, saving little, but lavishing nothing that was not his own to lavish,—understanding that his enjoyment was to come from the comfort and respect of others, for whose welfare, as he understood it, the good things of this world had been bestowed upon him. . . . An only son had died just as he had reached his majority. When the day came on which all Humblethwaite and the surrounding villages were to have been told to rejoice and make merry because another man of the Hotspurs was ready to take the reins of the house as soon as his father should have been gathered to his fathers, the poor lad lay a-dying. . . . Sir Harry bore the blow bravely, though none who do not understand the system well can conceive how the natural grief of the father was increased by the disappointment which had fallen upon the head of the house. But the old man bore it well . . . still spending money, because it was good for others that it should be spent. . . . He was still constant with Mr. Lanesby, the steward, because it was his duty to know everything that was done on the property. . . . While his boy had lived, the responsibility of his property had had nothing for him but charms . . . he would have taught that son, had already begun to teach him . . . that all this was to be given to him, not that he might put it into his own belly, or wear it on his own back, or even spend it as he might list himself, but that he might so live as to do his part in maintaining that order of gentlehood in England, by which England had become—so thought Sir Harry—the proudest and the greatest and the justest of nations.[41]

The benevolently paternalistic feudalism of this ideal is close to the theories of Disraeli and his friends of the "Young England" movement in the early 1840s; they, in turn, drew on the novels of Walter Scott, which celebrated the bonds of mutual loyalty and obligation between landlord and tenant, chieftain and follower. In *Sybil* (1845), Disraeli praised "the territorial constitution of England as the only basis and security for local government"[42]—that is, a government not

---

41. *Sir Harry Hotspur of Humblethwaite* 1:1-5.
42. Benjamin Disraeli, *Sybil, or, The Two Nations* (New York: P. F. Collier and Son, n.d.) 4:14:281.

dominated by the commercial interests of the metropolis, with profit rather than the people's good as their chief aim, and not centralized in order to suppress local needs and local loyalties. England's "territorial constitution" meant to Disraeli that political power should belong primarily to those who owned and cared for the land. They should have power not for that self-aggrandizement against which Sir Harry Hotspur warned his son, ". . . not to gratify the pride or pamper the luxury of the proprietors of land," as Disraeli told the House of Commons in 1846,

> but because in a territorial constitution you and those whom you have succeeded have found the only security for self-government, the only barrier against that centralizing system which has taken root in other countries.[43]

In Disraeli's novels, the heroes endorse these theories, and realize that, as Coningsby told his grandfather, "the essence of all tenure is the performance of duty,"[44] a theory Disraeli reemphasized when he wrote a general preface to his novels in 1870: "The feudal system may have worn out, but its main principle, that the tenure of property should be the fulfillment of duty, is the essence of good government."[45] Disraeli's Tancred thinks often of his "duties as a

43. Quoted in Blake, *Disraeli*, p. 281.
44. *Coningsby* 8:3:374. See note 39, above.
45. Benjamin Disraeli, "General Preface," *Lothair* (New York: P. F. Collier and Son, n.d.), p. 5. Compare *Doctor Thorne* 1:11-12: ". . . the old symbols remained, and may such symbols long remain among us; they are still lovely and fit to be loved. They tell us of the true and manly feelings of other times; and to him who can read aright, they explain more fully, more truly than any written history can do, how Englishmen have become what they are. England is not yet a commercial country in the sense in which that epithet is used for her; and let us still hope that she will not soon become so. She might surely as well be called feudal England, or chivalrous England. If in western civilized Europe there does exist a nation among whom there are high signors, and with whom the owners of the land are the true aristocracy, the aristocracy that is trusted as being best and fittest to rule, that nation is the English. Choose out the ten leading men of each great European people . . . and then select the ten in England

great proprietor of the soil,"[46] and the heroes of *The Young Duke, Henrietta Temple, Venetia*, and *Lothair* all settle down on their estates to perform these duties. Characters in many of Trollope's later novels make the same decision to live on their estates, as in *Ralph the Heir, The Way We Live Now, Is He Popenjoy? The American Senator, The Duke's Children*, and *John Caldigate*. Both Disraeli and Trollope saw the gentleman settled on his own estate as one whose sense of belonging to a specific place would preserve him from the attractions of false and ephemeral ideas. He has an instinctive moral and social steadiness, which works to preserve the traditional social order.

This is a conservative doctrine, but neither Disraeli nor Trollope saw the aristocratic or land-owning class as a closed one, nor did they consider that the ownership of land by the old families was necessarily a permanent thing. They both recognized and endorsed slow but continual change. The first and last passages below are Trollope's; the others are Disraeli's:

> . . . the broad-acred squire, with his throng of tenants, is comparatively a modern invention. The country gentleman of two hundred years ago farmed the land he held. As years have rolled on, the strong have swallowed the weak,—one strong man having eaten up half-a-dozen weak men. And so the squire has been made. Then the strong squire becomes a baronet and a lord,—till he lords it a little too much, and a Manchester warehouseman buys him out. The strength of the country probably lies in the fact that the change is ever being made, but is never made suddenly.[47]

> . . . the new member of a manufacturing district has his

---

whose names are best known as those of leading statesmen; the result will show in which country there still exists the closest attachment to, the sincerest trust in, the old feudal and now so-called landed interests."

46. Benjamin Disraeli, *Tancred, or, The New Crusade* (New York: P. F. Collier and Son, n.d.), p. 5.

47. *Ralph the Heir* 2:49:252.

eye already upon a neighboring park, avails himself of his political position to become a county magistrate, meditates upon a baronetcy, and dreams of a coroneted descendant.[48]

It is not true that England is governed by an aristocracy in the common acceptation of the term. England is governed by an aristocratic principle. The aristocracy of England absorbs all aristocracies, and receives every man in every order and every class who defers to the principle of our society, which is to aspire and to excel.[49]

". . . Our peerage is being continually recruited from the ranks of the people, and hence it gets its strength."
"Is it so?"
"There is no greater mistake than to suppose that inferiority of birth is a barrier to success in this country."[50]

Gradual change preserves the health of the little rural commonwealth which is often, in Trollope's novels, "the State in miniature, the kingly power being represented, in the present instance, by Lord Lufton and his mother at Framley Court. Between the Court and the Parsonage the relations described reflected the union of the civil and the spiritual authority."[51]

It is true that at heart Trollope is a conservative who dislikes that change he recognizes as inevitable and even desirable. He claims that he "always regarded" Julian the Apostate's return to the pagan gods "as good old fashioned conservatism, but Xtians have always been so very bitter mouthed against those who have left us or would not come to us."[52] Like Disraeli's, his "territorial constitution" in

---

48. Benjamin Disraeli, "The Spirit of Whiggism" (1836), in *Whigs and Whiggism*, ed. William Hutcheon (London: John Murray, 1913), p. 349.
49. Benjamin Disraeli, *Lord George Bentinck; a Political Biography* (1852; London: Longmans, Green, 1881) 27:400.
50. *The Duke's Children* 48:390.
51. Escott, pp. 138-139.
52. *Letters* (Trollope to an unknown correspondent, 29 March 1867), p. 198.

practice is closely bound up with "traditionary influences" as guarantors of England's "honour, her liberty, her order, her authority, and her wealth."[53] John Caldigate suffers because he sells the right to inherit his family estate, and Trollope mourns when Humblethwaite goes from the Hotspur family. In *Ralph the Heir*, *Cousin Henry*, and *Mr. Scarborough's Family* he is critical of the character who tries to alter the entail of an estate—the legal instrument that determines the inheritance of the land—and in each of these novels, such tampering leads to evil results. Despite his endorsement of change, he prefers continuity. He arranges things to save Greshamsbury from the full consequences of Squire Gresham's inability to perform his duties properly; the "new men," the Scatcherds who control the estate financially, die; their money goes to Mary Thorne, who marries the Squire's heir and ensures that the Greshams will flourish again on their ancestral lands. In the final analysis, he is emotionally attached to tradition. So is Plantagenet Palliser, even though he is a leader of the Liberal party. Palliser approvingly tells the American girl, Isabel Boncassen, that the peerage is "continually recruited from the ranks of the people," but Trollope tells us that "in discussing such matters generally," Palliser never mingled "his own private feelings, his own pride of race and name, his own ideas of what was due to his ancient rank with the political creed by which his conduct in public life was governed."[54] Palliser strenuously resists the recruitment of Isabel and of Frank Tregear into his own family.

Trollope's conservative principles make him antipathetic to some modern readers but he offers coherent reasons for holding them. He believed that "equality," and most of the other social solutions offered by the reformers of his day, were based on unprovable theories—on a rigid Benthamite rationality that did not understand the real world. Cicero, he tells us, wisely "loved the affairs of the world too well to

53. Blake, *Disraeli*, p. 282.
54. *The Duke's Children* 48:390.

trust them to philosophy."[55] Disraeli's Contarini Fleming, who distrusted "imaginary principles" which "establish systems that contradict the common sense of mankind,"[56] would have agreed, and the last sentence of *Coningsby* hopes that the young man and his friends will "denounce to a perplexed and disheartened world the frigid theories of a generalizing age."[57]

Trollope was not convinced that the theoretical reforms offered by some of his contemporaries would solve society's problems, and they could create new problems. He is not always fair in arguing this: in *The Three Clerks* he attacks competitive examinations for Civil Service positions by making Alaric Tudor, the successful candidate, a speculator and embezzler; such an examination will promote the man who is clever but unprincipled. Until practical and certain social solutions could be found, it seemed best to adhere to traditional methods. Writing to the Australian historian George William Rusden in 1872, Trollope praised the apparent contradictions of the British Constitution, "worked by usage in direct opposition to the theory," and argued that because "apparent contradictions are admitted, . . . a gradual development of the power of the people is enabled to go on without abrupt changes in our traditional theories, [so] that we have no revolutions and remain loyal and contented."[58]

For Trollope, the gentleman made society stable, and so it is essential that a gentleman share society's values, and conform to society's ways. He must think and act as do his peers. Like Tennyson's Sir Balin, he must feel "his being move / In music with his order."[59] This endorsement of

55. *Life of Cicero* 2:315.
56. Benjamin Disraeli, *Contarini Fleming* (New York: P. F. Collier and Son, n.d.), p. 5.
57. *Coningsby* 9:7:432.
58. *Letters* (4 June 1872), pp. 293-294.
59. *Idylls of the King*, "Balin and Balan," lines 207-208. Tennyson makes the Knights of the Round Table conformists; in one of their most exalted moments, each loses his individual identity and they all share "A momentary likeness of the King" ("The Coming of Arthur," line 270). Compare

conformity finds its antithesis in Trollope's unfavorable treatment of the individualist. When Trollope approves of a character who is independent or rebellious, it is almost invariably in a context of marriage. Some of his men and women refuse to mary as their guardians recommend, and sometimes he endorses these refusals. But this endorsement does not indicate an approval of the social rebel. It often turns out that the guardian has projected a marriage that would in some way be socially wrong. The young man or woman in question is so placed that there is some discrepancy between their apparent and their true social status, usually because their habits and associates are not those to which they are formally entitled. In such cases, they "rebel" by conforming to their sense of their true social identity, and the general society eventually accepts them at their own valuation. For example, Lady Anna has been brought up in the household of a tailor, and chooses to marry the tailor's son rather than the earl her family prefers; despite her title, she does not feel at home among aristocrats. Mary Masters, in *The American Senator*, has spent much of her time with Lady Ushant; though her stepmother urges her to marry a rich farmer, she refuses and makes a more appropriate match with the local squire. In other cases, a selfish guardian opposes a marriage out of neurotic possessiveness, as when Mrs. Bolton opposes her daughter's marriage with John Caldigate, or Mr. Whittlestaff, in *An Old Man's Love*, tries to keep his young ward for himself. A young man or woman conforms to society's general practices in rebelling against this kind of opposition.

Those who read Byron attract Trollope's disapproval—mild disapproval for Johnny Eames (*The Small House at Allington*), strong disapproval for Lizzie Eustace. In all his

Carlyle, "Independence, in all kinds, is rebellion," *Sartor Resartus* (New York: Charles Scribner's Sons, n.d.), 3:5:186. For discussions of Trollope and Carlyle, see *The New Zealander*, ed. N. John Hall (Oxford: The Clarendon Press, 1972); Wilson B. Gragg, "Trollope and Carlyle," *Nineteenth-Century Fiction* 13 (1958): 266-270; N. John Hall, "Trollope and Carlyle," *Nineteenth-Century Fiction* 27 (1972): 197-205.

works, he is hostile toward characters who possess traits associated with the Byronic hero, the individualist who refuses to conform. Such a character is, admittedly, more interesting than the ordinarily worthy hero or heroine. We are more interested in Melmotte and Sir Felix Carbury than in Roger Carbury, more interested in bad Lizzie Eustace than in good Lucy Morris. But the very fact that these characters do stand out shows that they are refusing to conform. To attract interest is to be unusual. To be unusual is to be something other than an ordinary gentleman. "A man ought to be common," the hero of *An Old Man's Love* tells himself, in a remark that sums up Trollope's own belief. "A man who is uncommon is either a dandy or a buffoon."[60]

The modern reader must remind himself that the man of ordinary goodness and ordinary talents who is endorsed in Trollope's novels represents a social ideal, just as Achilles and Odysseus do. The impulsive warrior, or the prudent explorer, were ideal types in Homeric Greece; the Victorian ideal was the decent, unobtrusive English gentleman, who sustained the nation morally and economically:

> Most blameless is he, centered in the sphere
> Of common duties, decent not to fail
> In offices of tenderness. . . .[61]

The romantic Ulysses sounds a little patronizing about the stolidly Victorian Telemachus. Despite Disraeli's success as novelist and politician, Victorians usually distrusted flamboyance and brilliance, the signs of the romantic hero. "Dullness is our line," Trollope declared, "as cleverness is that of the French. Woe to the English people if they ever forget that."[62]

A distrust of the romantic hero begins to appear in Europe after the first post-Napoleonic generation had

---

60. *An Old Man's Love* 2:21-22. See, however, Donald D. Stone's argument that Trollope is ambivalent about Byronism, in "Trollope, Byron, and the Conventionalities."

61. Tennyson "Ulysses," lines 39-41 (written c. 1833, published 1842).

62. Quoted in Briggs, *Victorian People*, p. 113.

grown old enough to examine the events of 1790 to 1815 with some detachment. We are not surprised to find in Byron, who did so much to define the romantic hero, an enthusiasm for Napoleon, while Newman and Tennyson, who tried to define the modern gentleman, both admired the unspectacular Duke of Wellington. The reaction against the Napoleonic-Byronic-romantic hero, which on the Continent produced Pushkin's *The Queen of Spades*, the *Comédie humaine*, *Le Rouge et le noir*, *War and Peace*, and *Crime and Punishment*, finds its British expression in Thackeray's "novel without a hero," Dickens's romantic wastrels, and in the quietly decent protagonists of Trollope.

Trollope's acceptance of the world as he found it, and his dislike of romantic heroics, can easily become an impediment to taking him seriously as an artist. The modern reader is accustomed to regarding the artist as an outsider, a rebel. We have almost lost the ability to deal with writers who accept social and artistic conventions and create their art out of that acceptance. If we discuss them, we tend to emphasize their value as indices to social and cultural attitudes rather than as artists. Trollope does have undoubted value as a guide to the attitudes of his age, but he is not a passive recorder. In a sense, he is a propagandist, positively committed to the Victorian ideal of order, and his art is continually and systematically pervaded by this ideal. He saw Victorian civilization as a positive achievement, though it could be manipulated by outsiders and adventurers. Even these could often be routed by the exercise of collective common sense. Civilization was vulnerable, and it had enemies within and without. Its defenders could be fooled or corrupted, or could simply give up the fight. "It may be well, even for us, to look around us, and see whether our walls are all sound"; he wrote in *The New Zealander*, "whether our towers stand fast; if our watchman be always awake, and our powder always dry."[63] Nevertheless, Trollope believed in his society and in its ability to enforce its

63. *The New Zealander* 1:4.

standards and solve its problems. He believed that a man lived most freely when he conformed to the generally accepted idea of decent behavior.

Among his contemporaries, Trollope is perhaps closest to Tennyson, for both are laureates of society, and celebrate society's epitome, the just and decent gentleman. The pattern of the *Idylls of the King* seems repeated in some of Trollope's novels. There are resemblances between the stern and just King Arthur, the preserver of order, and such men as Palliser and Roger Carbury; between the usurping and romantic Lancelot and Trollope's Fitzgeralds, Lopezes, Vavasors, and George Hotspurs; and between the frivolous Guinevere and women like Lady Glencora, Hetta Carbury, Lizzie Eustace, and Arabella Trefoil. If Tennyson created King Arthur by putting Prince Albert into armor, Trollope reversed the process, for his Plantagenet Palliser is King Arthur in a well-tailored Prince Albert.

Trollope provides his own reading of *Idylls of the King* in *The Eustace Diamonds*, when he makes Frank Greystock point out to the enthusiastic Lizzie the impracticability of a "fanatic and foolish" romantic quest:

> ". . . Arthur did not go on the search, because he had a job of work to do, by the doing of which the people around him might perhaps be somewhat benefited."
> "I like Launcelot better than Arthur," said Lizzie.
> "So did the Queen," replied Frank.
> "Your useful, practical man, who attends vestries, and sits at Boards, and measures out his gifts to others by the ounce, never has any heart. Has he, Frank?"
> "I don't know what heart means. I sometimes fancy that it is a talent for getting into debt, and running away with other men's wives."[64]

What Trollope represented to his contemporaries as an artist and as a defender of social order is summed up in a passage from the autobiography of W. P. Frith, the famous Victorian painter. Frith is describing one of those documen-

64. *The Eustace Diamonds* 1:19:174.

tary pictures of public events that earned him his popularity: "The Private View of the Royal Academy, 1881," which shows the leaders of Victorian society inspecting the year's new paintings. Gladstone, Browning, Lily Langtry, and many others are present. But the picture is a moral statement as well as a record of an event. Frith uses his canvas to attack those individualists who were beginning to rebel against Victorian society's public art and conformity:

> I therefore planned a group, consisting of a well-known apostle of the beautiful [Oscar Wilde], with a herd of eager worshippers surrounding him. He is supposed to be explaining his theories to willing ears, taking some picture of the Academy walls for his text. A group of well-known artists are watching the scene. On the left of the composition is a family of pure esthetes absorbed in affected study of the pictures. Near them stands Anthony Trollope, whose homely figure affords a striking contrast to the eccentric forms near him.[65]

The picture becomes one of the manifestoes of Victorian realism, a proclamation and an example of an aesthetic theory that defined the artist's mission as the objective portrayal of the material world together with a clearly defined moral attitude toward that world. Trollope is chosen to symbolize that theory.

Mere objective realism is not enough: when Ralph Newton visits the Royal Academy, Trollope is gently sardonic about his taste:

> "That's a fine picture," he said, pointing up at an enormous portrait of the Master of the B B, in a red coat, seated square on a seventeen-hand high horse, with his hat off, and the favourite hounds of his pack around him. "That's by Grant," said Gregory. "I don't know that I care for that kind of thing." "It's as like as it can stare," said Ralph, who appreciated the red coat, and the well-groomed horse, and the finely-shaped hounds. . . .

65. W. P. Frith, *My Autobiography and Reminiscences* (New York: Harper and Brothers, 1888) 1:441.

"That gentleman in the red coat is my cousin's favourite," said Gregory.

"I don't care a bit about that," said Clarissa.

"That's because you don't hunt," said Ralph.[66]

Writing on "The Genius of Nathaniel Hawthorne" in the *North American Review* (September 1879), Trollope emphasizes the moral purpose of realistic art; photographic realism is not enough. He describes his own attempts to draw "'Little pictures" which would make his readers "feel that they were dealing with people whom they might probably have known, but so to do it that the every-day good to be found among them should allure, and the every-day evil repel."[67]

Frith's famous "Derby Day" (1858) offers some suggestive parallels to a Trollope novel in content, composition, and moral attitude. When "Derby Day" was first shown, the *Athenaeum* called it "a panoramic epitome of English character in the year 1856."[68] Though he was meticulously accurate, Frith did not paint an event. He chose instead to paint a picture of English society and its attitudes. He ignored the race itself to show us the fashionable spectators, who are participating in one of society's rituals. The canvas is full of apparently irrelevant details—like Trollope, Frith was often criticized for an alleged lack of organization and structure. But the apparently unrelated portraits and episodes that make up "Derby Day" are all part of a varied but carefully organized pattern, which a twentieth-century critic has called "a wonderfully harmonious, decorative and indivisible unity of design."[69] Trollope's panoramic novels are simi-

---

66. *Ralph the Heir* 2:49:256-257. Sir Francis Grant (1803-78) specialized in equestrian portraits, especially of huntsmen.

67. *North American Review* 274 (September 1879): 204-205. In this essay, Trollope declared that American writers are less realistic than British writers: "On our side of the water we deal more with beef and ale, and less with dreams" (p. 207).

68. *Athenaeum* (1 May 1858), p. 565.

69. S. C. Kaines Smith, *Painters of England* (London: The Medici Society, 1934), p. 85.

larly patterned and similarly unified. And both the painter and the novelist celebrate conformity, and pity or condemn those who are excluded.

"In "Derby Day" the whole of English society is presented; "The Private View" portrays only what we now call the Establishment. Both pictures organize reality, and use pictorial analogies to emphasize moral and social doctrine, as Trollope uses his multiple plots analogically. In "Derby Day" two self-absorbed lovers dressed in white echo the white shirts of some absorbed picnickers; they are paralleled by color and attitude. In "The Private View," Frith has placed Wilde near the observer's extreme right of the canvas, and Trollope near the extreme left. Each man wears a top hat, and each holds the Academy catalogue. (Trollope is writing notes in his, while Wilde seems to be commenting on the text.) At Wilde's left, and at Trollope's right, at the extremities of the picture, there are women dressed in russet clothing; at Wilde's right there is a woman in a very full rose gown, at Trollope's left a child in muted red. The two groups are paralleled by color and stance to force the viewer to recognize the antithesis between them.

Trollope's remarks about making "subsidiary plots . . . take their places as part of one and the same work," and the simile he uses, "many figures on a canvas which shall not . . . seem to form themselves into separate pictures,"[70] seem to echo Frith's boast that he never had "difficulty in composing great numbers of figures into a more or less harmonious whole."[71] Both men use their recurrent figures to create a sense of a complex and interrelated social world. They celebrate the homogeneity of upper class society, and show how uncomfortably the occasional eccentric stands out. They exalt society's power of suppressing the rebel. In "The Private View," Wilde and the "pure aesthetes" to Trollope's left are excluded from the world of Gladstone, Huxley, Ellen Terry, Henry Irving, John Bright, Browning,

70. *An Autobiography* 12:238-239.
71. W. P. Frith, *My Autobiography and Reminiscences* 1:192.

Archbishop Thomson, Lord Chief Justice Coleridge, Tenniel, Sir William Harcourt, Sir Julius Benedict, and Baroness Burdett-Coutts, who surround the rebels to diminish their importance and stress their isolation.

Trollope's rebels and outsiders fail to disturb society very much. They are either absorbed by society, or in some way they become incapable of causing further trouble. Trollope rarely treats them melodramatically; he domesticates them, so that they can fit into the real world of his novels. Wilkie Collins makes his weak wicked baronet, Sir Percival Glyde, die in a burning church; Trollope's Sir Felix Carbury, equally weak but capable of very little wickedness, goes tamely off to Germany to live on a small remittance. Dickens's Rochester is invaded by murder, but Barchester's invaders are a vulgar bishop's wife and an unscrupulous chaplain. Melmotte, in *The Way We Live Now*, may be named for the tormented hero of Charles Maturin's *Melmoth the Wanderer* (1820), but Trollope replaces pacts with the devil and terror with financial chicanery and vulgarity; a shady financier is a probable social and moral threat.

When Trollope portrays such characters as Lopez and Melmotte as morally objectionable, and implies that they are Jews, he seems open to the charge that he is using racial slurs and stereotypes. In fact, Trollope never does tell us unequivocally that either of these men is a Jew. He simply says that their origins are mysterious and not English, and that society believes them to be Jews and so treats them with suspicion. He is portraying—uncritically, to be sure—a social prejudice, rather than himself endorsing that prejudice. Madame Max Goesler *is* Jewish and he portrays her as a person of high honor and courage. Even Lopez and Melmotte are not portrayed as Jewish stereotypes in the way that Fagin is portrayed. They are simply adventurers who may be Jewish; the rumor makes them a little more exotic and mysterious, and a little more like the despised Disraeli. In *Nina Balatka* (written 1865) Trollope makes it clear that for him the issue is between the man who belongs and the rootless adventurer. Although he disapproves of the marriage between Emily Wharton and Lopez in *The Prime Minister*, here he approves of one between the Christian Nina and his Jewish protagonist, Anton Trendellsohn. Lopez is unscrupulous, and Trendellsohn is honest, but Trendellsohn is also a man with a recognized place in society. His family have lived in Prague—the setting of the story—for many years, and "all who knew Prague well, knew the house in which the Trendellsohns lived." Trollope reminds the reader of the stability of the Jewish community in Prague, and their just pride in their synagogue, "the oldest place of worship belonging to the Jews in Europe, as they delight to tell you."[72]

In his novels, Trollope says little about the great political and intellectual issues of his day. He believed that both sides in any controversy were likely to be right; a contemporary reviewer of *Phineas Redux* said that the novel illustrated "another form of the immortal thesis that there are two sides to every question, and that there is so much to be said for each of them that it is really rather hard to tell them apart."[73] Though he stood for Parliament as a Liberal, he does not show the two political parties as essentially very different: Liberals are committed to moderate progress, Conservatives keep that progress from too rapid an acceleration. Lord Silverbridge cannot see much difference between Palliser, who is a conservative Liberal, and Frank Tregear, a liberal Conservative,[74] and the reader is inclined to agree. Escott describes Trollope's own "natural prejudices" as "always those of aristocratic and reactionary Toryism,"[75] and adds that he was able to "pass for a Liberal . . . when Liberalism took its principles from the reactionary moderates rather than the progressives."[76] Like his hero, Lord

---

72. *Nina Balatka* 1:9.
73. Edith Simcox, *Academy* 5 (7 February 1874): 141.
74. *The Duke's Children* 55:438-439. See also 76:600.
75. Escott, p. 166.
76. Escott, p. 177.

Palmerston, he could be described as "a Whig more Tory than the Tories."[77] Perhaps his lack of sharply defined political doctrine is one more way in which he reflects the period. From 1852 until shortly before Trollope's death, the most important political issue often seemed to be the personal antipathy between Gladstone and Disraeli, which dominated public life for a generation.[78] Many of Disraeli's contemporaries believed that he had no political principles or program except the desire to gain and retain office; Gladstone often saw political problems in moral rather than practical terms.

In the Palliser series, though Palliser is a Liberal politician we have only a vague notion of his politics. The important thing is his personal worth, and his desire to serve the nation. He proves that society can produce decent leaders, who can run the government competently. Society in fact governs itself. What happens in the House of Commons is simply a ratification of society's collective decisions: ". . . there is an outside power,—the people, or public opinion . . . the country will have to go very much as that outside power chooses. Here, in Parliament, everybody will be as Conservative as the outside will let them."[79]

Nor do the less immediate issues of the day receive much attention in the novels. Trollope does not, for example, mention the Darwin controversy—in an 1868 letter he declared himself quite ignorant of the subject[80]—and he is only desultorily interested in the specifics of Women's Rights in *Is He Popenjoy?* Father Barham, in *The Way We Live Now*, has become a Catholic because of the Tractarian Movement, but Trollope satirizes him because he cannot be easy in society rather than because of his doctrine. Trollope was a member of the Established Church, but in the novels he was interested in the Church as a social organization

77. Blake, *Disraeli*, p. 436.
78. Blake, *Disraeli*, pp. 345-346. Disraeli died in April 1881.
79. *The Duke's Children* 76:600. This is Lord Silverbridge talking. Frank Tregear replies, "I never heard a worse political argument in my life."
80. *Letters* (Trollope to Mr. Taylor, 25 September 1868), p. 229.

rather than as a respository of religious truth. "In my days I have written something about clergymen but never a word about religion,"[81] he tells us in *South Africa*, and refuses to discuss the controversy surrounding Bishop Colenso of Natal. He even endorses the advice that Cicero gives in his essay on divination, that the man whose education has freed him from a belief in superstitious practices should feign such belief rather than separate himself from his fellows: "It seems necessary to make allowance for the advancing intelligence of men, and unwise to place yourself so far ahead as to shut yourself out from that common pale of mankind."[82]

In effect, Trollope does not offer much commentary on the more complex political and intellectual issues of his day. His view of a coherent and placid social order, threatened by a few insignificant upstarts, would not find much agreement among modern students of the period. The class that he saw as essential to England's well-being, the landed gentry, was already in decline when he began to write, though this decline was not really apparent until the seventies; capital had already replaced land as the determinant of wealth and power. Trollope was improvising a social creed and ideal. Like the other great Victorian writers, he wrote with an awareness that the eighteenth century's optimism about the prevalence of order in the world was no longer possible. Revolution and the Romantic movement had shown him that order was neither universal nor permanent. There is a nostalgic element in his celebration of the gentleman, and in his attempt to define the gentleman by uniting the older insistence on gentle birth and "blood" to the Victorian insistence on virtuous behavior. His political and social theories were not very profound, and his ideal of the gentleman was not comprehensive enough or definite enough to perform the task of guaranteeing the social system. It remains a literary improvisation, like Newman's celebrated definition of

81. *South Africa* 1:258.
82. *Life of Cicero* 2:363. See apRoberts, *The Moral Trollope*, pp. 110-111, which cites similar passages where Trollope agrees with Cicero's position.

the gentleman, and Trollope, like Newman, insists on a certain passivity. Newman's comment, that the gentleman "concurs with . . . movements rather than takes the initiative himself,"[83] is one that fits a number of Trollope's protagonists. Trollope is not a deep or original thinker. But he is an accurate guide—in his very lack of political and intellectual analysis—to the opinions and attitudes of the average member of the middle and upper classes. "He reminds us," Max Beerbohm once said, "that sanity need not be Philistine."[84]

There is an artistic corollary to Trollope's celebration of the ordinary unobtrusive gentleman. His style has been called undistinguished by some critics, who have not realized how deliberately he avoided individuality and distinction in his writing. He is capable of very idiosyncratic writing, as we see whenever he has occasion to write a letter that will reveal the personality of one of his characters, but his narrative style is not distinctive. It is difficult to analyze or parody, for it calls no attention to itself.

The discussion of style in the *Autobiography* is confined to a demand for ease and clarity, and in *Thackeray* Trollope simply asks that "A novel in style should be easy, lucid, and of course grammatical."[85] But in discussing Thackeray's style he goes on to explain his own aims more fully:

> I hold that gentleman to be the best dressed whose dress no one observes. I am not sure but that the same may be said of an author's written language. Only, where shall we find an example of such perfection? Always easy, always lucid, always correct, we may find them; but who is the writer, easy, lucid, and correct, who has not impregnated his writing with something of that personal flavour which we call mannerism? . . . I have

83. John Henry Newman, *The Idea of a University* (New York: Longmans, Green, 1927) 8:208-209.

84. S. N. Behrman, *Portrait of Max* (New York: Random House, 1960), p. 283.

85. *Thackeray*, "English Men of Letters" (New York: Harper and Brothers, 1879) 9:181.

sometimes thought that Swift has been nearest to the mark of any—writing English and not writing Swift. But I doubt whether an accurate observer would not trace even here the "mark of the beast." Thackeray, too, has a strong flavour of Thackeray.[86]

To Trollope a distinctive style was a disagreeable assertion of self, a romantic eccentricity. In his work such a style would have been out of harmony with the subject matter. A novel that celebrates the ordinary and unobtrusive gentleman who conforms to society must be simply and clearly narrated in a style that is ordinary and unobtrusive. The denial of the right to be different must be accompanied by the author's abdication of the same right.

86. *Thackeray*, p. 197. Compare Arnold's disdain for the "*curious* and exquisite" style and his endorsement of "great plainness of speech" for poets. See *The Letters of wmatthew Arnold to Arthur Hugh Clough*, ed. Howard Foster Lowry (London: Oxford University Press, 1932), pp. 65, 124. Trollope's "plain style" has found its defenders in recent years. Hugh Sykes Davies, in "Trollope and his Style," *Review of English Literature* 1 (1960): 73-84, argues the appropriateness of Trollope's style to his moral attitudes, citing his leisurely manner and habit of circling around a question or issue as being in harmony with the tentative nature of his moral judgments; he considers Trollope a "passionate casuist." Davies examines the "cadences" created by Trollope's use of *and* and *but* in long sentences, often to qualify a discrepancy between moral theory and a specific situation. Geoffrey Tillotson suggests that Trollope's style can "sustain grace without its seeming too much a thing of art," and generally praises Trollope as a stylist. See his "Trollope's Style" in Geoffrey and Kathleen Tillotson, *Mid-Victorian Studies* (London: Athlone Press, 1965), pp. 56-61, reprinted from *Ball State Teachers' College Forum* 2 (1961-62): 3-6. David Aitken finds that Trollope does in fact have a personal style, and praises its conversational cadences and vocabulary; see his " 'A Kind of Felicity': Some Notes about Trollope's Style," *Nineteenth-Century Fiction* 20 (1966): 337-353. Ruth apRoberts summarizes these critics' comments, and cites the passage I have quoted from Trollope's *Thackeray*, in her defense of Trollope's style in *The Moral Trollope*, pp. 19-27. She praises its lucidity, and rightly sees Trollope's lack of stylistic idiosyncrasies as one of his great strengths as writer and novelist. Her remarks originally appeared as "Anthony Trollope, or the Man with No Style at All," *Victorian Newsletter* 35 (1969): 10-13.

✳ PART TWO ✳

❋ IV ❋

STUDIES IN DEFINITION
Sir Harry Hotspur of Humblethwaite,
Ralph the Heir, An Eye for an Eye,
Lady Anna, and *Harry Heathcote of Gangoil*

> Those great men, who have . . . risen to guide
> the helm of our government . . . knew that the
> foundation of civil polity is Convention, and that
> everything and every person that springs from that
> foundation must partake of that primary character.
> They held themselves bound by the contracts of
> their forefathers, because they wished their pos-
> terity to observe their own agreements. . . . They
> looked upon the nation as a family, and upon the
> country as a landed inheritance. Generation after
> generation were to succeed to it, with all its conve-
> nient buildings, and all its choice cultivation, its
> parks and gardens, as well as its fields and meads,
> its libraries and its collections of art, all its wealth,
> but all its incumbrances.
>
> —Disraeli, *Vindication of the*
> *English Constitution* (1835) 5

WHEN he had freed himself from his Post Office duties and
other public commitments, late in 1868, Trollope continued
to work on the Palliser cycle, but between 1868 and 1873 he
also completed several novels that are brief, direct, and simple in structure, each concerned with a single moral and
social problem: *Sir Harry Hotspur of Humblethwaite, An Eye
for an Eye, Lady Anna,* and *Harry Heathcote of Gangoil.*
Though considerably longer, *Ralph the Heir* belongs in this
group chronologically and structurally.

Except for *Harry Heathcote of Gangoil,* these novels are all
concerned with inheritance as a moral and social problem.

109

Ralph the Heir and the hero of *An Eye for an Eye* are destined to inherit estates and responsibilities, but by irresponsible behavior both disqualify themselves from the proper performance of their duties. The heroines of *Sir Harry Hotspur of Humblethwaite* and *Lady Anna* are heiresses whose inheritances involve them in a conflict of duties. These short novels seem to have been written partly as experiments in a more tightly organized structure, partly as an attempt to examine the same theme from several different angles, and partly as relief from larger projects—Trollope wrote *The Eustace Diamonds* between *Ralph the Heir* and *An Eye for an Eye*, and *Phineas Redux* between *An Eye for an Eye* and *Lady Anna*. These shorter novels have few characters, and for the most part they depend on a simple confrontation between two directly antithetical characters or ideas. There are two antithetical characters named Ralph Newton in *Ralph the Heir*, and directly conflicting sets of duties in the other novels.

I. *Sir Harry Hotspur of Humblethwaite*

> Even now, methinks, I see your lordship's house
> Haunted with suitors of the noblest rank,
> And my young lady, your supposed heir,
> Tir'd more with wooing than the Grecian queen,
> In the long absence of her wandering lord.
> There's not a ruinous nobility
> In all this kingdom, but conceives a hope
> Now to rebuild his fortunes on this match.
> —Thomas May, *The Heir* (1620) 1:1

> "There are few things more pleasing to me than an ancient place," said Mr. Temple.
> "Doubly pleasing when in the possession of an ancient family," added his daughter.
> —Disraeli, *Henrietta Temple* 2:5

Trollope wrote *Sir Harry Hotspur of Humblethwaite* in about two months (December 1868 to January 1869), just after he had completed *The Vicar of Bullhampton* and returned from his unsuccessful attempt to represent Beverley in Parliament. The novel was serialized in *Macmillan's Magazine* (May to December 1870) and appeared in book form at the end of 1870. Contemporary reviewers noticed the effects of Trollope's newfound leisure on his style. "The style of *Sir Harry Hotspur* shows signs of greater care than Mr. Trollope always finds it worth while to take," declared the *Saturday Review*, ". . . we note perhaps fewer of certain tricks of rapid writing";[1] an American critic, writing in *Harper's Magazine* (October 1871), called the novel "the saddest story, and at the same time the simplest, that Anthony Trollope has ever written," and suggested that its "very simplicity" made it effective.[2] Trollope himself noted the deliberately limited nature of his story in his *Autobiography*, describing "its object" as "the telling of some pathetic incident in life rather than the portraiture of a number of living human beings."[3]

Sir Harry Hotspur is the story of two people who are destroyed by their excessive devotion to duty. Emily Hotspur, Sir Harry's only daughter, shares her father's devotion to the Hotspur family and its glories, "and through his family to his country, which, as he believed, owed its security and glory to the maintenance of its aristocracy."[4] Both of them strive to preserve the family name, honor, and territorial influence, even at some risk to their personal honor. Instead they destroy the Hotspurs of Humblethwaite forever.

Sir Harry is a baronet. Faced with a problem, he is attracted by an easy solution. The death of his son has left him with no male heir to his estates. His daughter can

---

1. *Trollope: The Critical Heritage*, ed. Donald Smalley, p. 345. The review appeared in *Saturday Review* 30 (10 December 1870): 753-755.
2. *Trollope: The Critical Heritage*, p. 339.
3. *An Autobiography* 18:335.
4. *Sir Harry Hotspur of Humblethwaite* 20:195.

inherit the estates, which are no longer entailed, but the Hotspur name will vanish when she marries, while the heir to the title and name, a cousin, will have no estate to support his dignity. "It would perhaps have been better . . . had some settlement or family entail fixed all things for him,"[5] Trollope comments after explaining the problem. In the absence of such a prior settlement, Sir Harry is tempted to marry Emily to her cousin, George Hotspur, and keep the title and estates together, even though George has a bad reputation. "Was his higher duty due to his daughter, or to his family?" the baronet asks himself. "Would he be justified,—justified in any degree,—in subjecting his child to danger in the hope that his name and family pride might be maintained?"[6] But Emily desires the marriage even more strongly than her father does. When she falls in love with George, it is primarily in terms of her father's familial obsession:

> It was not only that he was young, clever, handsome, and in every way attractive, but that, in addition to all this, he was a Hotspur, and would some day be the head of the Hotspurs. Her father had known well enough that her family pride was equal to his own. Was it not natural that, when a man so endowed had come in her way, she should learn to love him?[7]

Emily is one of Trollope's most complex good women, willing to risk contact with evil to perform what she sees as her duty: to rescue the future head of her family from his profligate life, to give herself and her fortune to him for the preservation of the family's importance. When she realizes his unworthiness, she is not repelled, but dangerously in-

5. 1:6. An entail is a legal instrument for regulating the inheritance of an estate, usually to insure that the estate will remain intact and will descend in the male line. The inheritor of such an estate can only possess it during his lifetime. He cannot sell it or any portion of it. He cannot leave it to a daughter in his will, or otherwise choose its next inheritor. He must see it go automatically to the next male heir.

6. 20:195.   7. 16:163-164.

spired to save him. "I think I love him more because he is—so weak," she tells her father. "Like a poor child that is a cripple, he wants more love than those who are strong."[8] She begins to dream of acting as a kind of angel in George's life, praying for him, bringing him grace, washing him clean. She is also attracted—an aspect Trollope handles very delicately—by George's close resemblance to her father. If she marries him, she will take her mother's place and rank as Lady Hotspur.

Emily's determination, and her conviction that George can be redeemed, combine with Sir Harry's own hopes to persuade him that the marriage should take place after a period of probation, during which George is to prove his worthiness, but the project fails. He adds a conspiracy to cheat at cards to his other vices—drinking, a mistress, heavy debts, and the deliberate cheating of money-lenders. The marriage is clearly impossible. George is unworthy of Emily, and incapable of ruling justly at Humblethwaite. Despite his family name and rank, he does not belong there. Emily dresses in mourning, as if sensing her own and her family's approaching end. She spends her time in prayer and good works, determined to remain unmarried. No other possible husband will do, for no other can inherit the Hotspur baronetcy. Then the news comes that George has married his mistress. Emily pines away until she dies. Her father sinks into a "worn-out, tottering old man,"[9] and the estates become part of the vast possessions of a distant relative.

Emily's devotion to George and to the Hotspur family has been suicidal, and her unwavering loyalties destroy the family forever. She has learned her creed from her father, so that he is both instigator and victim of all that occurs. Father and daughter differ only in the degree to which they are obsessed and rigid in their concept of duty. Emily never

8. 17:170. Cockshut remarks (*Anthony Trollope*, p. 126) on the "family likeness" between Emily and Sir Harry.
9. 24:245.

wavers from her double loyalty to George and the Hotspurs, but her father at times hesitates between family loyalty and his daughter's well-being. Sir Harry is initially guilty of too literal a definition of his duty. He mistakes the letter for the spirit by insisting that the Hotspur estates must be preserved intact and the name with them. This makes the marriage with George dangerously attractive to him, and he vacillates, first encouraging it, then forbidding it, then half-heartedly agreeing even though George's vices have become apparent, then forbidding it again. He attempts to help George, then to buy him off, then to reform him. His strong sense of duty, and his uncertainty between two equally compelling duties, end in a failure to preserve either Emily or his house.

Trollope makes ironic use of this tendency to vacillation by showing it as one of the most obvious family resemblances between Sir Harry and his cousin. George, too, vacillates, first between self-indulgence and the great reward that will be his if he reforms, later between persevering in his attempt to win Emily and allowing himself to be bought off by Sir Harry. Ironically, in this novel in which the social value of a family and the continuation of that value is a central concern, two shared traits emphasize the relationship of the Hotspur men—their physical resemblance and their habit of vacillation. These shared traits help to destroy the family.

Trollope's use of analogies is more literal in *Sir Harry Hotspur* and the other novels of this period than it is in later work. George and Sir Harry are literally alike. They share a name and features, and George will inherit his cousin's title. Throughout the book Trollope's method is simple: to double characters and events in order to develop his story. George has two parallel and similar creditors, and two lady friends who resemble one another in their tolerance for him and in the advice they give him. Sir Harry introduces two other suitors to Emily, both alike in their worthy dullness. There are two important confrontations between Sir Harry and

George, the engagement is twice established and twice broken off, and George is guilty of two serious crimes. Trollope's mind seems to be gradually working toward analogical and contrasting techniques in this novel, even though the technique is used here primarily to contrast characters. The structure of the novel is direct and linear.

His own comment on *Sir Harry Hotspur* in the *Autobiography* indicates the rather limited aims he had set for himself: "There is much of pathos in the love of the girl, and of paternal dignity and affection in the father."[10] He placed his characters in an inexorable moral and social trap and watched their virtues bring about their doom. He was to use a similar method in the next few short novels, organizing not around character or locale but in terms of a moral and social conflict—usually a conflict between good and good rather than between good and evil.

II. *Ralph the Heir*

> Let it stand firm both in thy thought and mind,
> That the duke was thy father, as no doubt
> He bid fair for't, thy injury is the more;
> For had he cut thee a right diamond,
> Thou had'st been next set in the dukedom's ring,
> When his worn self, like age's easy slave,
> Had dropt out of the collet into th' grave.
> What wrong can equal this?
> —Cyril Tourneur,
> *The Revenger's Tragedy* (1607) 1:1

After completing *Sir Harry Hotspur*, Trollope spent February and March, 1869, in an even more experimental task: he attempted to turn *The Last Chronicle of Barset* (written 1866) into a play called *Did He Steal It?*[11] Early in April he

---

10. *An Autobiography* 18:335.
11. Trollope published *Did He Steal It?* privately, in a sixty-four page pamphlet (1869). There is a modern facsimile edition (Princeton: Princeton University Press, 1952).

returned to his own trade and began *Ralph the Heir*, finishing by early August. The novel appeared as a supplement to *Saint Paul's Magazine* from January 1870 to July 1871, and was published in three volumes in April 1871.

Ralph the Heir is an early experiment in combining several plots so that they comment on each other. Trollope suggests implicit parallels or contrasts between events and characters, but he also struggles to connect his four discrete plots in explicit ways. These explicit connections are at times rather forced, and they are so intricate that they sometimes distract the reader from recognizing the more important implicit relationships.

Each of Trollope's plots is organized around a social and moral question. First there is the question of who is to inherit the family estate of the Newtons, Newton Priory. The estate is entailed on Ralph Newton, Squire Newton's nephew, but the Squire has an illegitimate son, also named Ralph Newton. The Squire tries to break the entail by purchasing his nephew's right to inherit, so that he can leave the estate to the illegitimate Ralph. This attempt to break the entail violates tradition and social order, which depend on estates descending to legitimate heirs. And Trollope sees a moral issue in a parent trying to gain for his child a social rank to which that child is not entitled by birth. The second plot centers on Mr. Neefit, a wealthy breeches-maker, who tries to make his daughter a lady by marrying her to Ralph the Heir. Again the moral problem is that of an unjustified rise in social rank, while Polly Neefit will not be able to perform the duties of a squire's wife, and will dishonor the Newton family. In the third plot, Sir Thomas Underwood stands for Parliament, wins the election, and is then unseated because his agent had bribed some of the electors. Here the social problem is electoral corruption, which Trollope blames on Disraeli's recent extension of the franchise to include poor men who are easily bribed—another violation of social order, and an assignment of social duties to those not able to perform them properly. Sir Thomas himself is

Tichborne

morally at fault because he tries to gain a position for which he is intellectually and temperamentally unfit, and so his ambitions for himself resemble the ambitions that the Squire and Mr. Neefit have for their children. The fourth plot is a conventional set of love stories: Clarissa Underwood is wooed by Ralph the Heir and his brother, the Reverend Gregory Newton, while Mary Bonner, her cousin, is wooed by Ralph the Heir and by the illegitimate Ralph. The social and moral issues here are Ralph's illegitimacy, Mary Bonner's lack of fortune, the excuses that society makes for the Heir because of his rank.

Trollope carefully created explicit links between these four plots. Sir Thomas Underwood is Ralph the Heir's guardian and Squire Newton's legal advisor. He is linked with the Neefit plot because his electoral opponent, Ontario Moggs, is Polly Neefit's other suitor, a rival of Ralph the Heir. The Heir proposes to Sir Thomas's daughter, Clarissa, and to his niece, Mary Bonner. These young women, in turn, eventually marry; Clarissa marries the Reverend Gregory Newton, and Mary Bonner marries the illegitimate Ralph.

Trollope further organizes his book by showing us implicit contrasts or resemblances between some of his characters. Squire Newton and Mr. Neefit are devoted fathers, while Sir Thomas ignores his daughters. Ralph the Heir, Clarissa Underwood, and Ontario Moggs are all three impulsive and irresponsible. The illegitimate Ralph is serious and sensible, as are Polly Neefit and Mary Bonner. The two Ralphs' antithetical temperaments are emphasized by their shared name and their rivalry for the estate and for Mary Bonner. Sir Thomas and Ontario Moggs are political opponents, but each discovers he has been duped by his party workers.

Trollope connects his plots more organically by tracing a number of events back to one social and moral transgression, the Squire's fathering of an illegitimate child. He does not condemn the Squire, who loved Ralph's mother but

117

needed time to reconcile his family to a marriage, and then saw her die before this could take place. The Squire's father had created the entail, settling the estate on the Heir, solely to prevent the illegitimate Ralph from ever inheriting Newton Priory, and this entail has divided the remaining members of the Newton family. The Squire hates the Heir, who is the barrier to his own son's inheritance, and has refused to let him come to Newton Priory. As a result, the Heir knows very little about the estate he is to inherit. The Squire's hostility has left him with nothing to do except wait for his inheritance, and this idle waiting has led to extravagance. Without responsibilities he has become irresponsible. His debts lead to borrowing from Mr. Neefit, who sees his hold over the Heir as a chance to make him marry Polly. Squire Newton sees in these same debts a chance to purchase the Heir's rights, so that the illegitimate Ralph can someday own the estate. Of the novel's four plots, only that involving Sir Thomas's parliamentary ambitions is unrelated to the Squire's earlier transgression.

Trollope looks at the issue of the succession to Newton Priory in the light of this transgression, which violates moral and social order. The illegitimate Ralph is a better man than the Heir. He is prudent, hard working, and devoted to the estate and its people—but he is not the legitimate heir. He can never really be "Newton of Newton." The Heir is weak, idle, and foolish. He is ready to betray the family by pawning the estate—but he is the legitimate heir. "Perhaps his errors have arisen as much from his unfortunate position as from any natural tendency to evil on his own part," Sir Thomas argues, defending the Heir. "He has been brought up to great expectations . . . taught . . . to think that a profession was unnecessary for him . . . he has been debarred from those occupations which generally fall in the way of the heir to a large landed property by the unfortunate fact of his entire separation from the estate which will one day be his."[12] The illegitimate Ralph is a

12. *Ralph the Heir* 1:10:122.

usurper, though an involuntary and virtuous one. His very existence has estranged the Squire and the Heir and perhaps caused the Heir's weaknesses. It is therefore impossible to condemn the Heir outright, despite his weaknesses. It is equally impossible to overlook the illegitimate Ralph's conspicuous virtues, and his unique qualifications to rule the estate, but to prefer him as heir to Newton Priory is to ignore the central fact of his false position. For him to inherit would be a violation of "the English order of things,"[13] which prefers the legitimate Heir, however personally unworthy.

Trollope seems unreasonably devoted to the principle of legitimacy, and he has made this devotion seem perverse by endowing the illegitimate Ralph with every virtue proper to a country gentleman, while the Heir proves himself a bad landlord after he does inherit. The development of the story seems to justify the charge that Trollope prefers birth to merit. But Trollope is not really judging between the legitimate and illegitimate heirs. He shows us that each has strong arguments in his favor, but he is really interested in the moral implications of the Squire's attempts to tamper with the entail and take the succession into his own hands. The competition between the Heir and the illegitimate Ralph is seen in terms of the Squire's egoism and pride as he tries to break with traditional ways and to replace law with his own will—as he has already done in fathering the illegitimate Ralph.

The Squire feels guilt, but he is not really able to repent. Instead, he tries to allay his guilt by obtaining for his son the very place from which his birth excludes him, giving him a kind of legitimacy in defiance of objective facts. "His boy was as dear to him, as though the mother has been his honest wife," Trollope says. " . . . He would do anything in order that his child might be Newton of Newton after him."[14] Like Sir Harry Hotspur, he is too narrowly specific in planning the continuation of his name and estate. "Of

13. 1:28:337.   14. 1:11:128.

course it has been my fault," he admits to Ralph, after his plan to buy the entail seems to have succeeded, "but I do feel now that I have in a great measure remedied the evil which I did . . . for the first time in my life I can look you in the face, and not feel a pang of remorse."[15] In all other matters, the Squire is an honest and sturdy upholder of tradition. Much can be said in favor of an arrangement that will give Newton Priory to the illegitimate Ralph, and Trollope says it all by portraying him as the Heir's superior in every way, but the arrangement is still wrong, for it violates social and moral law. "You know he can't be the real squire," one of the tenants tells another. "They may hugger-mugger it this way and that; but this Mr. Ralph can't be like t'other young gentleman." Although the tenants know and love the illegitimate Ralph, he is warned that "There will be a feeling"[16] at his accession, and when the Heir does in fact succeed the tenants are "not upon the whole ill-pleased." They do not know him, but they feel it is "in proper conformity with English habits and English feelings that the real heir should reign." The neighboring gentry agree that,

> personally popular as was the other man, it was clearly better than a legitimate descendant of the old family should be installed at Newton Priory. The old Squire's son . . . was loved by all; but nothing that all the world could do on his behalf would make him Newton of Newton. . . . He might live among them as a general favourite; but he could not under any circumstances have been, — Newton of Newton.[17]

The Squire's efforts to win the estate for the illegitimate Ralph bring about his own death. In his exaltation at the Heir's agreement to sell the entail, he hunts recklessly until his horse kills him, and all his efforts result in nothing at last. "He would have given me his flesh and blood;—his

15. 1:28:339, 345.   16. 1:28:347, 346.   17. 2:35:85-86.

very life," Ralph says to the butler, as they stand beside the Squire's lifeless body. " 'I think no father ever so loved a son. And yet, what has it come to?' . . . 'It ain't come to much surely,' said old Grey to himself, as he crept away to his own room; 'and I don't suppose it do come to much mostly when folks go wrong.' "[18] Trollope is showing society's instinctive preference for sustaining general principles even though individuals suffer; it is more important that traditional order be maintained than that an individual have his way.

Trollope does not take sides. He does not favor the Heir's succession and oppose that of the illegitimate Ralph, nor does mere aristocratic bias determine his handling of the plot involving Mr. Neefit's efforts to make his daughter a lady by marrying her to the Heir. Trollope does not ask us to decide whether or not the Heir should marry a girl of low birth. Instead, he attempts to show us a father whose ambitions parallel those of Squire Newton. The Squire wishes to make his illegitimate son a country gentleman, the master of Newton Priory. Mr. Neefit wishes to make his daughter a lady, and mistress of Newton Priory. Mr. Neefit's ambitions for Polly are as socially unacceptable and unrealistic as the Squire's ambitions for his son, and they too must fail. Polly is morally and intellectually superior to the vapid woman whom the Heir eventually marries, but she is not a lady. Society can never pretend she is one, any more than it can pretend that the illegitimate Ralph is truly Newton of Newton. She wisely refuses to marry a man who does not love her. But Trollope's emphasis is on her father and his analogous relationship to Squire Newton. Along with their efforts to improve the status of their children, both men share a common devotion to the hunt (Mr. Neefit has prospered because he makes the best hunting-breeches in London), and both recognize the importance of being master of Newton Priory. Both are undone by the accident that kills

18. 2:34:69-70. See Cockshut, *Anthony Trollope*, pp. 147-148.

the Squire; it prevents the purchase of the Heir's rights, and when he inherits he does not need to marry the breeches-maker's daughter.

Trollope's portrait of Mr. Neefit is careful and sympathetic. The novelist does not patronize the breeches-maker, but leaves him dignity even in his most absurd moments. In his groping efforts to gain for his daughter a position among people who would despise him and would despise her, in his rage and frustration when all is lost by the old Squire's sudden death, he emerges as a convincing character from a class that Trollope seldom portrayed.

Neefit is gauche and vulgar, but he is the Heir's moral superior. When he smashes the Heir's copy of the Apollo Belvedere, he is protesting against the handsome facade that masks the young man's emptiness. There is a subtle touch in Neefit's own awareness of how much the Heir despises him. He is boisterously willing to overlook this contempt while there is still a chance that the marriage with Polly will take place; later he exploits the Heir's contempt for him to annoy the young man, pursuing him after the marriage negotiations have broken off to proclaim publicly that the Heir has promised to marry his daughter.

The third in the trio of fathers is Sir Thomas Underwood, the most fully realized character in the novel and one of Trollope's most interesting creations. Unlike the Squire and Mr. Neefit, he is not much interested in the future of his children and cannot be induced to spend time with them. He is one of Trollope's morbidly isolated men, unfitted by temperament for the ordinary life of the world, and he has created for himself an almost total solitude from which he struggles vainly to escape.

Trollope had planned to call his novel *Underwood*,[19] and Sir Thomas is concerned in most of the book's events. It begins and ends with him, and the only plot not explicitly

19. Michael Sadleir, *Trollope: A Bibliography* (London: Constable and Company, 1928), p. 298.

connected with Newton Priory revolves around him—the Percycross election plot. His candidacy represents one last desperate attempt to break out of self-imposed isolation, and to find a place in the world of men as a member of the House of Commons, the society that represents all society.

The Squire and Mr. Neefit attempt to realize themselves in the lives of their children, but Sir Thomas aims at personal triumph. He fails just as the two ambitious fathers do, and for a similar reason: they have attempted to evade the realities of class and status; he has attempted to evade the reality of his own temperament, which excludes him from society as decidedly as Polly and the illegitimate Ralph are excluded by birth. "There are men who cannot communicate themselves to others," Trollope begins his tale.

> Sir Thomas Underwood . . . had never yet made a close friend. . . . And yet he was possessed of warm affections, was by no means misanthropic in his nature, and would, in truth, have given much to be able to be free and jocund as are other men. He lacked the power that way, rather than the will. . . . He had lamented it as an acknowledged infirmity; . . . but at the age of sixty he had taken no efficient steps towards curing himself of the evil.[20]

When the story begins, he has abandoned most of his legal practice, cut himself off from his two daughters, and even sleeps in his office, visiting home as seldom as possible. At his club, where he dines nightly, "it was said of him . . . that he had never been known to dine in company with another member."[21] His life is spent alone in his chambers, where he sleeps after dinner until ten, reads or writes until one, and then

> would prowl about the purlieus of Chancery Lane, the Temple, and Lincoln's Inn, till two or even three o'clock in the morning;—looking up at the old dingy windows,

20. 1:1:1-2.   21. 1:1:8.

and holding, by aid of those powers which imagination gave him, long intercourses with men among whom a certain weakness in his physical organisation did not enable him to live in the flesh.[22]

At the end of the book, Sir Thomas realizes that his campaign at Percycross was a final "renewed attempt . . . to enter the world and to go among men that he might do a man's work." Trollope analyzes his aspirations. He has dreamed of professional success and of something more, "something to be done over and above the mere earning of his bread."[23] That something was to be the writing of a life of Francis Bacon, but though Sir Thomas has brooded over his subject and gathered materials, he is unable to begin his book. Trollope's usual scorn for the slow or unproductive writer (he considered that Thackeray worked "not very quickly" in taking a little over four years to write *Pendennis*, *Henry Esmond*, and *The Newcomes*)[24] is replaced here by pity. Sir Thomas is ambitious, but "the fibre" is lacking and he finds himself condemned, like George Eliot's Casaubon (*Middlemarch* appeared in 1871-72, just after *Ralph the Heir*) to

> an agony protracted for years, always intending, never performing, self-accusing through every wakeful hour, self-accusing almost through every sleeping hour. The work to be done is close there by the hand, but the tools are loathed, and the paraphernalia of it become hateful. And yet it can never be put aside. It is to be grasped tomorrow, but on every morrow the grasping of it becomes more difficult, more impossible, more revolting. There is no peace, no happiness for such a man;—and such a one was Sir Thomas Underwood.[25]

Successful as a lawyer, he has failed in his political and in his literary ambitions. Both projects have been beyond his powers. His inability to succeed with Bacon drives him back to politics, and his failure at Percycross drives him

22. 1:1:11-12.   23. 2:51:275, 278.
24. Trollope, *Thackeray*, p. 38.   25. 2:51:278.

back to his books again, "hating himself and wretched."[26]
Alone with the notes for his unwritten book, he recalls the
figure of Trollope's father, the unsuccessful lonely barrister
toiling over his vast projected ecclesiastical encyclopedia.
(The hostility between Squire Newton and the Heir echoes
Mr. Trollope's inability to get along with the relative from
whom he was to inherit an estate; these expectations seem to
have crippled Mr. Trollope and made him a failure.)

Sir Thomas's inability to live an ordinary life has led him
into vain ambition, into failure and loneliness. At the last,
he is driven to question his whole life in a moment of self-
awareness brought on by the mournful sounds of a flute,
heard as he sits alone. "Why should he have dared to arrange for himself a life different from the life of the ordinary
men and women who lived around him?" he wonders.

> . . . he had ventured to think himself capable of some-
> thing that would justify him in leaving the common cir-
> cle. He had left it, but was not justified. . . . He was
> simply a weak, vain, wretched man, who, through false
> conceit, had been induced to neglect almost every duty of
> life! . . . why had he dared to leave that Sunday-
> keeping, church-going, domestic, decent life, which
> would have become one of so ordinary a calibre as him-
> self? . . . To walk as he saw other men walking around
> him,—because he was one of the many; to believe that to
> be good which the teachers appointed for him declared to
> be good; to do prescribed duties without much personal
> inquiry into the causes which had made them duties; to
> listen patiently, and to be content without excitement;
> that was the mode of living for which he should have
> known himself to be fit.[27]

In Sir Thomas, Trollope has created another of his tragically isolated men who have cut themselves off from life by
not living in an ordinary way.

26. 2:51:279.
27. 2:51:285-286. L. and R. Stebbins suggest Sir Thomas's resemblance
to Trollope's father, *The Trollopes*, p. 262.

The violence and near madness present in many of Trollope's solitary figures is missing from Sir Thomas. His flaws seem minor ones: a fatal combination of weakness and ambition, and a debilitating shyness. But the pity and terror of isolation, which always moved Trollope deeply, are no less present here because the man is so ordinary and the reasons for his isolation so common. Sir Thomas is fully and precisely analyzed. He is not a type but a believably suffering individual, and Trollope's careful dissection creates sympathy for a man defeated by the ordinary demands of life itself, one who cannot quite function among men.

The election at Percycross is Sir Thomas's last attempt to reenter the world of affairs and gain the honors that his ambition craves. In these episodes Trollope made use of his own experiences at Beverley,[28] in a campaign so corrupt that Beverley, like the fictional Percycross, lost its right to be represented in Parliament (like Percycross, Beverley was once associated with the Percy family). Trollope later had to testify before a parliamentary committee, and Sir Thomas finds himself before a similar committee as it investigates charges that his agent had spent election day purchasing votes for twenty shillings apiece. The inquiry into the Beverley election discovered that the Conservative candidate had purchased between eight hundred and a thousand voters for the same price.[29] Trollope had hated the sordid work of canvassing, and Sir Thomas shares this dislike as he is dragged about from voter to voter by his agent.

28. The chronology of Trollope's own candidacy probably explains a confusion in the chronology of the novel. Sir Thomas arrives at Percycross on Monday, 16 October (1:25:296) and is told that there are ten days to canvass the electors (p. 306). He then spends about two weeks at this uncongenial task. Elsewhere (1:23:278) Trollope says that the election takes place on Tuesday, 17 October. Trollope himself arrived in Beverley on 1 November 1868. On the next day the *municipal* elections were held, and his opponents' manager paid fifteen to twenty shillings a head to about eight hundred voters to purchase their votes for *both* the municipal elections and the parliamentary election two weeks later.

29. L. and R. Stebbins, *The Trollopes*, p. 259. Trollope describes his adventures as a candidate in *An Autobiography* 16:297-306.

The election episodes allow Trollope to comment directly on contemporary politics, and it is not surprising that he blames much of the corruption at Percycross-Beverley on the changes Disraeli brought about by his Household Suffrage Bill of 1867. Like the Squire's attempt to tamper with the entail, and Mr. Neefit's aspirations for his daughter, this Bill foolishly disregards social and moral realities, and tries to substitute an aspiration for facts. The old boroughs were corrupt, and Percycross was accidentally left untouched by earlier Reform Bills, but Disraeli's new voters from the laboring class make it more corrupt than ever. They are poor enough to be easily tempted by a small bribe, or else they cannot vote in opposition to the wishes of their employers. None of the old electoral abuses have been solved, and a few new ones have been added. Trollope suggests that no reforms would change human behavior very much, and, on the whole, a gentleman is probably less likely to choose a bad M.P. than a group of uninformed and easily bribed laborers.

Trollope's command of pattern and structure are not yet fully developed in *Ralph the Heir*. He is more sophisticated in the creation of his characters, introducing several of them as rather conventional caricatures or types and then allowing them gradually to grow until they seem convincing. His treatment of Mr. Neefit is a good example of this practice. The breeches-maker first appears as crude and ambitious, but gradually we become aware of the intricate relationship between his ambitions for Polly and his awareness of his own crudity, his desire that she should marry someone better, and the self-knowledge that makes him realize how much the Heir despises him. Neefit grows out of a caricature in the course of the book. Polly Neefit is developed in a similar way. She begins as a cliché, a tradesman's daughter excited at the possibility of marrying a gentleman. She turns into another cliché, the principled girl of the lower classes who realizes that she is not fit for a gentle marriage and so relinquishes the Heir. But when Trollope analyzes

Polly and her motives, she too has grown into a real person, who makes her decision to reject the Heir on specific and intelligent grounds, and who is fully and clearly motivated.

The various love stories are the least successful part of *Ralph the Heir*, as Trollope himself pointed out in the *Autobiography*. "I have always thought it to be one of the worst novels I have written," he remarks candidly, "and almost to have justified that dictum that a novelist after fifty should not write love stories . . . of the young ladies . . . she who was meant to be the chief has passed utterly out of my mind without leaving a trace of remembrance behind."[30] He presumably means Mary Bonner, who is so secretive and uncommunicative that the reader can hardly take much interest in her. The Heir says almost all that can be said about her when he tells his brother that she is beautiful like "that thing at Dresden" (presumably the Sistine Madonna). He can only explain her attractions in external terms:

> I don't know what it is. It's the way her head is put on. Upon my word, to see her turn her neck is the grandest thing in the world. I never saw anything like it. I don't know that she's proud by nature,—though she has got a dash of that too. . . . I don't know whether you can understand a man being proud of his wife. . . . I don't mean of her personal qualities, but of the outside get-up. . . .[31]

Despite his efforts to make Mary sympathetic, Trollope shows us little more of her than this. As for the two Ralph Newtons, neither is portrayed very fully, and the novelist even seems unsure which of them is his hero: in the novel itself he assigns this role to the Heir,[32] but in the *Autobiography* he says that the illegitimate Ralph "is intended to be the real hero"[33] and remarks that he is lifeless. *Ralph the Heir* is not a successful novel, though it is of considerable interest

---

30. *An Autobiography* 19:343. 31. 2:42:164-165. 32. 2:41:150.
33. *An Autobiography* 19:343.

as an important experiment in one of Trollope's major themes, that meaningless self-imposed exclusion from life which in his work becomes the equivalent of Hell.

III. *An Eye for an Eye*

> Ear! Ear! Not ay! Eye! Eye! For I'm at the heart of it. Yet I cannot on my solemn merits as a recitativer recollect ever having done of anything of the kind to deserve of such. Not the phost of a nation! Nor by a long trollop! I just didn't have the time to. Saint Anthony Guide!
>
> —James Joyce, *Finnegans Wake*

The dangers of isolation play an even more important part in *An Eye for an Eye*, a brief, carefully organized novel that Trollope wrote in a little less than a month, between 13 September and 10 October, 1870 (it was not published for some years, appearing eventually in the *Whitehall Review* from 24 August 1878 to 1 February 1879, and in book form in January 1879). Here too we find that device of doubling characters and events which is marked in *Ralph the Heir*, and a use of pairing as device and as theme which is an important step in Trollope's development of his analogical method. The book is a further expedition into that shadowy area between moral reality and social reality which is implicit in his whole concern with the definition of the gentleman. In *Ralph the Heir* Trollope examined the impossibility of the Squire's attempt to alter the fact of Ralph's illegitimacy and make him Newton of Newton Priory; in *An Eye for an Eye* he places his young hero between the moral reality of an obligation to the girl he has ruined and the social reality of his rank as earl, which would be dishonored by an unsuitable marriage—the dilemma Squire Newton had presumably faced as a young man. The two novels share these preoccupations, but there is an added dimension to *An Eye for an Eye*—a stern indictment of romanticism, the romantic hero, and the romantic wish to live a life that is out of the ordinary. Trollope had just finished a comic treatment of this theme in *The Eustace Diamonds*, the book that had occupied a large portion of his time (4 December 1869 to 25 August 1870) between the completion of *Ralph the Heir* and the commencement of work on *An Eye for an Eye* (he also completed his translation of *The Commentaries of Caesar* during this period).

Foolishly romantic dreams are at the heart of *An Eye for an Eye* as they are at the heart of *The Eustace Diamonds*. But this time they lead to tragedy rather than comedy, and the little book forms a kind of grim pendant to the raffish adventures of Lizzie Eustace. She sees Lord George Carruthers as a Byronic Corsair, a role he is not really fitted to play. Fred Neville, the hero of *An Eye for an Eye*, sees the West of Ireland as a wild country of adventure and romance, and hopes to "indulge in that wild district the spirit of adventure which was strong within him."[34] When he meets Kate O'Hara and her mother, two ladies in reduced circumstances who live in a lonely cottage, their good looks, their poverty, their Roman Catholicism, and their isolation excite him until he transforms them into romantic heroines and dreams of Kate as "the girl who lived out of the world in solitude on the cliffs of Moher."[35] He sees Father Marty, the humdrum local priest, as a character out of Monk Lewis or Anne Radcliffe, so that a simple dinner at the priest's house becomes an indulgence in "the spirit of adventure."[36] Fred never really escapes

> from the idea that because Father Marty was a Roman Catholic priest, living in a village in the extreme west of Ireland, listening night and day to the roll of the Atlantic and drinking whisky punch, therefore he would be found to be romantic, semi-barbarous, and perhaps more than semi-lawless in his views of life. Irish priests have been made by chroniclers of Irish story to do marvellous

34. *An Eye for an Eye* (Leipzig: Bernhard Tauchnitz, 1879) 2:28.
35. 8:97.   36. 7:88.

things; and Fred Neville thought that this priest, if only the matter could be properly introduced, might be persuaded to do for him something romantic, something marvellous, perhaps something almost lawless.[37]

Trollope knew Ireland well from his years as a Post Office Surveyor there (1841-51); Ireland was his home until 1859. He began his novel-writing career with two novels set in Ireland, and thereafter he wrote three "Irish" novels at intervals of ten years: *Castle Richmond* (written 1859-60); *An Eye for an Eye*, and *The Landleaguers* (written 1882). Trollope probably knew Ireland and the Irish better than any other non-Irish writer, and he was also well read in the Irish novelists, from Maria Edgeworth through Carleton and Griffin to his own friend Charles Lever. These novelists reflected the reality around them by portraying a lawless and disorganized society, without the codes, loyalties, and sanctions that sustained English society. In Ireland, landlords and tenants were usually separated by religion and race as well as class, and the peasant population felt themselves to be oppressed and exploited. Tenants often hated their landlords, landlords often feared their tenants. Troops were stationed all over the country to maintain order; the rollicking heroes of Lever's *Harry Lorrequer* (1837) and his other early novels are British officers whose regiments are in Ireland for this purpose, and so is Fred Neville's regiment.

Trollope's Irish novels show Irish life as violent and anarchic, and in tone they resemble the work of Carleton, Gerald Griffin, and the Banim brothers; Trollope found Carleton's *Fardorougha the Miser* (1839) "really stimulating,"

---

37. 14:178. Mrs. Trollope's *Father Eustace: A Tale of the Jesuits* (1847) presents a sinister and "lawless" priest. See Anthony Trollope, "Father Giles of Ballymoy" (1866) in *Lotta Schmidt, and Other Stories* (London: Alexander Strahan, 1867): "My mother, who was a strict woman, had warned me vehemently against the machinations of Irish priests. . . . . There was something pleasant in the romance of sleeping at Pat Kirwan's house in Ballymoy, instead of in my own room in Keppel Street, Russell Square" (p. 146). Trollope was born in Keppel Street, Russell Square, in 1815; his family moved to Julians, near Harrow, a year later.

and he also studied the same writer's *Valentine M'Clutchy, the Irish Agent* (1845), *The Tithe Proctor* (1849), and *The Squanders of Castle Squander* (1852).[38] In these novels, a persistent theme is the insecurity of Irish life. Cruel landlords or their agents are assaulted or murdered; the owners of estates feel no responsibility toward their tenants; tenants suddenly lose their houses and property; neither public opinion nor justice can restrain tyrannical police officers and magistrates; Irishmen who protest are sometimes outlawed or exiled on false charges; young Irish women are used by British officers or by irresponsible Anglo-Irish landowners—two of Trollope's Irish heroines, Feemy Macdermot and Kate O'Hara, are sexually exploited in a way that would seem like deliberately allegorical propaganda if they had been created by an Irish novelist. These young women are unprotected as no young English lady would be unprotected, and in their misadventures, Trollope portrays life in the absence of generally accepted values and of an organized and supportive society.

Fred Neville looks on Irish anarchy less critically than Trollope, and imagines it as exciting and attractive. He has imagined romance where there is none. But when he succeeds his uncle as Earl of Scroope, he tires of his romantic daydreams, only to find that they have assumed a reality. Kate has believed in his romantic infatuation. By yielding to him, she has become a romantic heroine. Father Marty solemnly curses him when he refuses to make the young woman Countess of Scroope. The cliffs of Moher become a place of romance and melodrama indeed when Mrs. O'Hara

38. Escott, *Anthony Trollope*, pp. 52-54. William Carleton (1794-1869) is best known for *Traits and Stories of the Irish Peasantry* (1830-33). Griffin's major work is *The Collegians* (1829); a young Anglo-Irishman murders his peasant wife so he can marry a wealthy woman of his own class. John (1798-1842) and Michael (1796-1874) Banim wrote *Tales of the O'Hara Family* in two series (1825, 1827). See Doris R. Asmundsson, "Trollope's First Novel: A Re-Examination," *Éire* 6 (1971): 83-91, for a discussion of *The Macdermots of Ballycloran* as a novel of social criticism dealing with England's exploitation of Ireland.

takes her revenge by pushing the young Earl to his death on the rocks below. Another romantic cliché is fulfilled when Mrs. O'Hara then goes mad. Life is transformed into a deadly kind of romance.

This neat movement and counter-movement make *An Eye for an Eye* one of Trollope's most tightly organized novels. Fred Neville flees the dull respectability of Scroope Manor and his responsibilities to seek adventure, but when he finds adventure he becomes more and more attracted to those responsibilities. He swears to marry Kate; at the same time he swears to his uncle that he will never bring a penniless and obscurely born Irish Catholic to Scroope as his Countess. The Irish landscape, which he had seen as wild and romantic, becomes "ugly . . . to his eyes as he now saw it . . . he could hear the melancholy moan of the waves, which he had once thought to be musical and had often sworn that he loved. Now the place with all its attributes was hideous to him, distasteful, and abominable."[39] "What an ass had he made himself, coming thither in quest of adventures!" he meditates, just before his death. "He began to see now the meaning of such idleness of purpose as that to which he had looked for pleasure and excitement. Even the ocean itself and the very rocks had lost their charm for him . . . there was neither beauty nor variety. How poor had been the life he had chosen!"[40] His fluctuating attitudes toward the girl, the priest, and the landscape are closely connected.

"Father Marty . . . was certainly not romantic in his manner of managing such an affair as this," Fred realizes with dismay, when the priest insists on a public marriage:

No doubt he might marry the girl. . . . But were he to do so, he would disgrace his family, and disgrace himself by

39. 16:196.

40. 23:179. Trollope's use of the Irish landscape in *An Eye for an Eye* is commented upon by Sadleir, p. 192; Cockshut, p. 200; apRoberts, p. 18; and by Ellen W. Witting, "Trollope's Irish Fiction," *Éire* 9 (1974): 97–118.

breaking the solemn promise he had made . . . he would
be held by all his natural friends to have ruined himself
by such a marriage . . . he could, no doubt, throw the
girl over. . . . But he was not hard, and he did feel that
so escaping, he would have a load on his breast which
would make his life unendurable. Already he was beginning to hate the coast of Ireland, and to think that the
gloom of Scroope Manor was preferable to it.[41]

But this neatly reversed situation is not the whole of the
story. Fred's refusal to see the O'Haras as they really are,
and his deliberate romanticizing of these two poor and
commonplace women, have a counterpart when his aunt,
the Countess of Scroope, also sees Ireland and the O'Haras
unrealistically. She despises Catholics, the Irish, and anyone not of noble blood. Father Marty becomes a sinister
emissary of Rome in her eyes, and Kate a dangerous adventuress. Ireland and Kate are viewed falsely, with Fred's
romantic prejudices and with the religious and class prejudices of Scroope Manor. Fred is caught between these two
false points of view. He accepts both and finds himself in a
psychological, moral, and social dilemma that destroys him.

The neatness with which these two "eyes" or points of
view first conflict and then coalesce to bring about the final
disaster is one way in which the title is meaningful throughout the book. The phrase is also used literally. Mrs. O'Hara
believes that she has carried out the biblical ideal of justice
by hurling Fred over the cliffs, and she repeats "an eye for
an eye" constantly during her subsequent years of madness.
The title, and the idea of substitution or equivalence it implies, actually governs the book in almost every detail. Fred
substitutes Ireland for Scroope, freedom for responsibility,
romance for reality, the impulsive Kate for the prudent and
respectable bride chosen for him by his relatives. He entertains an impossible "confused notion of an Irish bride, a
wife who should be half a wife and half not."[42] Later he

41. 14:181.   42. 8:97.

reverses himself, replacing his love and duty toward Kate with love and duty toward his rank and title. The two antithetical oaths he has taken have equivalent power over him.

Fred and the Countess are both incapable of seeing truly, unable to free themselves from their preconceptions. Disparate in other ways, their shared blindness makes them analogical characters, and both come to grief in an effort to perform what they consider to be their duty. Fred tries to fulfill both his oaths, and so destroys himself, Mrs. O'Hara, and Kate. The Countess's rigid belief in family honor leads her to condone any dishonorable treatment of Kate, and she comes to realize that the oath she has exacted from Fred creates a dilemma which can be solved only by his death. Her realization of her own responsibilities for what has happened eventually brings her to a self-confinement as close and gloomy as the madhouse where Mrs. O'Hara spends her last years.

The Countess attributes her actions to the highest motives. Trollope makes of her a carefully observed study of a woman whose sense of duty brings about her own downfall and that of others. She is devoted to the cult of Scroope and its glories "with a duty that was almost excessive. Religious she was, and self-denying," Trollope explains, "giving much and demanding little; keeping herself in the background, but possessing wonderful energy in the service of others. Whether she could in truth be called good the reader may say when he has finished this story."[43] Her belief in nobility and her devotion to the Earldom of Scroope lead her to argue that the family would be dishonored by accepting a girl who has been dishonored by the heir. The Countess is caught in that confusion between nobility of rank and nobility of conduct which is so often a central issue in Trollope's novels.

43. 1:17. See Cockshut's discussion of the parallels between Fred and the Countess, p. 201.

As for Kate, there is really no room for a romantic heroine in this anti-romantic novel. Though she lives in solitude, amid the wild scenery that surrounds the protagonists of Lady Morgan's *The Wild Irish Girl* (1806) or Lever's *Luttrell of Arran* (1865), she is not romantic by temperament, and describes the isolation of her cottage on the cliffs as "life within a tomb."[44] She is passive, less sinner than occasion for sin. Her naiveté and lack of vivacity, the fact that the whole episode took place "some years past,"[45] and the smallness of her role, make her remote from the reader, and emphasize the way that Fred has imposed romantic attributes upon her.

Fred must act ignobly in order to be considered noble; he must act dishonorably toward Kate to preserve his family's honor. These discrepancies finally become clear to the Countess in the chapter ironically named "Sans Reproche," the motto of the Earls of Scroope. If Fred "had given to this girl a promise that he would marry her, if he had bound himself by his pledged word, as a nobleman and a gentleman, how could she bid him become a perjured knave?" she asks herself. "Sans reproche! Was he thus to begin to live and to deserve the motto of his house by the conduct of his life?" But at the same time, she believes that if Kate were to become Countess, then "that proud motto" must "be taken down from its place in the hall from very shame." Moral clarity comes when she must recognize that she herself is deliberately lying, and that she must tell Fred "to lie, and having resolved so to tell him, must use all her intellect to defend the lie,—and to insist upon it."[46] She realizes that she has imposed an oath upon Fred by which he will break another sacred oath:

> she, who could not divest herself of a certain pride taken in the austere morality of her own life, she who was now a widow anxious to devote her life solely to God, had persuaded the man to this sin, in order that her successor as Countess of Scroope might not be, in her opinion,

44. 5:69.   45. 1:7.   46. 19:234-235, 236.

unfitting for nobility! The young lord had promised her that he would be guilty of this sin, so damnable, so devilish, telling her as he did so, that as a consequence of his promise he must continue to live a life of wickedness! [Fred plans to live with Kate, but not to marry her] In the agony of her spirit she threw herself upon her knees and implored the Lord to pardon her and to guide her. But even while kneeling before the throne of heaven she could not drive the pride of birth out of her heart. That the young Earl might be saved from the damning sin and also from the polluting marriage;—that was the prayer she prayed.[47]

Her prayer is ironically answered when Fred is murdered.

That isolation which is often dwelt upon in *Ralph the Heir* is an even more insistent theme in *An Eye for an Eye*. The introductory chapter shows us Mrs. O'Hara confined in a madhouse, in the total isolation of the insane. She can neither understand nor communicate. The gloom and isolation of her madhouse is matched by the gloom and isolation of Scroope Manor, a large house which no one ever visits, turned away from its village and cut off from it by a "high, gloomy wall"—a symbol, perhaps, of that unwillingness to share in ordinary life which is to play so large a part in the characters of Fred and the Countess. The park is large, but the drives through it are overgrown and unusable. No one ever touches the books in the library, "huge volumes of antiquated and now all but useless theology."[48] Nor does anyone ever visit the village of Scroope itself, which is isolated, eleven miles from the nearest railroad station. The old Earl never leaves his domain; every day he sits alone in the gloomiest room. Though there are many servants, "beyond his valet and the butler, he hardly knew the face of one of them."[49]

Fred has looked upon isolation as one more element of romance. He has sought it and enjoyed it, and the romantic isolation of the cliffs where he meets Mrs. O'Hara for their

47. 19:243-244.   48. 1:9-10.   49. 1:14.

final interview is an ironic factor in his death. But at the same time, Fred cannot isolate himself sufficiently. He seeks freedom until he comes to realize that he is not free, that he cannot be considered apart from his family and his title. If Kate is to be his wife, she must also be his countess. Fred tries to evade the social and moral realities of his life. Like Squire Newton in *Ralph the Heir*, he dies because these imperatives cannot be disobeyed.

IV. *Lady Anna*

Love had he found in huts where poor men lie;
His daily teachers had been woods and rills . . .
Nor did he change; but kept in lofty place
The wisdom which adversity had bred.
—Wordsworth, "Song at the Feast of
Brougham Castle" (1807): 161-168

I think that a girl who is a lady, should never marry a man who is not a gentleman. You know the story of the rich man who could not get to Abraham's bosom because there was a gulf fixed. That is how it should be;—just as there is with royal people as to marrying royalty. Otherwise everything would get mingled, and there would soon be no difference. If there are to be differences, there should be differences. That is the meaning of being a gentleman,—or a lady.
—*Lady Anna*, 22

After completing *An Eye for an Eye*, Trollope returned to the Palliser cycle to spend the next five months (23 October 1870 to 1 April 1871) writing *Phineas Redux*. In May he sailed for Australia to visit his son Fred, a sheep-herder in New South Wales, and on the two months' journey in the *Great Britain* he wrote *Lady Anna* "day by day—with the intermission of one day's illness—for eight weeks, at the rate of 66 pages of manuscript in each week, every page of manuscript containing 250 words. Every word was counted."[50] The new novel was finished on 19 July, the day before the ship landed at Melbourne, and came out in the *Fortnightly Review* from April 1873 to April 1874; a two-volume edition followed.

In *Lady Anna* Trollope reversed the plot of *An Eye for an Eye*, for one book almost mirrors the other. In place of the young Earl of Scroope, ashamed to marry the girl he loves because she is not his social equal, there is Lady Anna Lovel,[51] an earl's daughter, who insists on marrying a tailor, even though all those about her consider the match unworthy. Fred Neville is weak and easily led, so much so that he swears two irreconcilable oaths, promising Kate O'Hara that he will marry her and promising his relatives that he will do no such thing. Lady Anna is strong-minded enough to resist advice, tears, and threats from her relatives when she refuses to go back on her promise to marry the tailor. Weakness, a foolish yearning for romantic wildness, and a belated sense of his rank are the unspectacular flaws that destroy young Neville; strength and steadfastness, a commitment to living an ordinary life, and a refusal to value rank over honor are Lady Anna's chief virtues. The two novels also share certain elements with each other and with *Ralph the Heir*, notably a preoccupation with illegitimacy. Squire Newton had loved the illegitimate Ralph's mother, but he failed to marry her, yielding to family pressures like those that inhibit Fred Neville from marrying Kate O'Hara. Kate's mother had herself made a bad marriage; so has Lady

50. *An Autobiography* 19:346.
51. At this period, Trollope often named some of his characters out of Shakespeare, generally using names associated with rebellion: Hotspur, Scroop (*Richard II*, *Henry IV*, prologue to *Henry V*), and Lovel, the murderer in *Richard III* (3:4:80). Lovel, however, may also come from Massinger's *A New Way to Pay Old Debts*; from Robert Lovel, an associate of Coleridge and Southey in their scheme for a "pantisocracy"; or from the old ballad of "Lord Lovel." Sir William Patterson cites Malvolio (*Lady Anna*, 30:318), who dreamed of marrying a lady of high rank: "The Lady of the Strachy married the yeoman of the wardrobe" (*Twelfth Night* 2:5:36-37).

Lovel, the mother of Lady Anna. Both women cherish great hopes for their daughters, and are disappointed. Mrs. O'Hara kills Fred Neville because he has seduced her daughter; Lady Lovel tries to kill Daniel Thwaite, the tailor, when it becomes certain that her daughter is going to marry him. The two mothers end their lives in solitude.

Trollope's readers seem to have been as outraged by the misalliance with the tailor as Lady Lovel. "This is a sort of thing the reading public will never stand, except in a period of political storm and ferment," thundered the *Saturday Review*:

> There are Radicals in the abstract, but a man must be embittered by some violent present exasperation who can like such disruptions of social order as this. . . . In the interest both of male and female novel-readers we protest against Lady Anna's match; for their sensibility's sake, we expose at once the main feature of the story, that they may not be betrayed unawares into reading what will probably leave a disagreeable impression . . . who can be pleased here? Not middle-class readers midway between earls and artisans, determined at least to hold their own; not earls and countesses, unless they are disloyal to their order; not tailors, if they are wise men, for what sensible man wants a wife who is ashamed of him?[52]

This response suggests the intensity with which social prejudices could be held in Trollope's day—and not only then—and endorses the accuracy of his depictions of such prejudice in *The Prime Minister*, *The Way We Live Now*, and other novels. In *Trollope: A Bibliography*, Michael Sadleir comments on the unusually large number of copies of the first edition of *Lady Anna* that survived, and on the few signs of normal wear-and-tear they reveal, adding that the novel's "unsuitable flouting of mid-Victorian propriety left *Lady Anna* more immaculate in her brown-grained cloth than in her matrimonial dignity."[53] Trollope's annoyance at critics

---

52. *Saturday Review* 37 (9 May 1874): 598-599. Reprinted in Smalley, *Anthony Trollope: The Critical Heritage*, p. 387.
53. Sadleir, *Trollope: A Bibliography*, p. 303.

who condemned this apparent departure from his social principles caused him to discuss the book more fully than was his custom, both in letters and in the *Autobiography*. Writing to his friend and fellow novelist, Lady Wood, he is very clear about his intentions:

> Of course the girl has to marry the tailor. It is very dreadful, but there was no other way. The story was originated in my mind by an idea I had as to the doubt which would, (or might) exist in a girls [sic] mind as to whether she ought to be true to her troth, or true to her leneage [sic] when, from early circumstances the one had been given in a manner detrimental to the other—and I determined that that [sic] in such case she ought to be true all through. To make the discrepancy as great as possible I made the girl an Earls [sic] daughter, and the betrothed a tailor. All the horrors had to be invented to bring about a condition in which an Earls daughter could become engaged to a tailor without glaring fault on her side.[54]

In the *Autobiography* he is even more specific as he summarizes the novel:

> But the feeling that she is bound by her troth to the man who had always been true to her overcomes everything,—and she marries the tailor. It was my wish of course to justify her in doing so, and to carry my readers along with me in my sympathy with her. But every body found fault with me for marrying her to the tailor. What would they have said if I had allowed her to jilt the tailor and marry the good-looking young lord? How much louder, then, would have been the censure! The book was read, and I was satisfied. If I had not told my story well, there would have been no feeling in favour of the young lord. The horror which was expressed to me at the evil thing I had done, in giving the girl to the tailor, was the strongest testimony I could receive of the merits of the story.[55]

54. *Letters* (Trollope to Lady Wood, 21 June 1873), p. 308.
55. *An Autobiography* 19:347.

Lady Anna, then, is to be admired because she keeps her word, but Trollope is eager to justify her socially as well as morally. In the novel itself he reminds us that the misalliance is not quite as "horrible," "abominable," and "incongruous"[56] as Lady Anna's critics make it out to be. He creates Sir William Patterson, a Solicitor-General whose interest in truth rather than in the niceties of law makes him Trollope's ideal lawyer. Sir William argues that the marriage really does not violate society's laws, and can be reconciled with them. The situation bears him out. Lady Anna's father, the wicked Earl Lovel, has repudiated her mother, pretending that their marriage was invalid. He has denied the Countess any right to her name and title, and branded his child as illegitimate. For many years the mother and daughter have been nameless and penniless. The Lovel family has not recognized any of their claims. Their only recognition, and their entire support, has come from old Thomas Thwaite, a radical tailor, and Lady Anna has grown up with Daniel, his son. This is the "condition in which an Earls daughter could become engaged to a tailor without glaring fault on her side" which Trollope tried so hard to achieve. It is true that society's laws demand that like should marry like, that a girl of noble blood should marry an equal. But too literal a view of these laws ignores Lady Anna's real background. She is as equal to the tailor as she is to her cousin, the young Earl Lovel. The Earl has long been her legal enemy. A marriage between them is suggested by his lawyers as a way of securing for him his uncle's fortune should the courts recognize Lady Anna's legitimacy and allot that fortune to her as her father's direct heir. This marriage, and the equality of interests that it presupposes, is only an artifice of the lawyers, with little relevance to the real people involved.

The central problem around which Trollope organized *Lady Anna* is the problem of identity. For a large part of the book, the characters are concerned with the question of

56. *Lady Anna* 30:318.

Lady Anna's legal identity: is she the legitimate daughter of the late Earl Lovel, and as such entitled to prefix the courtesy title of *Lady* to her Christian name? The question allows Trollope to maneuver in his favorite semantic area, where social and moral usage seem to conflict. For the word *lady*, like those two other words that he so thoroughly explores, *noble* and *gentleman*, is elusive. Anna has always been Lady Anna, as it turns out. There is no legal case against her legitimacy. But throughout her childhood and adolescence her title has not been recognized. She has been shabby and poor. Lacking social and legal recognition, the title has been meaningless.

While the Countess has had the chief role in the girl's upbringing, Anna has shared with Daniel the environment of the Thwaite cottage. They are really equals. He is as much of a gentleman as she is a lady, a fact that cannot be altered by the decrees of the court which award her her title. "I don't think a tailor can be a gentleman," exclaims one of her new friends, and Anna replies,

> I don't know. Perhaps I wasn't a lady when I promised him. But I did promise. . . . Supposing that mamma hadn't been the Countess. . . . So they say now;—but if they had said that she was not, nobody would have thought it wrong then for me to marry Mr. Thwaite. . . . I will tell you the truth. . . . I am ashamed to marry Mr. Thwaite,—not for myself, but because I am Lord Lovel's cousin and mamma's daughter. And I should be ashamed to marry Lord Lovel. . . . Because I should be false and ungrateful! . . . He [Daniel], too, can command. He, too, is noble.[57]

Here Lady Anna is herself wrestling with the novel's central question. Does an individual change in essence when he or she undergoes a change of legal, and consequently of social status? Is Lady Anna a different person, with different needs and obligations, after her status is recognized, or does she remain the same? Is it right for her to

57. 22:233-234.

remain the same? Do her new obligations to her rank take precedence over her old obligations to herself and to her lover? A change in rank can often bring about a corresponding personality change, as in the case of Shakespeare's Prince Hal. But Anna has not risen. Her true status has simply been recognized at last. She has always really been Lady Anna, and so she has always been taught to consider herself. And she has always been the friend and dependent of Daniel Thwaite. "Do you think that you could be happier as the wife of such a one as Daniel Thwaite," the Countess demands angrily, "a creature infinitely beneath you, separated as you would be from all your kith and kin, from all whose blood you share, from me and from your family, than you would be as the bearer of a proud name, the daughter and the wife of an Earl Lovel,—the mother of the earl to come?"[58] The question cuts two ways. Anna's implicit answer is that her ways are already determined. She can be happier with the man she has always known and loved than with new friends who have been her enemies during most of her life. The Lovels have never loved her nor helped her, but now they suddenly demand her love and assistance as their right. They have never recognized her rank; now they demand that she be acutely aware of it. Trollope has balanced the accident of birth that makes it wrong for her to marry a tailor with an accident of upbringing that makes it right and natural that she should do so. She and Thwaite are at the same time unequal and equal, and the novel is an explanation of this paradox.

"Horrors had to be invented to bring about a condition in which an Earls daughter could become engaged to a tailor without glaring fault on her side."[59] Trollope invented these horrors by making the background of his story romantic, even melodramatic, by writing an historical novel set in the 1830s and reminding the reader that life was lived differently "in those days." By setting events in the thirties, and

58. 22:226.   59. *Letters*, p. 308.

Lady Lovel's marriage and misfortunes even earlier, between 1810 and 1819, Trollope makes his story more convincing. The wicked Earl Lovel is a conventional eighteenth century or Regency type. The novelist perhaps felt that he could not make such a character convincing as a contemporary of his readers—a challenge to himself he was later to take up by creating the wicked Marquis in *Is He Popenjoy?*

The romantic atmosphere is increased by allusions to legends of wicked noblemen, or of rightful heirs who have dwelt in obscure poverty before gaining their ranks and fortunes. Trollope describes the complicated story of the wicked Earl's previous Italian marriage as "that Sicilian romance,"[60] and Anne Radcliffe's *A Sicilian Romance* (1790) contains many of the elements in the Lovel case: a mistreated wife, a wicked nobleman, a daughter who is at last rescued. In the course of the novel, Lady Anna and her cousin visit Bolton Abbey, where the reader is explicitly reminded of Wordsworth's *The White Doe of Rylstone*, containing the story of the "shepherd lord" whose claim to the barony of Clifford was unrecognized for many years.[61]

Nor is this the only reference to the Romantic poets. The Lovel estate is in the Lake Country. Thomas Thwaite, the Keswick tailor, a friend of Wordsworth and Southey, retains their early philosophic radicalism. The Countess's romantic temperament is shown by her love of the Lake Country. She finds there some of that exciting wildness which Fred Neville seeks in Ireland, and Lizzie Eustace tries to evoke by reading Shelley on the Scottish coast. Lovel Grange is

> very lovely, from the brightness of its own green sward and the luxuriance of its wild woodland, from the contiguity of over-hanging mountains. and from the beauty

60. *Lady Anna* 5:43.
61. The "shepherd lord" is also celebrated in Wordsworth's "Song at the Feast of Brougham Castle."

of Lovel Tarn, a small lake . . . studded with little is-
lands, each of which is covered with its own thicket. . . .
The house itself is poor, ill-built, . . . a sombre, ill-
omened looking place. When [the Countess] was brought
there as a bride she thought it to be very sombre and
ill-omened; but she loved the lakes and mountains, and
dreamed of some vague mysterious joy of life which was
to come to her from the wildness of her domicile.[62]

The landscape and that "vague mysterious joy" are alike
Wordsworthian.

The Lake Poets are more decidedly introduced when
Daniel Thwaite visits Southey to ask for his help and advice. Trollope does not identify the poet by name, but the
account given of the man, his home, and his works can fit no
one else. Southey lived at Greta Hall, on the edge of Keswick, at the time of the story, and there Daniel finds his
poet. The man was once a radical critic of classes and titles,
but when the tailor tells of his love for Lady Anna, he is
advised to look elsewhere for a bride. The democratic poet
has become conservative, acknowledges class distinctions,
and testily repudiates Daniel's quotations from his own
earlier writings. There is strong sarcasm in the episode, an
echo of the bitterness with which Byron castigates
Southey's change of heart in *The Vision of Judgment*.

These evocations of the Lake District define the two different romantic traditions that determine the characters of
Lady Lovel and Daniel. Her love of romantic scenery helps
to identify her as a heroine out of Coburg melodrama and
Sir Walter Scott. She is one of the "the right Murrays,"[63] of
the romantic family of the Dukes of Atholl and the "bonnie
earl" of Moray. Her pride of blood is strong enough to make
her wish her daughter to die rather than marry unworthi-
ly, and to shoot at the tailor to prevent the match. Her
feudal loyalties and melodramatic conduct place her in that
Romantic tradition which depends on wildness and
excitement—a tradition that is deliberately pointed up in

62. *Lady Anna* 1:1-2.   63. 1:3.

the differences of temperament between the Countess and Lady Anna. The young girl is courageous about her love, but she is a quietly determined heroine rather than a romantic one. When she visits Bolton Abbey she is pleased at the beauty of the Stryd, the spot where the river narrows to rush between high rock walls, but she sensibly refuses the traditional leap across. Daughter of a Romantic heroine, she is herself a Victorian heroine. Trollope stresses the difference between the two women by portraying Lady Anna as less self-assertive and vivid. "She lacked the ambition which gave her mother strength," he comments,

> and would gladly have become Anna Murray or Anna Lovel, with a girl's ordinary privilege of loving her lover, had such an easy life been possible to her. . . . She was affectionate, self-denying, and feminine.[64]

A different strain of Romanticism is seen working itself out in the two Thwaites, father and son. Old Thomas Thwaite is a romantic democrat like the young Wordsworth. He is a Radical and an individualist with traces of the knight-errant: "To oppose an Earl, even though it might be on behalf of a Countess, was a joy to him; to set wrong right, and to put down cruelty and to relieve distressed women was the pride of his heart,—especially when his efforts were made in antagonism to one of high rank."[65] His political aspirations are fervent but vague. "He had dreams of a republic in which a tailor might be president or senator, or something almost noble. But no rational scheme of governance among mankind had ever entered his mind." Daniel holds essentially the same political doctrine, but for him it is more clearly defined. He has read More's *Utopia* and Harrington's *Oceana*. "He looked deeper into things than did his father, and was governed by wider and greater motives. . . . To diminish the distances, not only between the rich and the poor, but between the high and the low, was the grand political theory upon which his mind was

64. 3:28-29.   65. 4:31.

always running. His father was ever thinking of himself and of Earl Lovel; while Daniel Thwaite was considering the injustice of the difference between ten thousand aristocrats and thirty million of people, who were for the most part ignorant and hungry."[66] The Romantic Radical, eager to assert his own individuality, has given way to the Victorian reformer with schemes of social betterment. Trollope's treatment of the Lovels, mother and daughter, and of the Thwaites, father and son, is a commentary on the differences between representatives of the Romantic generation and their successors.

These Romantic evocations also have their central place in determining the plot. The Countess's feudal ideas have led her to marry the wicked Earl, while Daniel's sense of his own worth is a part of his radical Cumberland background. Trollope does not laugh at him as he laughs at Mr. Neefit and Ontario Moggs. Well read in political theory and in literature (he is able to bandy *Cymbeline* references with Southey and to discomfit the poet), chivalrous, intelligent, sure of his own worth, Daniel is the Wordsworthian and Jeffersonian ideal of the educated worker. Trollope does not look upon him as an interloper who threatens society by an attempt to force himself into a higher position than is his right. Daniel is proud of his own place in society, and unwilling to admit that that place makes him unworthy of marriage with Lady Anna. He is no Lopez. He refuses to deny his past and he does not intend to use his marriage as a means of improving his status. Instead, Lady Anna accepts his rank after the marriage. She abandons her title to become plain Mrs. Thwaite.

Trollope lets each apparently positive action lead to a negative result. Thomas Thwaite's good deed—his assistance of the Countess—has taken his fortune, and kept Daniel Thwaite in an inferior social position. His father has had little money to educate him and he has had to become a tailor—and unfit for Lady Anna. At the same time, old

66. 4:34-35. Compare Disraeli's discussion of the "two nations" in *Sybil*, II, v.

Thwaite's support of the Countess and her daughter has thrown the young people together, bringing about their love and eventual marriage. The Countess's victorious assertion of her right to the Lovel title and fortune sets up that title and fortune as an impediment to a marriage between her daughter and a tailor, but at the same time her victory restores to Daniel the money spent by his father in supporting her claims, making it possible for him to marry. Lady Anna's abdication of rank is an inevitable corollary of her mother's achievement of rank. At the end of the novel, the defeated Countess realizes that her final acceptance as Countess Lovel by the Lovel family and by society at large has brought her to isolation. Estranged from her daughter, she retires alone to Lovel Grange.

V. *Harry Heathcote of Gangoil*

> My hold of the colonies is the close affection which grows from common names, from kindred blood, from similar privileges, and equal protection. These are ties which, though light as air, are strong as links of iron.
>
> —Edmund Burke, quoted by Trollope in
> *Australia and New Zealand*, 1:1

At the end of *Lady Anna*, Trollope sends his hero and heroine to Australia, his own destination while he was writing the book. The voyage resulted in a travel book, *Australia and New Zealand* (1873), and a brief novel set in Australia. *Harry Heathcote of Gangoil* is based on the adventures of Fred Trollope, the novelist's younger son, who had settled in the colony in 1869. The events of the story occur in the two weeks before Christmas 1871, when Trollope was in Australia himself. The book ends with a proposal of marriage on Christmas day; Fred Trollope married in December 1871. Heathcote is a Queensland sheep farmer, the occupation Fred Trollope followed in New South Wales, though Heathcote is more successful than young Trollope. "I grieve

149

to say that several thousands of pounds which I had squeezed out of the pockets of perhaps too liberal publishers have been lost on [Fred's] venture," Trollope plaintively tells us in his *Autobiography*, adding, "But I rejoice to say that this has been in no way due to any fault of his. I never knew a man work with more persistent honesty at his trade than he has done."[67] Later he makes the relationship between Fred and Harry Heathcote more explicit: "I was not loth to describe the troubles to which my own son had been subjected, by the mingled accidents of heat and bad neighbours, on his station in the bush. So I wrote *Harry Heathcote of Gangoil.* . . ."[68]

Some of Trollope's personal reasons for writing this novel become clear when we know of Fred Trollope's situation, and Trollope's attitude toward his son seems to shape the incidents of the story. Harry Heathcote is strong and imperious. Through ceaseless industry and pluck he saves his estate from arsonists. The book is a kind of sermon to Fred, a celebration of courage, industry, and independence. In a letter to his Australian friend, George William Rusden, written from Fred's house at Mortray Station, Trollope hints that Fred had not quite attained these virtues: "Speaking as a colonist you seem to think, as sons so often think of their fathers, that enough has not been done because the father wishes the son to thrive by dint of his own mettle."[69] Harry Heathcote possesses a very generous share of that "mettle." At the same time, Trollope emphasizes the difficulties of a sheep-farmer's life, and the heavy demands made on his time and energy. The novelist seems to be wrestling with himself, partly exhorting Fred to be self-sufficient, partly admitting that all kinds of accidents can destroy the work of even the best farmer and that he can fail without being at fault. Trollope seems to be trying to work out, in the controlled situation of a novel, problems in his relationship with his son.

67. *An Autobiography* 19:348.
68. *An Autobiography* 20:357.
69. *Letters* (Trollope to George William Rusden, 29 October 1871), p. 288.

But *Harry Heathcote of Gangoil* is slight, limited in style and scope by the conditions of its publication. Written in June 1873, in a month taken from the writing of *The Way We Live Now*, the tale appeared as the Christmas number of *The Graphic* that same year. "Nothing can be more distasteful to me than to have to give a relish of Christmas to what I write," Trollope tells us in the *Autobiography*. "I feel the humbug implied by the nature of the order."[70] In *Harry Heathcote* there is a Christmas feast, but the subtitle—"A Tale of Australian Bush Life"—indicates how Trollope evaded the humbug. He dwells on the blazing heat of Christmas in semitropical Queensland, and his real interest is the wildness and strangeness of Australian life, a theme turned into melodrama by a group of villainous outcasts who try to burn Heathcote's estate. These exotic touches are balanced by a conventional courtship. Manners, climate, and landscape make Australia the antithesis of England, but the people who live there are at heart much like their relatives at home.

Trollope seems to be suffering from both a personal and an artistic feeling of dislocation. He is a little baffled by the size and the strangeness of the new country. He finds it difficult to adapt Australian life to the forms of a novel, almost impossible to place the inhabitants in those familiar and precisely defined social classifications on which his work so often depends. An Australian gentleman is much harder to define than an English one. Even familiar words and concepts change their meanings in this new world. "For miles around," the Gangoil estate "was divided into paddocks, as they were there called." But these are unlike the familiar small enclosures of the English counties. These paddocks are "so large that a stranger might wander in one of them for a day and never discover that he was enclosed." Harry's sheep are kept in "five or six paddocks . . . each of which comprised over ten thousand acres."[71] These enor-

70. *An Autobiography* 20:356.
71. *Harry Heathcote of Gangoil, A Tale of Australian Bush Life* (London: Sampson, Low, Marston, Low, and Searle, 1874) 1:20.

mous areas, which retain a familiar English name but are completely different in size and function, typify Trollope's Australia. They suggest the kind of difficulty that the colony posed for a novelist used to exploring the usual.

Trollope's ambivalence is obvious in his portrayal of the hero. Harry Heathcote is impulsive, quick to anger, self-centered, imperious. He dreams of "the excellence of absolute dominion and power . . . such power as Abraham, no doubt, exercised" when "the people were submissive and the world was happy."[72] "Not to be master of all around him seemed to him to be misery."[73] "You like too much to be governor over all,"[74] an employee warns him. Trollope generally condemns the excessively individualistic man, who cannot live submissively as part of orderly society. At times he seems about to condemn these traits in *Harry Heathcote of Gangoil*, to mount one more attack on the dangers of nonconformity. Harry is literally isolated by the frequently invoked "silence of the bush, and the feeling of great distances,"[75] but he is also temperamentally isolated. He quarrels with his few neighbors and with several of his employees, sometimes with good reason, but sometimes out of misanthropy. "Neighbours!" he exclaims. "I don't know any word that there's so much humbug about. The Samaritan was the best neighbour I ever heard of, and he lived a long way off, I take it."[76] He avoids society, remarking that friendship may be worse than enmity. "I suppose I'm fitted for bush life," he admits, "for I want to see no one from year's end to year's end but my own family and my own people."[77] Harry has the traits of the Ishmaelite. He lacks that ability to live in harmony with others which Trollope consistently values. He seems dangerously antisocial and individualistic, recalling the madness of Louis Trevelyan in *He Knew He Was Right* and of Robert Kennedy in *Phineas Redux*, the inane solitude of Lord Brotherton in *Is He Popenjoy?*, and Cousin Henry's guilty solitude.

72. 9:227-228. 73. 4:86. 74. 2:47. 75. 8:207.
76. 3:60. 77. 3:65.

But Australia is not England. Like the word *paddocks*, these traits do not mean quite the same thing in the new world. Harry is living where there are no social institutions to maintain the fabric of civilization. Police are few, and even when they come there is not much that they can do. Like Trollope's Ireland, it is a world of lawless and dangerous men. Harry's neighbors, the Brownbies, are ex-convicts, cattle-thieves, drunkards, and arsonists. He cannot count on that shared respect for order which is found among land-owners at home. Even Medlicot, a law-abiding neighbor, harbors one of Harry's discharged employees for a time. Medlicot refuses to recognize the dangerous lawlessness of the country. He tries to retain traditional English attitudes toward society, law, and justice, demanding absolute proof of guilt before he will dismiss Harry's ex-employee. As a result, Nokes, the employee, is able to plot against Harry, and Medlicot himself is injured.

In Queensland it is difficult, perhaps even dangerous, to behave in accordance with English customs. The kind of man Trollope would endorse in England may be unable to survive in this new land, where there is no established society to support him. When his employee rebukes him for liking "too much to be governor over all," Harry replies sharply that "Somebody must be governor, or everything would go to the devil."[78] Law and society cannot impose and maintain order here. Each man must do it for himself. In the asocial Australian world the man who can make his own laws is needed, even though such a situation dangerously encourages self-will and is a temptation to tyranny. "Men said [of Harry Heathcote] that he was too imperious, too masterful, too much inclined to think that all things should be made to go as he would have them."[79]

Although Harry's way is generally right in the rough conditions under which he must live, Trollope cannot quite bring himself to endorse it completely. He admits that Harry's enemies are rascals who threaten all society, but

78. 2:47.   79. 1:5.

suggests that it might be possible to live among such men diplomatically, ignoring them without arousing their enmity. Trollope cannot completely abandon his distrust of the nonconformist, nor his trust in a social order based upon man's ability to get along with his fellows. In *Australia and New Zealand*, however, he is somewhat more positive about the Australian squatter's life:

> I don't know that there can be a much happier life than that of a squatter, if the man be fairly prosperous, and have natural aptitudes for country occupations. He should be able to ride and to shoot,—and to sit in a buggy all day without inconvenience. He should be social,—for he must entertain often and be entertained by other squatters; but he must be indifferent to society, for he will live away from towns. . . . He must be able to command men, and must do so, in a frank and easy fashion,—not arrogating to himself any great superiority, but with full power to let those around him know that he is master. . . . The sense of ownership and mastery, the conviction that he is the head and chief of what is going on around; the absence of any necessity of asking leave or of submitting to others,—these things in themselves add a great charm to life. The squatter owes obedience to none, and allegiance only to the merchant. . . . He goes where he likes and nobody questions him.[80]

There is an intriguing whiff of self-awareness here. Trollope's literary admiration for the conforming, self-effacing gentleman may partially originate in his own inability to live up to this ideal. Escott, Edmund Yates, Henry James, and other contemporaries describe his loud, dominating social manner; James Russell Lowell found him "rather underbred. . . . A good roaring positive fellow who deafened me," and records Trollope's dialogue with Dr. Oliver Wendell Holmes:

80. Anthony Trollope, *Australia*, ed. P. D. Edwards and R. B. Joyce (St. Lucia, Queensland: University of Queensland Press, 1967) 6:131-132.

Dr. You don't know what Madeira is in England?

T. I'm not so sure it's worth knowing . . .

Dr. But you may be assured—

T. No, but I mayn't be asshorred. I don't intend to be asshorred (roaring louder)![81]

Trollope's success as a civil servant began only after he became in effect his own master, supervising his own districts in Ireland and later England with little interference from his colleagues, and comparatively little intercourse with them.

In *Harry Heathcote*, he suggests that Harry's imperious ways may have caused some of his problems. But nevertheless, Medlicot, the man who believes in social order and most closely resembles the typical Trollope hero, is wrong about Australian conditions. His inexperience leads him to treat Nokes as he would treat an accused but unconvicted man in England. In this society it is a man of law and order, like Medlicot, who is to Harry an "interloper,"[82] rather than the aggressive individualist who would be considered an interloper at home. In the southern hemisphere all the norms are reversed.

The new land, then, demands a differend kind of man than the old. The man who cannot get along in England, who feels restricted in English society, will probably prosper in Australia. Harry, like Fred Trollope, disliked school in England and rebelled against his guardian, but the traits

81. James Pope Hennessy, *Anthony Trollope* (London: Jonathan Cape, 1971), p. 284.

82. Harry is a squatter—that is, he leases his acres for grazing from the Crown. The Crown lands were for sale to any purchaser, however. Medlicot is a free-selector, a man who purchases Crown lands for farming rather than for sheep. The squatters resented the free-selectors because they took land that the squatters needed and had come to consider their own. Harry feels that the laws should forbid free-selecting. Trollope himself did not agree. "Personally, I love a squatter," he declared in *Australia and New Zealand*, ". . . I can make myself at home with him. . . . But on principle I take the part of the free-selector" (*Australia*, pp. 200-201). He saw the squatter as "the gentleman *par excellence* of the colony," but realized that only the farming free-selector would properly settle the land and civilize it.

that produce rebellion in England produce firmness in his new home.

Trollope does not rest content with so simple a theme. As the novel progresses, he allows Harry to become aware of his isolation and even to fear it and hate it. He begins to criticize his own misanthropy, even though events seem to justify it. Gradually he becomes aware of

> a terrible feeling of loneliness in his sorrow. He bore a brave outside to all. . . . He forced upon them all an idea that he was not only autocratic but self-sufficient also— that he wanted neither help nor sympathy. He never cried out in his pain, being heartily ashamed even of the appeal which he had made to Medlicot . . . and never acknowledged that his trials were almost too much for him. But he was painfully conscious of his own weakness. He sometimes felt, when alone in the bush, that he would fain get off his horse, and lie upon the ground and weep till he slept . . . he had no one with whom he could converse freely. . . . He had chosen to manage everything himself, without contradiction and almost without counsel; but, like other such imperious masters, he now found that when trouble came the privilege of dictatorship brought with it an almost insupportable burden.[83]

Something is working to change him, and he gradually becomes aware of the dangers that are implicit in his insistence on isolation and absolute power. The civilized norms are necessary, and at the end of the novel Harry begins to move toward an acceptance of society, symbolized by the amiable Christmas feast and certified by Harry's delighted consent when Medlicot proposes to his sister-in-law, accepting him gladly as neighbor, friend, and kinsman. In the novel, Trollope justifies the individualist, but at the end his hero is coming to terms with society. In time, perhaps (Harry, like Fred Trollope, is only twenty-four), as the land becomes more civilized and society becomes safe and orderly, Harry will approach the English norm. But in writing his novel,

83. *Harry Heathcote of Gangoil* 5:111-112.

Trollope conveyed primarily his own dislocation in Australia, as well as an uncertainty about the probable future of the transplanted Englishmen who lived there, a theme he returns to a few years later in *John Caldigate*. As traveler, father, novelist, and believer in the essential rightness of English society and its ways, he could not but be shaken by his experience of this new land, half parody, half repudiation of the old.[84]

Harry Heathcote of Gangoil is the last of those comparatively brief novels of 1868-73. In writing them, Trollope moved away from the loosely constructed novels of the fifties and sixties, and greater care in organization and composition is also evident in the portions of the Palliser cycle written during this period. Trollope was learning at last how to control his sprawling talent, how to order his material, and how to define the values that he wished to defend.

---

84. J. H. Davidson, in "Anthony Trollope and the Colonies," *Victorian Studies* 12 (1969): 305-330, discusses the contrast between Harry Heathcote's Australia and the sordid world of *The Way We Live Now*.

❋ V ❋

THE PAPER KINGDOMS
The Way We Live Now

> A gentleman in our days is supposed to have his
> hands clean; but there has got abroad among us a
> feeling that, only let a man rise high enough, soil
> will not stick to him.
>
> —Trollope, *The Life of Cicero* 1:4

> Are these your Pattern Men? *Great* Men? They
> are your lucky (or unlucky) Gamblers swollen *big*.
> Paltry Adventurers for most part; worthy of no
> worship . . . to the modern English populations,
> Supreme Hero and Supreme Scoundrel are,
> perhaps, as nearly as is possible to human crea-
> tures, indistinguishable. . . . Raise statues to the
> swollen Gambler as if he were great, sacrifice obla-
> tions to the King of Scrip,—unfortunate mortals,
> you will dearly pay for it yet.
>
> —Carlyle, "Hudson's Statue,"
> *Latter-Day Pamphlets*

THE WAY WE LIVE NOW is strikingly different in themes and
structure from the shorter novels we have been examining.
Written between May and December 1873, and published in
parts shortly afterwards (February 1874 to September 1875;
two-volume edition in July 1875), the work represents Trollope's most elaborate use of his panoramic and analogical
technique in a single novel, and the fullest exposition of his
moral and social values.

"Dishonesty magnificent in its proportions, and climbing
into high places . . . become . . . rampant and . . . splendid"[1] is Trollope's own description of his theme. The theme

---

1. *An Autobiography* 20:354.

is personified in Augustus Melmotte, a financial speculator who appears in London. No one knows his background or origins, but he soon becomes an object of veneration in the commercial, social, and political spheres, and even among unworldly religious people. Melmotte is really little more than rumor and illusion; his sudden rise is due less to any deep scheming or villainy on his part than to society's apparent inability to enforce its own standards, which implies an inability to recognize Melmotte's insubstantiality. Society, after all, welcomed Disraeli.

Trollope broadens his situation and extends his social panorama by introducing a number of analogues to Melmotte, minor frauds who successfully impose on various sectors of society. The motif of fraudulent imposition and an unwillingness to expose it is repeated again and again, until the particular becomes the typical. All society seems to move in a vast meaningless dance around illusions, a series of hollow centers.

The general details of Melmotte's career are probably based on the activities of several notorious nineteenth-century speculators: Henry Fauntleroy, John Sadleir, and especially George Hudson (1800-71), who was known as "the Railway King," "the Railway Napoleon," and "the Yorkshire Balloon."[2] Trollope had referred to Sadleir—and summarized the theme of *The Way We Live Now* nearly

2. Fauntleroy, a London banker, forged a power of attorney to keep his bank solvent; he was executed for forgery in 1824; Melmotte also forges a power of attorney. Like Melmotte, John Sadleir (1814-56) failed when the City lost confidence in him; he spent the last day of his life showing himself in the City and at his club, then committed suicide, as Melmotte does, with prussic acid. Trollope used certain incidents from the careers of these men in depicting Melmotte; he also uses incidents from Disraeli's career, and the falseness and reckless adventuring that Disraeli represented to Trollope are the novelist's major target. It was common knowledge that Disraeli, early in his career, had speculated in dubious Anglo-Mexican Mining shares, and had written pamphlets endorsing the company and its plans, even though the shares were worthless and the mining operation did not exist. He was also supposed to have once addressed the House of Commons while drunk. See Robert Blake, *Disraeli*, pp. 24-26, 344. For Fauntleroy and Sadleir, see R. B. Martin, *Enter Rumour* (New York: W. W. Norton, 1962).

twenty years before he wrote that novel—on the last page of *The New Zealander*:

> It is not of swindlers and liars that we need live in fear, but of the fact that swindling and lying are gradually becoming not abhorrent to our minds. . . . Could the career of that wretched man who has lately perished have been possible, had falsehood, dishonesty, pretences, and subterfuges been odious in the eyes of those who came daily in contact with his doings?[3]

Trollope rather reluctantly conceded the influence of Carlyle on *The Way We Live Now*,[4] and his treatment of Melmotte seems indebted to Carlyle's treatment of Hudson in *Latter-Day Pamphlets* (1850), where the Scottish sage sardonically suggests that a statue to Hudson would appropriately symbolize the degenerate values of contemporary Englishmen, "that our 'Religion' might be seen, mounted on some figure of a Locomotive, garnished with Scrip-rolls proper."[5] Hudson's railway empire, which existed chiefly on paper, had vanished in the financial panic of 1847, leaving investors with only worthless scrip. "We are a lost gregarious horde," thundered Carlyle, "with Kings of Scrip on this hand . . . presided over by the Anarch Old."[6] Carlyle anticipates Trollope in seeing society's adulation of "the swollen Gambler"[7] as more dangerous than the activities of the speculator himself; in *The Way We Live Now*, Trollope expresses the same idea through Roger Carbury, who represents traditional values. Roger describes Melmotte as

---

3. *The New Zealander* 13:211. This passage, written in 1856, helps to refute the notion that Trollope's view of contemporary life became more pessimistic as he grew older.

4. *An Autobiography* 20:354.

5. Thomas Carlyle, "Hudson's Statue," *Latter-Day Pamphlets* (New York: Charles Scribner's Sons, 1898), pp. 255-256. Trollope read *Latter-Day Pamphlets* in 1851, and declared that Carlyle's "grain of sense is so smothered up in a sack of the sheerest trash, that the former is valueless." See *Letters* (Trollope to Frances Trollope, 1851), pp. 14-15.

6. Carlyle, p. 283.   7. Carlyle, p. 287.

. . . a miserable imposition, a hollow vulgar fraud from
beginning to end;—too insignificant for you and me to talk
of, were it not that his position is a sign of the degeneracy
of the age. What are we coming to when such as he is an
honoured guest at our tables? . . . They who do set the
example go to his feasts, and of course he is seen at theirs
in return. And yet these leaders of the fashion know,—at
any rate they believe,—that he is what he is because he
has been a swindler greater than other swindlers. What
follows as a natural consequence? Men reconcile themselves to swindling. Though they themselves mean to be
honest, dishonesty of itself is no longer odious to
them. . . . It seems to me that the existence of a Melmotte is not compatible with a wholesome state of things
in general.[8]

Like Hudson, Melmotte gives parties attended by statesmen, noblemen, and members of the Royal Family; he is
elected to Parliament as a Conservative, as Hudson was in
1845, and enjoys Disraeli's friendship as did his real life
prototype.

In *An Autobiography*, Trollope characterizes *The Way We
Live Now* as a satire,[9] and describes the book as a general
assault upon the vices of the day; the title further indicates
an exhibition of English habits and morals in the 1870s.
There are many displays in this exhibition, and they all
show that fraudulence and sham has made truth an exile
from contemporary London. Trollope supplements this
main theme with other favorite ideas: the importance of
traditional values and their mainstay, the English gentleman; the danger outsiders pose to traditional values; the
similar danger posed by self-willed Napoleonic or Byronic
individuals.

As in other long novels of this period, especially *The Prime
Minister* and *The American Senator*, Trollope has employed a

8. *The Way We Live Now*, ed. Robert Tracy (Indianapolis: Bobbs-
Merrill, 1974) 55:446. All citations from *The Way We Live Now* will be from
this edition.
9. *An Autobiography* 20:355.

complex system of parallel plots which are analogical and mutually referential, continually commenting on each other and restating the main themes. Characters and events reappear in different forms as the novelist presents the complexity of real life and at the same time tries to keep his argument continually before the reader.

The book studies the interrelated affairs of several families, and Trollope develops his analogical structure across these familial relationships. He may have known and recalled Balzac's declaration, in the preface to *La Comédie humaine* (1842): "Aussi regardé-je la Famille et non l'Individu comme le véritable élément social."[10] Like the French novelist, Trollope depicts his families as miniatures of society. They resemble the larger social order which is based upon them, and which functions or fails to function much as they do.

First of all, there is the Carbury family: Sir Felix Carbury, a dissolute and penniless young baronet who needs a rich wife; his scheming mother, Lady Carbury, who writes worthless books and is an expert at getting them favorably reviewed; his sister Hetta; and their cousin, Roger Carbury of Carbury, a country gentleman and head of the family, who is Melmotte's moral opposite in the book. Next are the Longestaffes: Adolphus Longestaffe, a neighbor of Roger Carbury in Suffolk; his wife and elder daughter; his younger daughter, Georgiana, who has spent ten unsuccessful seasons in London searching for a rich and titled husband; and his foolish son Adolphus, or Dolly. Then there are the Melmottes: the financier himself; his foreign wife; and his daughter Marie, considered the richest heiress in London, pursued by a crowd of impoverished young noblemen. All three families are variously involved in one another's affairs: Sir Felix Carbury and Mr. Longestaffe sit on the do-nothing board of directors for Melmotte's nonexistent South Central Pacific and Mexican Railway, and

10. *L'Oeuvre de Balzac*, ed. Albert Béguin (Formes et Reflets, 1953), 15:375.

Georgiana Longestaffe lives in Melmotte's house for a time; Sir Felix is one of Marie Melmotte's suitors; Melmotte rents the Longestaffes' London house, and later Mr. Longestaffe sells him an estate, a transaction that involves Melmotte in forgery and helps to bring about his downfall.

Many of the basic physical and social relationships of the plot are determined by the organization and activities of these three families. All three families are as disorganized and falsely motivated as the larger society of which they are a part, and as ready to pursue illusions. All three are disintegrating families, in which battles rage between parents and children. Dolly Longestaffe and his father squabble over money, and cannot be civil to one another. Georgiana and her father are at war after he refuses to pay for another husband-hunting season in London. Like Melmotte, Mr. Longestaffe is supposed to be rich, but in fact is short of money. He is mostly appearance, "a tall, heavy man, about fifty, with hair and whiskers carefully dyed, whose clothes were made with great care . . . who thought very much of his personal appearance. . . ."[11] His involved finances, and his secrecy about them, emphasize his parallels with Melmotte.

The Carburys also depend on illusion. Lady Carbury's literary reputation is a manipulated fraud,[12] like Melmotte's financial empire. Infatuated with her son, she sacrifices everything to him; he takes her money and repays her with lies and empty promises, the same items Melmotte negotiates. Though he is a baronet, Sir Felix is not the head of the Carbury family and has neither money nor estate to support his title. He is openly scornful of Roger, who owns the family estate. Hetta Carbury respects Roger but rebels against her mother's wishes by refusing to marry him.

Melmotte operates in a larger world than that of his family, but at home his daughter Marie is illegitimate, and Madame Melmotte is not her mother. Marie is sullen and rebellious. Her father threatens her, and occasionally beats

11. *The Way We Live Now* 13:101.   12. 1:3-12.

her. She robs him and tries to run off with Sir Felix; later, in his extreme need, she denies him money that he had placed in her name.

Trollope's general attack on the relaxed morals of the day is further developed by continual commentary. Roger Carbury's complaints about "the degeneracy of the age"[13] are echoed by Mrs. Pipkin, a London boarding-house keeper, when her country-bred niece is fooled by Sir Felix's pretence of love, just as society is fooled by Melmotte's pretence of wealth and power. "We usen't to have our ways like that when I was young,"[14] the woman sobs. Even the depraved Sir Felix can point to the old days as a more moral time. "Fellows used to pay their gambling debts," he grumbles, in a conversation which emphasizes the similarities between Melmotte's activities and those of the idle young men who gather at the Beargarden, a London club. A companion replies,

> "They don't now,—unless they like it. How did a fellow manage before, if he hadn't got it?"
> "He went smash," said Sir Felix, "and disappeared and was never heard of any more. It was just the same as if he'd been found cheating. I believe a fellow might cheat now and nobody'd say anything!"
> "I shouldn't," said Lord Nidderdale. "What's the use of being beastly ill-natured?"[15]

Nidderdale's easy-going tolerance for wrongdoing underlines Roger's remarks about the weakening of society's moral sense: "Men reconcile themselves to swindling. Though they themselves mean to be honest, dishonesty of itself is no longer odious to them."[16]

Trollope reinforces his general condemnation of the age

---

13. 55:446.
14. 71:570. Tony Tanner discusses the novel's atmosphere of change in "Trollope's *The Way We Live Now:* Its Modern Significance," *Critical Quarterly* 9 (1967): 256-271.
15. 22:179.   16. 55:446.

by suggesting through parallel situations that there is nothing unusual about Melmotte or his actions. His financial manipulations depend on the circulation of meaningless bits of paper that represent non-existent property. In the miniature society of the Beargarden, an analogue to the great world, everything is permitted. It is a club without any of the traditional rules that maintain order,[17] and all day long its members gamble for IOUs, meaningless bits of paper which they all realize will never be redeemed. Trollope has sharpened the parallel to Melmotte by naming this club, for in commercial slang *bear* means stock that exists purely for speculation (the phrase "sell a bear," means to sell something one does not possess), and a garden is a place where one is betrayed and defrauded.[18] The City, where Melmotte operates, and the Beargarden are identical.

Trollope continually suggests that Melmotte is only a manifestation of evil, not its cause. The worlds of business, fashion, and politics flock to do him honor until all society is engaged in a dance around this "hollow vulgar fraud."[19] The representatives of religion are willing to tolerate his shady reputation and his unknown past. Because he donates to both the Church of England and the Catholic Church he is praised in almost identical terms by the worldly Bishop of Elmham and the zealous Roman Catholic, Father Barham. Both the Conservatives and the Liberals beg him to stand for Parliament. His hollowness is ignored because society wants to believe in him.

17. Trollope may have been thinking of the Marlborough Club, founded by the Prince of Wales in 1869 because he resented the limitations on smoking imposed at White's Club. See Philip Magnus, *King Edward the Seventh* (New York: E. P. Dutton, 1964), p. 105. "Smoke all over the house" is one of the Beargarden's chief attractions, along with "Not a vestige of propriety, or any beastly rules to be kept" (96:774).

18. See Eric Partridge, *A Dictionary of Slang and Unconventional English* (New York: Macmillan, 1970), 7th ed. A "bear" is also a stock manipulator who sells short; and "bearbaiting" is gambling. Cockshut (p. 207) suggests that the Beargarden "imitates" Melmotte.

19. 55:446. Tony Tanner (see note 14) speaks of "a society whirling around in the vortex of money-mad London."

Melmotte uniquely villainous. Respectable mem-
ciety are as greedy and fraudulent as he. Men of
ome directors of his South Central and Mexican
without ever asking about its real existence. Miles
ill, the nephew of a duke, becomes Melmotte's assis-
ne cheats at cards at the Beargarden, just as his
employer cheats on a larger scale. Miles's father acts as
Melmotte's social secretary. Lord Nidderdale and Sir Felix
pretend to love Marie Melmotte to obtain money, and lie to
Melmotte about their own fortunes. No one cares for
truth—Melmotte is doubted only by Dolly Longestaffe and
Roger Carbury, the fool and the old-fashioned man of
honor.

When the novel opens we find Lady Carbury writing to
book reviewers so that they will favorably review her worthless book, *Criminal Queens*—itself a fraud, concocted without any real knowledge of history, and without research.
Her letters immediately draw us into a world ready to accept that which is untrue. Lady Carbury's creation of a false
reputation is an overture to the book's whole theme of fraud
and its picture of a society circling joylessly and mean-
inglessly around the hollow idol it has made.

For this theme of meaninglessness to succeed, it is structurally essential that Melmotte never be revealed as more
than a hollow man, and this posed artistic problems for
Trollope. Because Melmotte must be a void he can have no
inner debate about his actions. Analogous characters must
provide us with this self-awareness and debate, just as Lady
Macbeth's nightmare shows us not only her own mental
state, but Macbeth's suffering as well. When we are shown
Lady Carbury's careful manipulation of the press to create a
favorable public image out of nothing, her tricks allow us to
understand how Melmotte's reputation came into being.
His lack of any inner life emphasizes his role as a projection
of society's wishes rather than as a ruthless man of will. He
must be empty, and when we are finally allowed behind the

facade and into his mind we find him busy only with that facade, thinking of ways to persuade the world that all is well. Lady Carbury's self-publicity, Sir Felix's irresponsible scheming, and Mr. Longestaffe's greed provide us with samples of behavior similar to Melmotte's, which can be explained, and through these explanations Trollope makes it possible for us to guess something of what happens inside the mystery man himself without filling that void which is essential to the book's theme. Melmotte cannot exist as a human being. To make him a real man would give the book's central void an inhabitant, and the whole point is that it has none. Society has venerated a mirage. It is a brilliant exercise in reticence, for by leaving Melmotte a void Trollope gives his satire its final emphatic point, that all is vanity.

Yet some introspection and some moral debate are necessary or the book would be little more than polemic. For the novel to have its full effect we must be made to understand the attraction of Melmotte's ways, the temptation that his fraud offers and to which so many people yield. Trollope manages this in two ways. First, he shows us how eagerly society cooperates in the creation of Melmotte—Carlyle's point in his essay about Hudson—and how consistently members of society employ fraud and illusion themselves. The novelist's second device is to tempt Roger Carbury toward falsehood. Roger is not tempted by the excitements or by the pinchbeck luxuries for which others sell themselves. He is rather tempted to falsehood itself.

Roger Carbury represents traditional morality, but he is also used to help us understand the attractions of immorality. Trollope develops him as a conventional moral spokesman, the good man opposed to all Melmotte represents. His commitment to tradition is continually emphasized. He is Carbury of Carbury Manor, and Carbury has been in the family since the Wars of the Roses. Roger is fittingly opposed to Melmotte's upstart splendor, but because he is one of Trollope's conventionally virtuous country gentlemen, it is easy to overlook his real role, and the way Trollope prevents him from becoming a cliché. Because Roger knows that he is right about Melmotte and about "the degeneracy of the age," it is easy for him to become self-righteous. He loves his cousin Hetta, and knows himself to be a better man than his rival, Paul Montague. Paul is weak and foolish. He is involved in Melmotte's railroad enterprise, and he has promised to marry an American, Mrs. Hurtle. When Hetta hears about this entanglement, she suspects that Paul is behaving dishonorably toward herself. She questions Roger about the situation, making him the arbiter of her destiny, Paul's, and his own—Hetta will marry him, as he hopes, if she cannot marry Paul.

Roger knows that Paul is guilty only of weakness and equivocation with Mrs. Hurtle; he lived with her in the United States, before he had ever known Hetta, and has since tried to break off the relationship. But the weakness is there, and Roger also believes that Paul has stolen Hetta from him. When Hetta asks Roger for advice, he is tempted to use the situation to gain her for himself. He does not even need to lie to her—a simple refusal to discuss the matter will ruin Paul in her eyes. Hetta will never question Roger's decision, for, though she does not love him, she trusts him absolutely.

Though he is convinced of Paul's unworthiness, Roger can only convince Hetta of it by allowing her to condemn Paul for the wrong reasons. Melmotte creates false appearances; all Roger needs to do is to tolerate them. He is tempted to build his life around an attractive lie, which is what Melmotte has done. Roger's struggle explores the moral issues of tolerating a lie, and living a lie, an exploration Trollope cannot provide in Melmotte's case because it is thematically essential that Melmotte not be capable of moral introspection. But the struggle turns Roger from a conventional spokesman for virtue to a real man. He is really tempted, and nearly yields. When he finally chooses to act well and tell Hetta the truth about Paul and Mrs. Hurtle, Trollope saves him from priggishness—and the reader's scorn—by allowing him to make the decision grudgingly. He gives Hetta the assurances she needs, but at the same time he entertains a very human resentment.

Although Trollope shows us Roger's temptation at length, he makes little of the actual decision, and even deemphasizes this decision with a final ironic twist. While Roger is struggling to act well, Mrs. Hurtle herself absolves Paul by telling Hetta that Paul has acted weakly but not dishonorably. Roger's battle is rendered irrelevant in terms of plot; its function is entirely thematic, to set out the moral problem that underlies the book, the temptation of the attractively untrue, and to make this problem real by allowing us to see it argued in the soul of a good man. After we have made the conventional response to Melmotte by condemning him, Trollope suddenly tempts us to condone Roger if he allows a false impression to go uncontradicted. We are reminded of how uncertain our own sense of morality—like Roger's—can be, when faced with a variant of Melmotte's temptation. Trollope uses the episode to engage the reader in the book's central moral issues.

Melmotte may take his name from the tormented hero of Charles Maturin's Gothic novel, *Melmoth the Wanderer* (1820), or perhaps from Balzac's ironic sequel, *Melmoth réconcilié* (1835); in *Melmoth the Wanderer*, the sinister hero, an Irishman as Melmotte is rumored to be, sells his soul to the Devil; Balzac describes the same man as selling the evil powers he has gained to the unscrupulous cashier of a Parisian bank, and subsequently they are traded like a commodity on the Paris exchange; Trollope's Melmotte, his name now gallicized, comes to London from Paris to speculate in the British capital. Balzac had brought the haunted Byronic hero and the "Corsair" up to date by attacking "les corsaires que nous décorons du nom de Banquiers."[20] Trollope

20. Balzac, *Melmoth réconcilié*, in *Oeuvres complètes* (Paris: Guy Le Prat, n.d.), 18:360.

shared the French writer's realization that the reckless adventurer was now to be found in banks and parliaments rather than on a pirate ship.

Mrs. Hurtle finds in Melmotte the qualities of Napoleon I, and admires both men because they are above the law:

> "I would sooner see that man [Melmotte] than your Queen, or any of your dukes or lords. They tell me that he holds the world of commerce in his right hand. What power;—what grandeur!"
>
> "Grand enough," said Paul, "if it all came honestly."
>
> "Such a man rises above honesty," said Mrs. Hurtle, "as a great general rises above humanity when he sacrifices an army to conquer a nation. Such greatness is incompatible with small scruples. A pigmy man is stopped by a little ditch, but a giant stalks over the rivers."
>
> "I prefer to be stopped by the ditches," said Montague.[21]

Mrs. Hurtle's reasons for admiring the Napoleonic type have a parallel in the theories of Dostoevsky's Raskolnikov, in *Crime and Punishment*, who dreams of a superman above all ordinary laws. Like many other nineteenth-century writers, who use the figure of the first Napoleon as an example of selfish and lawless individualism, Trollope and Dostoevsky agree in condemning the man who declares himself free from traditional moral restraints. Both novelists were drawing on the same source, a biography of Julius Caesar (published 1865-66) by the French Emperor, Napoleon III—"that most futile book,"[22] Trollope calls it, in *An Autobiography*. Napoleon III argued that great men can ig-

---

21. 26:211.

22. *An Autobiography* 18:338. See also *Letters* (Trollope to W. Lucas Collins, 6 April 1870), p. 260. Dostoevsky's awareness of the book is noted in Mikhail Bakhtin, *Problems of Dostoevsky's Poetics*, trans. R. W. Rotsel (Ardis, 1973), pp. 74-75. The words "Napoléon" and "Julius Caesar" in calligraphic form occur frequently in Dostoevsky's notebooks for *Crime and Punishment*. See Konstantin Mochulsky, *Dostoevsky: His Life and Work*, trans. Michael A. Minihan (Princeton: Princeton University Press, 1967), p. 278.

nore the laws. He justified the various illegal acts by which
Caesar established himself as dictator on these grounds, and
implicitly justified similar acts that he and Napoleon I had
performed in their own seizures of power. Since Trollope
tells us that Melmotte left France after the fall of Napoleon
III, he may intend us to perceive resemblances between the
financier—"the Napoleon of Finance"—and the Emperor;
like Melmotte, Napoleon III was an upstart and a gambler;
he successfully imposed on his countrymen for a time; he
lacked substance, and when this was realized he fell as
rapidly as Melmotte. Trollope may also have been thinking
of the resemblances between Napoleon III and Disraeli,
often pointed out at the time by Disraeli's political enemies,
who compared both men as unscrupulous adventurers.[23]

The most noticeable of Melmotte's analogues is Sir Felix,
a false Byronic hero, whose shifts and weaknesses are re-
lentlessly exposed. Unlike Paul Montague, who can feel
guilt, Felix can feel neither shame nor remorse. His last
moments of bravado at the end of the book, when he shows
himself at the Beargarden after he has been disgraced,
closely parallel Melmotte's conspicuous visit to the House of
Commons when his fall is imminent. Like Melmotte, Sir
Felix is for a time adored by those around him. He is loved
by his mother, by Marie Melmotte, and by Ruby Ruggles, a
farmer's daughter from Carbury Manor, and his behavior to
all three is equally deceitful. He lies to them, just as Melmotte lies to the general public. He takes his mother's
money and gambles it away; he accepts money from Melmotte as a bribe to leave Marie alone, and then prepares to
elope with her, which involves a betrayal of Ruby; later he

23. Blake, *Disraeli*, p. 404. Trollope expressed his opinion of Napoleon
III and modern Caesarism in a letter to *The Pall Mall Gazette*, dated 12 April
1865: "I do believe that educated men in Paris are beginning to be tired of
an Emperor, that they are opening their eyes to their own disgrace, and
that gradually is coming upon them once again the conviction that no
country can really thrive under a Caesar." See Bradford A. Booth, "Trollope and the *Pall Mall Gazette* (Part One)," *Nineteenth-Century Fiction* 4
(1949): 67-68.

gambles away the money that Marie has given him for their flight. Felix is so weak that Marie must plan her own elopement; after she arrives at their meeting place, she finds that Felix has not only lost the money, but has also got drunk—as Melmotte later does in his great crisis—and gone home to bed.

As for the farm girl, Ruby, Felix entices her away after he has caused her to rebel against her family's choice of a husband for her, just as he has caused Marie Melmotte to rebel. She comes to London, where Felix sees her but is unwilling to marry her or to help her. She is infatuated; he toys with her while he waits to elope with Marie, and finally attempts a seduction only to be trounced by her country lover, John Crumb. Felix's final degradation comes when he makes no attempt to defend himself against Crumb's anger. That staple of romantic Victorian fiction, the bad baronet, is turned to ridicule, shown as an empty sham. Like Melmotte, he cannot stand reality. John Crumb is, predictably, a tenant of Roger Carbury and reflects Roger's attitudes.

The role of Paul Montague has some affinities with those of Sir Felix and Melmotte, for he too is an unworthy object of veneration, weak, dangerously attractive, financially and morally insubstantial. But Paul can at least be ashamed of his conduct. He represents a kind of moral middle ground between Sir Felix—Melmotte and Roger Carbury. Sir Felix is as false as Melmotte; Paul's crime is to yield to that temptation which Roger withstands. He cannot bring himself to speak out and tell the truth. When he finally faces reality and explains himself truthfully to Mrs. Hurtle and to Hetta, he is saved.

Mrs. Hurtle also functions as an analogue to Melmotte, for each is an outsider who tries to gain a place in English society. Trollope ironically makes her a contrast to the great financier as well. She has killed a man in Oregon, and she threatens to bull-whip Paul Montague when he jilts her. She has the ruthless Napoleonic qualities that the empty

Melmotte lacks, a situation repeated in the relationship between Sir Felix and Marie Melmotte, when the weak baronet is temporarily attracted by Marie's daring. These two strong women reinforce each other thematically and provide the book with examples of a romantic heroic type to set against the false heroes. But these women have no place in an orderly society. Mrs. Hurtle remarks that "everybody here is either too humble or too overbearing. Nobody seems content to stand firm on his own footing and interfere with nobody else."[24] She rejects the values of an ordered and interdependent society in favor of that individualism which Trollope presents as inimical to order. At the end of the book she and Marie depart to the less organized society of the American West.

Mrs. Hurtle is an outsider, and her role as an outsider gives her another important thematic function, that of testifying to Melmotte's eminence by showing how even those who live outside his world, and outside society in general, are under his influence: Mrs. Hurtle; Father Barham, a Roman Catholic priest, whose conversion to an alien religion has cut him off from English society; and Mr. Brehgert, Georgiana Longestaffe's elderly Jewish suitor, whose race isolates him.

Each of these outsiders reflects some aspect of Melmotte. Mrs. Hurtle admires those very traits that his associates force themselves to overlook, his ruthlessness and criminality; her explicit attribution of Napoleonic qualities to the financier helps us to recognize him as a Romantic hero. Her obsession with heroism and excessive individualism make her vulnerable to Melmotte. She says all that can be said in his favor, and in favor of the hero who disregards conventional morality, just as Raskolnikov says all that can be said in favor of the amoral superman in *Crime and Punishment*. In both cases the defense is inadequate. Heroic herself, her

24. 71:573.

role is to exalt and defend Melmotte's apparent heroism, and to argue against the limitations that society imposes. Society's inability to find a place for her parallels its inability to assimilate Melmotte.

Father Barham also operates outside society's norms. He is incapable of an ordinary conversation, for he must turn it into an assertion of the claims of his church. He is attracted to Melmotte by the rumor that the great man is a Catholic. His obsession with conversion makes him vulnerable, and he becomes an apologist for the great man. Although his religious fervor contrasts him with the Bishop of Elmham, an easy-going man of the world, both clergymen are attracted by Melmotte, the Bishop because he is receptive to the opinions of society, the Priest because he is isolated and obsessed.

The role of Mr. Brehgert is more complex. He is a London banker involved in Melmotte's enterprises, although he is not a party to any fraud. When Melmotte falls, Brehgert suffers losses, and these losses lead to the break off of his projected marriage with Georgiana Longestaffe, a marriage opposed by her family because he is "an old fat jew."[25] Brehgert is shrewd, and a good man; he does not fall under Melmotte's spell, but even so he finds himself involved. His desire to marry Georgiana and become a part of established society reflects Melmotte's desire for assimilation, but Trollope has also used this projected marriage as a focus for some of his most ironic episodes. The fact that Melmotte is not a cause of society's corruption but a reflection of it is clarified by the treatment that the well-born Georgiana accords Brehgert. A typical Victorian reader may well have been repelled by such a marriage, but Trollope makes us see that the real victim would be Brehgert. Georgiana is the one who has the traditional attributes of greed and craftiness so often a part of the Jewish stereotype. Their exchange of letters, in which Brehgert offers honorable matrimony and Georgiana haggles about terms, is a commentary on the

25. 65:528.

society that has made Melmotte's career possible. Scorned by the mercenary Longestaffes and Monograms, Brehgert's conventional goodness emphasizes the fact that the moral man does not belong in contemporary society. His appearance at Lady Monogram's party, where everyone ignores him, is a commentary on a society that is no society at all. His invitation has been purchased by Georgiana in return for tickets to Melmotte's reception for the Emperor of China. The scene in which she and Lady Monogram barter these two social events forces us to realize that the social world and the business world are equally false and speculative:

> Miss Longestaffe was seated in Lady Monogram's back drawing-room, discussing the terms on which the two tickets for Madame Melmotte's grand reception had been transferred to Lady Monogram . . . and the terms also on which Miss Longestaffe had been asked to spend two or three days with her dear friend Lady Monogram. Each lady was disposed to get as much and to give as little as possible . . . the ordinary practice of all parties to a bargain. . . . Lady Monogram was to have the two tickets, . . . such tickets at that moment standing very high in the market. In payment for these valuable considerations, Lady Monogram was to undertake to chaperon Miss Longestaffe at the entertainment, to take Miss Longestaffe as a visitor for three days, and to have one party at her own house during the time, so that it might be seen that Miss Longestaffe had other friends in London. . . . At this moment Miss Longestaffe felt herself justified in treating the matter as though she were hardly receiving a fair equivalent. The Melmotte tickets were certainly ruling very high. They had just culminated. They fell a little soon afterwards, and at ten p.m. on the night of the entertainment were hardly worth anything. At the moment which we have now in hand, there was a rush for them.[26]

Brehgert's admission to Lady Monogram's party is part of

26. 60:482-483. See also Cockshut, p. 206.

the bargain, but it does not include any welcome for him. "I'm big enough to hold my own, and so is Sir Damask," Lady Monogram remarks as she refuses to do anything more, "But we ain't big enough to introduce new-comers."[27] Admission to such a society is hardly admission into an Eden, and Brehgert acts as witness to its falseness.

Melmotte's fall comes when he tries to create a place for himself in that society which he dominates. He understands the importance of those roots he does not have, and decides to purchase Pickering, one of Mr. Longestaffe's country estates. But when the man of illusion tampers with the land, with real property, he is destroyed. The entrance of reality into his game disrupts it, and the counters are seen for what they are, meaningless bits of paper. Melmotte converts Pickering into such a piece of paper when he forges the title deed and tries to use it in his intrigues. He is exposed by Dolly Longestaffe, who has suspected him from the start because Dolly is too stupid to fall under his spell.[28]

Throughout Trollope's novels, land and landed property are the abiding reality that stabilizes society. It is not sur-prising that Melmotte's fall comes when he lays sacrilegious hands upon this reality. Sir Felix commits the same crime when he tries to use Carbury Manor as a counter in his bargaining for Marie Melmotte and as a base of operations from which to woo her. He misuses the estate again when he attempts to seduce Ruby. He is punished for both ac-tions, and they bring about his downfall.

Melmotte's attempt to become a part of the social order rather than just its hollow center is only partly dependent on acquiring an estate. His campaign also depends on his great reception for the Emperor of China, which will estab-lish him socially. But it is impossible for Melmotte to per-form the trick of turning himself from an illusion into a real man. The system cannot tolerate him. When rumors of his fall begin to spread, fashionable society avoids him. His

27. 60:483-484.
28. See Cockshut's similar observation, p. 218.

satellites flee, and the complicated system of interlocking relationships on which social and financial credit depends is closed to him. He cannot draw on the good will and assistance of his peers, for he has none. At first splendidly isolated, he finds himself friendless and alone when his wealth is questioned. No one really causes his fall, for it is implicit in the illusory nature of his whole position.

There is one more important analogue for the great man, the Emperor of China. The Emperor is Melmotte's guest at a magnificent dinner, and throughout the episode Trollope stresses the resemblances between the monarch and his host. Both are alone amid the splendor and, like Melmotte, the Emperor is awesomely isolated. He, too, is a hollow man, a mere uniform and facade. "Prince Frederic says that he's stuffed with hay, and that he's made up fresh every morning at a shop in the Haymarket," says Lord Nidderdale. "He opens his mouth, of course. There is machinery as well as hay."[29] No one can communicate with him, for he speaks only Manchu—a pair of interpreters attend, one to translate his rare remarks from Manchu to Chinese, the other to translate from Chinese to English. Melmotte is unable to speak to the Emperor or the other royal guests because of protocol. The remaining guests refuse to address their host because of rumors about him. No one will answer his questions when he asks the reason for the many empty chairs at the table. His party is a failure. Rumor, which has made Melmotte a great man, begins to work against him. The leaders of the political, financial, and social worlds are alike unwilling to be seen at the house of a man when reports say his fortune is a sham, and his arrest is expected at any moment.

Trollope underlines the Emperor's role as an analogue for Melmotte by devices that link the two figures. He reminds us of the Emperor's isolation and unreal qualities to reinforce our sense of Melmotte's isolation and unreality, and places both men at the center of meaningless movement and

29. 62:502.

excitement. Both are passive objects of attention. For the Emperor, Trollope employs phrases like "the awful, quiescent solemnity of the celestial one[30] . . . impassible and awful dignity. . . ."[31] The Emperor seems to have no will or personality. He is moved about to provide a show, and Trollope generally employs the passive voice to chronicle his movements:

> The unfortunate Emperor . . . was marshalled into the room on the ground floor, whence he and other royalties were to be marshalled back into the banqueting hall. Melmotte, bowing to the ground, walked backwards before him, and was probably taken by the Emperor for some Court Master of the Ceremonies especially selected to walk backwards on this occasion. . . . He sat . . . for more than two hours, awful, solid, solemn, and silent, not eating very much—for this was not his manner of eating; nor drinking very much—for this was not his manner of drinking; but wondering, no doubt, within his own awful bosom, at the changes which were coming when an Emperor of China was forced, by outward circumstances, to sit and hear this buzz of voices and this clatter of knives and forks. . . . For another hour after he had returned to his place, the Emperor sat solemn in his chair; and then, at some signal given by some one, he was withdrawn. . . . According to the programme arranged for the evening, the royal guests were . . . to be paraded upstairs before the multitude . . . and to remain there long enough to justify the invited ones in saying that they had spent the evening with the Emperor and the Princes and the Princesses. The plan was carried out perfectly. At half-past ten the Emperor was made to walk upstairs, and for half an hour sat awful and composed in an armchair that had been prepared for him. How one would wish to see the inside of the mind of the Emperor as it worked on that occasion![32]

On public occasions Melmotte is equally remote, an object of attention but not a participant. At the Longestaffes'

30. 54:443.   31. 59:476.   32. 59:476-481.

party, where he himself is the guest of honor, no one feels able to speak. The occasion is another parody of social intercourse, arranged because Mr. Longestaffe needs Melmotte's money. "In accordance with the treaty, Madame Melmotte had been entertained civilly for four entire days." Melmotte "put his thumbs into the arm-holes of his waistcoat, and was impassible,"[33] reducing everyone to glum silence, and this party too is a failure. Neither Melmotte nor the Emperor can be assimilated, neither can communicate. Both exist chiefly for show. The parallel between them is particularly emphasized after the imperial reception, when Melmotte, alone in the empty house, "threw himself into the chair in which the Emperor had sat."[34] There he meditates on the wonder that he should have had an Emperor as a guest in his house, just as Trollope has earlier imagined the Emperor speculating on how odd and wonderful it is for him to be in such a house. And then, characteristically, Melmotte devotes this period of meditation to considering what face he had better show the world.

To portray Melmotte's fall, another social setting is used, the House of Commons. Melmotte is elected a Member despite the dinner fiasco, and makes his first entrance into the House in the company of Disraeli, the leader of his party.[35] There all society is represented: the fashionable world, the commercial world, and the political world. Melmotte has been revered by them all; on his second and last appearance in the House, he falls literally and symbolically.

33. 20:162.   34. 62:503.

35. 69:554. "The very leader of the party, the very founder of that new doctrine of which it was thought that Melmotte might become an apostle and an expounder . . . Mr. Melmotte was introduced to the House by the head of his party!" Trollope characterizes the "new doctrine" as "that hitherto hazy mixture of radicalism and old-fogyism, of which we have lately heard from a political master, whose eloquence has been employed in teaching us that progress can only be expected from those whose declared purpose is to stand still" (p. 552). "Melmotte was not the first vulgar man whom the Conservatives had taken by the hand, and patted on the back, and told that he was a god" (54:439).

The episode takes place when Melmotte appears to shore up his tottering position by a show of bravado. What happens is a miniature version of his entire career. At first he strikes awe in all the Members, and is the center of attention as he has always been. When he enters "there came a silence over the House which was almost audible. . . . Everybody looked up, but everybody looked up in perfect silence. . . . Augustus Melmotte, the member for Westminster, was walking up the centre of the House." He is asserting himself once more, and Trollope shifts from the effect this has on the Members to Melmotte's own desperate effort to create and maintain that effect. The illusion that he has created is explained as he struggles to maintain it:

> At this moment he was more determined than ever that no one should trace in his outer gait or in any feature of his face any sign of that ruin which, as he well knew, all men were anticipating. Therefore, perhaps, his hat was a little more cocked than usual, and the lappels of his coat were thrown back a little wider, displaying the large jewelled studs which he wore in his shirt; and the arrogance conveyed by his mouth and chin was specially conspicuous. . . . He was a big man, who always endeavoured to make an effect by deportment, and was therefore customarily conspicuous in his movements. He was desirous now of being as he was always, neither more nor less demonstrative, —but, as a matter of course, he exceeded. . . .[36]

No one will speak to him, but he is firmly resolved to go through with his performance. He remains in his place until the House adjourns for dinner, then goes to the dining-room where he sits through a solitary meal, alone as he has been on all social occasions where we have seen him. The other Members avoid sitting near him as the guests avoided his dinner for the Emperor.

After drinking until he is "brave enough almost for anything," Melmotte returns to the House and attempts to get

36. 83:673-674.

the floor during a debate. "But it seemed on that occasion that the Speaker was anxious to save the House from disgrace. . . . As long as any other member would rise he would not have his eye caught" by Melmotte. The financier's notoriety takes precedence, in the Speaker's mind, over the fact that he is a Member and has an undoubted right to speak. He is no longer worshipped, but is still Melmotte and the center of attention. Finally the Speaker is forced to recognize him.

> Melmotte standing erect, turning his head round from one side of the House to another, as though determined that all should see his audacity, propping himself with his knees against the seat before him, remained for half a minute perfectly silent. He was drunk . . . he had forgotten in his audacity that words are needed for the making of a speech, and now he had not a word at his command. He stumbled forward, recovered himself, then looked once more round the House with a glance of anger, and after that toppled headlong forward over the shoulders of Mr. Beauchamp Beauclerk, who was now sitting in front of him. . . . There was much commotion in the House. . . . The House resumed its business, taking no further notice of Melmotte . . . the member for Westminster caused no further inconvenience.[37]

With this abrupt fall the Great Financier becomes merely a drunken member of Parliament, and his fall over Mr. Beauclerk's shoulders symbolizes his fall as a public figure. A few minutes later he leaves the House "watched in silence." His notoriety, his pretenses, his isolation, his collapse, and his final ignominious exit make up a brief summary of his role in the entire book. He disrupts Parliament, a symbol of society, and then Parliament and society reassert themselves.

On his arrival home Melmotte shrinks to something less than an inconvenience. He

37. 83:676-678.

got into his own sitting-room without difficulty, and called for more brandy and water. Between eleven and twelve he was left there by his servant with a bottle of brandy, three or four bottles of soda water, and his cigar-case. . . . But at nine o'clock on the following morning the maid-servant found him dead upon the floor. Drunk as he had been,—more drunk as he probably became during the night,—still he was able to deliver himself from the indignities and penalties to which the law might have subjected him by a dose of prussic acid.[38]

With Melmotte's fall the spell he has exerted is broken. At the end of the book the world has returned to some semblance of order. A sterner reality succeeds the old license; reality, and real money, take the place of imaginary credit. The new order is felt in the Beargarden Club, where the manager, Herr Vossner, a miniature Melmotte, swindles the members by suddenly decamping, leaving them with a heavy burden of debt. His flight parallels that of one of Melmotte's associates, whose departure ruined Melmotte's credit and hastened his fall. The result of both flights is a tightening of financial laws. Melmotte is asked for cash, and after Vossner's disappearance, those who gamble at the Beargarden must pay cash. This demand for real money ends the Beargarden, as it ends Melmotte's financial empire. The club has been a miniature of an anarchic society, with "not a vestige of propriety, or any beastly rules to be kept."[39] Dolly Longestaffe pronounces an epitaph for the whole disordered world that it has reflected. "I think every-

---

38. 83:678. P. D. Edwards, in "Trollope Changes his Mind: The Death of Melmotte in *The Way We Live Now*," *Nineteenth-Century Fiction* 18 (1963): 89-91, cites Trollope's working papers in the Bodleian Library as proof that the novelist originally planned a trial for Melmotte. Edwards suggests that Trollope perhaps changed his mind because a trial might have placed Melmotte too much in the center of the stage. Roger L. Slakey, in "Melmotte's Death: A Prism of Meaning in *The Way We Live Now*," *ELH* 34 (1967): 248-259, argues that Melmotte simply cannot survive into the reality after his exposure.
39. 96:774.

thing is going to come to an end." he mourns. "I do indeed.
. . . Vossner has gone off, and it seems everybody is to pay
just what he says they owed him. . . . I feel as though there
were no good in hoping that things would ever come right
again."[40] Lord Nidderdale has understood the meaning of
all that has happened, and he accepts a new and sterner
morality:

> I don't think anybody has liked the Beargarden so
> much as I have, but I shall never try this kind of thing
> again. I shall begin reading blue books to-morrow. . . .
> Next session I shan't miss a day in the House, and I'll bet
> anybody a fiver that I make a speech before Easter. I shall
> take to claret at 20s. a dozen, and shall go about London
> on the top of an omnibus.[41]

The disappearance of this foolish club, built on illusion
and disorder, signals the destruction of the idle dreams on
which so many of the characters have lived for so long. "I
hate swells," says Marie Melmotte to Hamilton K. Fisker,
her American friend. "They never mean a word that they
say."[42] Ruby Ruggles relinquishes her hopes of Sir Felix,
realizing that "a loving heart is better nor a fickle tongue,"
and her aunt reminds her that honest John Crumb "means
what he says, and I call that the best of good manners."[43]
Even Lady Carbury, "sick of her own vanities and little-
nesses and pretences," finds "real peace . . . within her
reach" when she abandons her life of creating illusions to
become the wife of a newspaper editor, and gains "that
tranquillity which comes from an anchor holding to a firm
bottom."[44] Her conversion is a significant one, for she has
set the tone of pretence and falsehood at the beginning of
the book. She has been both an advocate and a victim of the
Melmotte world and its lies, and we should not disregard
entirely Trollope's statement that she is the "chief *charac-*

---

40. 74:600.   41. 96:778-779.   42. 92:745.
43. 94:762.   44. 99:801-802.

ter."[45] She has suffered from false stories (her late husband spread unpleasant rumors about her), she has manufactured stories—her novel and her potted histories—and she has sold them with contrived reviews, but now she turns to reality. In one sense the whole book is about her and her eventual abandonment of that pursuit of the false and worthless which Trollope shows as characteristic of "the way we live now."

45. See Trollope's working plan for *The Way We Live Now*, printed in my edition (pp. 33-35) and in Michael Sadleir, *Trollope: A Commentary*, pp. 426-428.

VI

THE NOBLE KINSMEN
Is He Popenjoy?

> "What do you suppose is the use of a child
> without any meaning?"
> —Lewis Carroll, *Through the Looking-Glass*

AFTER COMPLETING *The Way We Live Now*, Trollope returned to the Palliser cycle to write *The Prime Minister* (April to September 1874). Then he began *Is He Popenjoy?* a novel that represents a shift in technique and subject matter. The tale deals with private life rather than public affairs, and marks Trollope's abandonment of the panoramic novel about political or financial intrigue. Even Plantagenet Palliser makes his final appearance, in *The Duke's Children*, as a family man occupied with domestic relationships; *The Landleaguers* is about a political issue, but Trollope is interested in showing how that issue affects a single family.

Is He Popenjoy? is less interesting technically than *The Way We Live Now* and *The Prime Minister*, partly because Trollope makes comparatively little use of analogical or contrasting characters and situations, and partly because he seems less interested in structural innovations. In *The Way We Live Now*, he used several disintegrating families to show us a society no longer able to maintain its values; here he focuses on a single family and its chances of survival. His ambiguous presentation of his theme of family life and family continuation is the most conspicuous feature of the book.

Trollope began *Is He Popenjoy?* on 12 October 1874, and worked on the novel until his departure for Australia at the end of the following February. After a cold journey by rail to Brindisi, a voyage to Alexandria, and a trip "in the cars across the desert"[1] to Suez, he embarked on the P and O

---

1. *Letters* (Trollope to Rose Trollope, 10 March 1875), p. 337.

steamer *Peshawar* and resumed his writing. He wrote as he sailed down the Red Sea from Suez to Aden, he wrote as the ship rounded Arabia and passed the Indian coast, he wrote in the intervals of his tour of Ceylon, and he finished this "tale of modern English life"[2] in the Indian Ocean between Ceylon and Australia, on 3 May 1875. Two years later it was serialized in *All the Year Round* (13 October 1877 to 13 July 1878), and appeared in three volumes in April 1878.

The plot is simple. Mary Lovelace, daughter of the Dean of Brotherton, is rich but not well born. She marries Lord George Germain, who is well born but poor. He is the brother and heir presumptive of the unmarried Marquis of Brotherton, and the Dean hopes that his daughter will one day be marchioness. But soon after the wedding, news arrives that the Marquis, who lives abroad, has apparently been secretly married for some time. He even has an infant son and heir, who has the right to bear his father's second title and be known as Lord Popenjoy. There are, however, doubts about Popenjoy's legitimacy. Lord George, urged on by the Dean, begins an investigation, but before it is completed, Popenjoy and the Marquis die, and George becomes Marquis.

The threat that little Popenjoy offered to George's inheritance is paralleled by a double threat to his marriage. Handsome young Jack De Baron tries to begin an affair with Mary, and the scheming Mrs. Houghton encourages this while she herself tries to seduce Lord George. Mary and George are temporarily estranged, but both resist temptation. As the novel ends they are reunited, and Mary bears a son, a new and undeniable Popenjoy.

The plot is therefore exclusively concerned with the affairs of the Germain family, and the subject of the book is family life and family ambition. The pun on germane/Germain and the family title of Brotherton emphasize this preoccupation, and the two central questions of the book are questions of familial relationship. The title questions the

2. *Letters* (Trollope to George Bentley, 10 February 1875), p. 333.

186

legitimacy of the Marquis's infant son and asks what place, if any, this child has in the family tree. The other important question is also a question of family: how will Popenjoy's existence affect Lord George and Mary? Will their marriage survive the various assaults upon it, and will they be able to carry on the family?

Most of the characters range themselves on one side or the other of these family questions. They are opponents or defenders of family ties and of the family's continued existence. To Lord George, the house and the family are objects of worship, for which he willingly sacrifices himself throughout the book. He thinks chiefly of his duties to the family and urges Mary to share his values. His mother and sisters are equally devoted to the Germain family and its fortunes, and the Dean of Brotherton shares their reverence, though for slightly different motives. The Dean's ambitions are entirely familial. He has no ambition for higher ecclesiastical office. He wants only to be the grandfather of a Marquis of Brotherton, and his dream is that of Massinger's Sir Giles Overreach:

> All my ambition is to have my daughter
> Right honourable, which my lord can make her:
> And might I live to dance upon my knee
> A young lord Lovell, born by her to you,
> I write *nil ultra* to my proudest hopes.[3]

Mary wishes to be loved by her husband, and to love her father. She suffers when these two relationships and duties become for a time irreconcilable. Lord George, Mary, and the Dean all finally triumph in terms of the family, when Lord George succeeds to the title and at almost the same moment becomes the father of a future Marquis.

The Marquis, Mrs. Houghton, and Jack De Baron pose a threat to the existence and stability of the family. The Marquis lives apart from his relatives, rarely corresponds with them, and refuses to assume any of the duties of his rank.

3. Philip Massinger, *A New Way to Pay Old Debts* (1633), 4:1.

His first act in the book is to order his old mother to leave his house, and just before his death he threatens her again with expulsion. Mrs. Houghton and Jack De Baron eventually join with the Marquis to threaten the Germain marriage. De Baron himself is not malevolent, for he loves Mary, or thinks he does, and Trollope suggests that he is simply irresponsible and incapable of family life. In the course of the book he reluctantly allows himself to be engaged to a girl he cannot afford to marry. Then he falls in love with Mary because she is safely married and he is sure that she will never betray her marriage. He is used by Mrs. Houghton and the Marquis in their plots against the couple. As for Mrs. Houghton, she once refused to marry Lord George and does not love him. Impelled by spite and jealousy, she urges Jack to seduce Mary while she herself attempts George's seduction from the same motives. The Marquis hopes that Jack, by running off with Mary, will end George's hopes of continuing the family. He even leaves Jack a legacy to help him accomplish this. Jack De Baron, Mrs. Houghton—whose loveless marriage is a parody of husband and wife relations—and the Marquis are all incapable of happy marriages or of family life.

This central concern with the stability of family life explains the role of the Baroness Banmann, Dr. Olivia Q. Fleabody of Vermont,[4] and the other feminists. By deploring female "Disabilities" and demanding careers and equality with men, they pose a comic threat to George and Mary, and to the continuity of family life. They are portrayed as arid, and their drab meetings contrast with Mary's eventual

---

4. Henry James's *The Bostonians* (1886) may owe something to these scenes and characters. James also introduces a woman who is a doctor (Dr. Prance); his heroine's first name is Olive (Chancellor). In *Henry James, The Middle Years: 1882-1895* (Philadelphia: J. B. Lippincott, 1962), Leon Edel describes (pp. 142-143) how James's relatives and friends accused him of lampooning the well-known reformer Elizabeth Peabody (1804-94) in his character of Miss Birdseye. Trollope seems to have named Olivia Fleabody after her; he probably met her in Boston (1861-62). See Anthony Trollope, *North America*, ed. Donald Smalley and Bradford Allen Booth (New York: Alfred A. Knopf, 1951), pp. xxvi, 535.

triumph, achieved when she insists on her own equality in the marriage—to Trollope the only desirable feminine success. The Baroness is taken up by the Marquis toward the end of the story, to unite all the forces opposed to family life.

These opponents, rather than the fact at issue, give the question expressed in the title its importance, for most of the action depends on the characters' attitudes toward this question. Everyone wonders whether or not the dark, unhealthy little child is really the son of the Marquis and his Italian wife, and if so, whether or not he is legitimate. Even the Marquis is not quite sure. But this question is never explicitly answered. It becomes irrelevant when the child dies. "There are two Popenjoys in the book," Trollope remarks in his *Autobiography*, "but as they are both babies, and do not in the course of the story progress beyond babyhood, . . . readers . . . will not be much interested in them."[5] The novel is about the behavior of a group of people troubled by a question, and their attitudes toward it, just as *The Way We Live Now* is concerned with the agitation that surrounds Melmotte rather than with the man himself. In his later novels, Trollope often involves his characters in a mystery and then invites the reader to observe their actions, at the same time suggesting that the solution to the mystery is not very important.

Little Popenjoy, then, is of no importance in the book that bears his name—or, more precisely, which questions his right to that name. He exists only as a challenge to the ideas of family pride, duty, and ambition which pervade the entire book. As A. O. J. Cockshut suggests, he is simply a pawn,[6] valued or hated by different people in the book not for himself but because he is useful or destructive to various

5. *An Autobiography* 20:362. Charles Dickens, jun., suppressed certain passages in *Is He Popenjoy?* when it appeared in *All the Year Round*; they were restored in book publication. See T.C.D., "Victorian Editors and Victorian Delicacy," *Notes and Queries* 187 (2 December 1944): 251-253. Dickens played down De Baron's flirting and references to Mary's pregnancy.

6. A. O. J. Cockshut, *Anthony Trollope*, pp. 153-154.

schemes. Even the Marquis's vague feelings of paternity are of much less account than his desire to use Popenjoy as a way of excluding George and George's children from the title and estate. The Dean and others do not look upon Popenjoy as a child at all, only as an impediment which must be destroyed.

Popenjoy barely exists, and to some extent this is also true of his father. If the son is a dim, uncertain figure, the father is an empty one, and his role in the book is negative. He blusters and storms, but he accomplishes nothing at the last. If we never really know the truth about Popenjoy's identity, we never know the truth about the Marquis either. As we have seen, he rejects family life, and he is a villain because he sins against every possible family relationship. He is a bad son, a bad brother, a bad brother-in-law, a bad husband, and a bad father, and he hates his unborn nephews and nieces. Mrs. Houghton is his cousin, but he cares for her only because she helps him conspire against those more closely related to him. Even his very remoteness is a kind of domestic crime, for he evades family duties, and he hates England. He communicates with his mother, brother, and sisters only to banish them from his house so that he may stay there with a wife and son whose existence he has not bothered to announce to them. The whole imbroglio about Popenjoy's legitimacy is based on the Marquis's refusal to supply any information to his family. Lord George insists that his motives in seeking proof of the child's legitimacy are only to ensure that it will not be challenged later on, for he argues that unnecessary mystery about the Marquis's marriage and his son's birth could impede Popenjoy's later entrance into the title. By living mysteriously, apart from his home and family, the Marquis imperils the whole future of that family. To many of the characters in the book, his obsessive refusal to recognize family ties and duties is evidence that he is mad.

There are vague hints of other crimes and irregularities, but they remain hints. The Marquis may not be married at all. His Italian wife may have been his mistress, and she may be guilty of bigamy. Popenjoy may not be legitimate, and may not even be his child. The Marquis apparently drinks heavily, and frequents odd and probably shady company. But Trollope is careful to keep his villain from the center of the stage, denying him even that measure of desperate courage allotted to Melmotte and Lopez. The villainy we see is of a petty and dreary sort.

Brotherton represents a further stage in Trollope's attack on the Byronic hero. After examining the type in *The Prime Minister* and *The Way We Live Now*, in *Is He Popenjoy?* he reduces it to meaningless blustering malevolence. The Marquis is so unheroic that at one point he is knocked into his own fireplace by the Dean, a clergyman considerably his senior. In some ways, the career of this miserable figure draws on that of Lord Byron himself, for the Marquis's long residence in Italy, the relationship with an Italian noblewoman, and his lonely death all recall Byron's life.[7] His child dies suddenly, as did Byron's daughter Allegra. The initial letters of Brotherton's family name, Germain, and his title recall Gordon and Byron; the book's concern with the fraternal relationship recalls Byron's *Cain*; and Mary Lovelace bears the name of Byron's grandson, the Earl of Lovelace.

But *Is He Popenjoy?* contains no echo of the excitement that surrounds the traditional Byronic hero. The life of the Marquis is empty and desolate. "Everything is dull after a certain time of life, unless a man has made some fixed line for himself," he tells his only friend, old Mr. De Baron:

> "Some men can eat and drink a great deal, but I haven't got stomach for that. Some men play cards. . . . The sort of things that a man does care for die away from him, and of course it becomes dull. . . . I think I made a mistake . . . in not staying at home and looking after the property."

7. Donald D. Stone, in "Trollope, Byron, and the Conventionalities," pp. 179-203, notes Brotherton's Byronic "path of exile" (p. 194).

"It's not too late, now."

"Yes it is. I could not do it. I could not remember the tenants' names, and I don't care about game. I can't throw myself into a litter of young foxes, or get into a fury of passion about pheasants' eggs. It's all beastly nonsense, but if a fellow could only bring himself to care about it, that wouldn't matter. I don't care about anything."

"You read."

"No, I don't. I pretend to read—a little. If they had left me alone I think I should have had myself bled to death in a warm bath."[8]

A few hours after this bleak confession, a telegram announces that the question of Popenjoy's identity has been settled by the child's death. The Marquis's inability to feel very much about the death of his son, or to summon any emotion other than spite, exposes the man as completely empty, and reveals his own dawning awareness of his terrible vacuity. "It's all over with little Popenjoy," he tells Mr. De Baron.

"He has got away from all his troubles—lucky dog! He'll never have to think what he'll do with himself. They'd almost told me that it must be so, before he went."

"I grieve for you greatly, Brotherton."

"There's no use in that, old fellow. . . . I don't understand much about what people call grief. I can't say that I was particularly fond of him, or that I shall personally miss him. They hardly ever brought him to me, and when they did, it bothered me. And yet, somehow it pinches me—it pinches me."

"Of course it does."

"It will be such a triumph to the Dean and George. That's about the worst of it. But they haven't got it yet. Though I should be the most miserable dog on earth I'll go on living as long as I can and keep my body and soul

8. *Is He Popenjoy?* 2:52:194-195.

together. I'll have another son yet, if one is to be had for
love or money. They shall have trouble enough before
they find themselves at Manor Cross. . . . Poor little
boy! You never saw him. . . . They weren't very proud
of showing him. He wasn't much to look at. Upon my
soul I don't know whether he was legitimate or not, according to English fashions. . . . What a rumpus there
has been about a rickety brat who was bound to die."[9]

This mixture of half-recognized grief and explicit bitterness
is as close as the Marquis ever comes to an ordinary human
emotion. For the rest he is negative. His life and personality
remind us that evil may be defined simply as the absence of
good. The Marquis has lost all taste for human intercourse
and normal human pleasures. He is incapable of life, and
even his decadent cultivation of his own sensibility turns
out to be meaningless:

> The Marquis had his flowers, and his fruit, and his
> French novels on his way up to town. . . . I think that, in
> his way, he did grieve for the child who was gone, and
> who, had he lived, would have been the intended heir of
> his title and property. They must now all go from him to
> his enemies! And the things themselves were to himself
> of so very little value! Living alone at Scumberg's was
> not a pleasant life. Even going out in his brougham at
> nights was not very pleasant to him. He could do as he
> liked at Como, and people wouldn't grumble—but what
> was there even at Como that he really liked to do? He had
> a half worn out taste for scenery which he had no longer
> energy to gratify by variation. It had been the resolution
> of his life to live without control, and now, at four-and-
> forty, he found that the life he had chosen was utterly
> without attraction. He had been quite in earnest in those
> regrets as to shooting, hunting, and the duties of an En-
> glish country life. Though he was free from remorse, not
> believing in anything good, still he was open to a convic-
> tion that had he done what other people call good, he

9. 2:53:201-202.

would have done better for himself. Something of envy stirred him as he read the records of a nobleman whose political life had left him no moment of leisure for his private affairs; something of envy when he heard of another whose cattle were the fattest in the land.[10]

Trollope's description of the Marquis, and of the emptiness that he found in a life devoted to the barren pursuit of aesthetic pleasure, can perhaps be read as his comment on the controversy aroused when Walter Pater's *Studies in the History of the Renaissance* appeared in 1873. Pater seemed to justify a life spent entirely in the pursuit of aesthetic experience, and he was attacked as a hedonist. The Marquis's taste which should be gratified by "variation" seems to echo one of the rhetorical questions in the celebrated final chapter of the *Studies*: "A counted number of pulses only is given to us of a variegated, dramatic life. How may we see in them all that is to be seen in them by the finest senses?"[11] Trollope has drawn a picture of Byronism—to him a life of antisocial individualism, lived without the restraint of duty or law—at the moment when it began to turn to the aestheticism of Axël, Des Esseintes, and eventually of Oscar Wilde. Trollope is arguing that the Aesthetic Movement, which refused to involve itself with social values, was simply a variant of the old antisocial Byronism he had ridiculed so long.

In a sense, *Is He Popenjoy?* also attacks some cherished conventions of the popular Victorian novel. The death of a child, fraternal and filial loyalty, the wicked peer, the nonprodigal son who stayed at home, the marriage that combines fortune and blood, the paternal clergyman—all these conventions are neatly inverted. Trollope maintains a sardonic tone which he had not before used throughout a

10. 2:53:204-205.

11. Walter Pater, *The Renaissance: Studies in Art and Poetry* (London: Macmillan, 1912), p. 236. Contemporary attacks on the book's concluding chapter caused Pater to remove it from the second edition (1877). He restored it in 1888, because he believed he had answered his critics and explained his views more fully in *Marius the Epicurean* (1885).

whole novel. Nor does Trollope organize any other novel so thoroughly in terms of anticonventions.

The sardonic point of Popenjoy's death is that it causes pleasure rather than grief. When it is announced, those who dislike Mary begin to revise their opinion as they realize that she will become marchioness. The child's nonappearance in the novel, where he is only talked about, stresses his irrelevance. In the same way, the meaninglessness of the Marquis, which is basic to the plot, is reinforced by the way in which his story is only tangential to the main story. We know just enough to pity him and to see the contrast between his purposelessness and the life that Lord George lives—a trivial life, perhaps, but one that can have meaning, that lacks the terrible irrelevancy of the Marquis's life. "Some people manage to live so that everybody will be the better for their dying."[12] remarks Mrs. Jones of the Marquis, and the comment sums up his role.

The Marquis's chief antithesis and opponent in the book is the Dean, Mary's father, fervently committed to society and its ways, to the importance and glory of titled families. The Marquis, despite his high social rank, has chosen isolation; the low-born Dean has devoted his life to achieving social acceptance. Their lives and aims are consistently opposed, for it is the Dean who initiates the inquiry into Popenjoy's legitimacy, and he has arranged the marriage that will make his grandchildren heirs to the Brotherton estates and honors. On first meeting the Marquis, he proclaims his commitment to the world and its ways, angrily informing the disdainful nobleman that "the usual courtesies of life are pleasant to me."[13] The remark is this worldly clergyman's creed. He and the Marquis oppose one another throughout. The Marquis's death brings the Dean all he wants, and at the end of the book he has a moment of almost religious exaltation as he contemplates his own family fortunes—from son of a stable-owner to father of a mar-

12. 2:58:249.   13. 1:22:212.

chioness and grandfather of a marquis to come. To Mary he
delivers a sermon which celebrates her rank and his:

> All that I have wished has come about. . . . It is a grand
> thing to rise in the world. The ambition to do so is the
> very salt of the earth. It is the parent of all enterprise, and
> the cause of all improvement. They who know no such
> ambition are savages and remain savage. . . . I am proud
> that by one step after another, I have been able so to
> place you and so to form you that you should have been
> found worthy of rank much higher than my own. And I
> would have you proud also and equally ambitious for
> your child. Let him be the Duke of Brotherton. Let him
> be brought up to be one of England's statesmen, if God
> shall give him intellect for the work. Let him be seen
> with the George and Garter, and be known throughout
> Europe as one of England's worthiest worthies. . . . And
> that he may be great you should rejoice that you yourself
> are great already.[14]

And a little later, when his grandson is born, he weeps with
joy, like Simeon in the Temple:

> He had seen the happy day; and as he told himself, in
> words which would have been profane had they been
> absolutely uttered, he was now ready to die in peace.
> Not that he meant to die, or thought that he should die.
> That vision of young Popenjoy, bright as a star, beautiful
> as a young Apollo, with all the golden glories of the
> aristocracy upon his head, standing up in the House of
> Commons and speaking to the world at large with modest
> but assured eloquence, while he himself occupied some
> corner of the gallery, was still before his eyes.[15]

And yet, it all seems wrong at the last. We are allowed to
suspect that the Dean's ambitions have been noble only in a
very restricted sense of the word. The glory of being a
marquis's grandfather has perhaps been more to him than

14. 2:61:285-287.   15. 2:63:297.

his daughter's happiness; he is not an evil man, but he worships the wrong gods. Mary reminds him that his triumph, and hers, is, after all, based on the death of a child who offended merely by existing. We can sense what status means in a society where a relative's death confers rank and fortune. "Every stick is entailed," someone says of a rich nobleman, "and they say he's likely to have gout in his stomach, so that everything will go pleasantly."[16] The real nature of the Dean's triumph is unmistakably asserted when a final episode mocks the whole cult of family feeling: he acts as agent in selling the right to be Popenjoy's godmother to old Miss Tallowax for £20,000.

The great cold empty house of Manor Cross, the Brotherton seat, is the empty shrine of that cult of the noble family which the Dean serves so enthusiastically as priest and whose values he expounds. The name of the house suggests that confusion of religious fervor with rank and property which defines his life. Michael Sadleir complains that Manor Cross is "hardly sketched at all" because the mansion is "of a different epoch from that of the tale so that [its] qualities have no bearing on the characters presented."[17] But the house is, in fact, a successful extension of the values it symbolizes. Its atmosphere is realized with all its discomforts, all its depressing effects on the spirit. Trollope has not failed to describe Manor Cross. He has declined to do so, to emphasize its hollowness, just as he has declined to analyze

16. 2:58:248.
17. Michael Sadleir, *Trollope: A Commentary*, p. 192. Elizabeth I once slept at Manor Cross, and Trollope's treatment of the house as a kind of shrine is reminiscent of the way her courtiers thought of the great houses they built as shrines for the Queen's Majesty, as embodiment of the nation and epitome of its whole social system. See Ian Dunlop, *Palaces and Progresses of Elizabeth I* (London: Jonathan Cape, 1962). "That piece of furniture will always be sacred to me, because I believe it did once afford rest and sleep to the gracious majesty of England" (1:5:43), exclaims Lady Susanna Germain, during a tour of the house. Trollope may have modeled Manor Cross on Hatfield House, the Cecils' seat, not far from his own house at Waltham Cross.

the Marquis. This barnlike house, grand but cold, symbolizes the truth about the cult that the Dean expounds, that it is grandeur without intimacy, Family exalted at the cost of warmth or domesticity.[18]

Both the Dean and Manor Cross are used to undercut that system of values embodied in the family which seems so positive at first, especially when seen in contrast to the aridity of the Marquis's life. There is no doubt about that aridity, but is Lord George's commitment to family duty a valid alternative? Trollope seems to raise the ideal of the family only to destroy it, leaving us with a bitter statement about the meaninglessness of human effort, human pride, and human aspiration. The lives lived by the wicked Marquis and Lord George seem only different in detail. One lives an empty life, the other performs dull and apparently useless duties.

As for Mary, she does not really enjoy her new rank and title. Her greatest triumph is that, as the mother of future lords, she is no longer snubbed by her noble relatives. But she triumphs because of a fortuitous and pitiful death, and because she gives birth to an heir. Although she is portrayed as a stronger character than any of the Germains, she is not accepted for herself, that is, for her forceful sense of justice and her pride in her father. Her victory is almost victory by default. Her mother-in-law conveniently lapses into senility, and the Italian marchioness vanishes, leaving Mary without a rival.

It is true that Mary avoids the snares set for her by Mrs. Houghton and the Marquis, but even this is done passively.

18. Trollope underlines this with a symbol he was to use again in *The American Senator*. There, a hunted fox is a symbol of Arabella Trefoil's frantic search for a husband and home. In *Is He Popenjoy?* the hunted fox is an "old vixen" long established at Manor Cross, "the mother of four litters," who is "killed ignominiously in the stokehole under the greenhouse" while the old Marchioness looks on. The vixen suddenly breaks just as some of the characters are discussing the Marquis's cruelty in hunting his mother from the house. See 1:7:66-70.

Mary is never seriously tempted by Jack De Baron; she wants only the approval of her husband. But her marriage is not a particularly happy one, nor do Mary and Lord George ever find any strong satisfaction in it. It is adequate, but no more.

Mary does triumph in another way, and that she does so provides us with a clue to Trollope's aims in *Is He Popenjoy?* At the beginning of the novel, she is her father's means toward an alliance with a noble family, while the Germains see her as a considerable addition to their fortunes. No one is interested in her own desires. But she soon begins to insist on her rights. She will not be confined to the drab sewing-circle of George's sisters, nor will she avoid dancing and harmless frivolities. She declines to accept unreasonable criticism without argument, or to obey unreasonable rules of conduct. Her father urges her to assert herself, even as her husband urges her to subservience, but soon she begins to make her own decisions. "One cannot know what a girl is as long as a girl is a girl," Mrs. Houghton comments. "It is only when she's married that she begins to speak out."[19] Mary begins to speak out within two months of her marriage, when she argues against joining her sisters-in-law in making petticoats for the poor women of the parish:

> She made one petticoat, and then gently appealed to her husband. Did not he think that petticoats could be bought cheaper than they could be made? He figured it out, and found that his wife could earn three-halfpence a day by two hour's work. . . . Was it worth while that she should be made miserable for ninepence a week—less than £ 2 a year? Lady George figured it out also, and offered the exact sum, £ 1 19s., to Lady Sarah, in order that she might be let off for the first twelve months. Then Lady Sarah was full of wrath. Was that the spirit in which offerings were to be made to the Lord? Mary was asked, with stern indignation, whether in bestowing the

19. 1:25:241.

work of her hands upon the people, whether in the very
fact that she was doing for the poor that which was distasteful to herself, she did not recognise the performance
of a duty? Mary considered awhile, and then said that
she thought a petticoat was a petticoat, and that perhaps
the one made by the regular petticoat-maker would be
the best.[20]

Mary's important triumph is not her accession to the title,
but her success in demanding her husband's respect and
support, her refusal to be dominated. She even leaves him
for a time after he has behaved unreasonably. In the course
of the book, she grows from a naive girl into a woman. At
the end, she listens to her father and to George, then makes
her own decisions. Mary grows because she insists on being
her own woman.

She does not achieve this by joining the Baroness Banmann and the other feminists. Trollope did not approve of
their definition of women's rights. "Let women say what
they will of their rights," he announced in *North America*
(written in 1861-62),

or men who think themselves generous say what they
will for them, the question has all been settled both for
them and for us men by a higher power. They are the
nursing mothers of mankind, and in that law their fate is
written with all its joys and all its privileges. It is for men
to make those joys as lasting and those privileges as perfect as may be. That women should have their rights no
man will deny. To my thinking neither increase of work
nor increase of political influence are among them. The
best right a woman has is the right to a husband, and that
is the right to which I would recommend every young
woman here and in the States to turn her best attention.[21]

20. 1:3:27.
21. Anthony Trollope, *North America* 17:265. See also *Letters* (Trollope to
Adrian H. Joline, 4 April 1879), pp. 417-418: "You cannot, by Act of

Trollope endorses marriage as the only desirable life for a woman, but he does not endorse subservience to a husband. After her marriage, Mary is offered three models for her behavior: she can be totally subservient, like the other Brotherton ladies; she can become a feminist; or she can play the coquette, like Mrs. Houghton. She rejects all three, and makes a commitment to equality in marriage. She shows Lord George that there are limits to his control over her. Marriage need not be stifling. Mary attends a feminist lecture about women's "Disabilities" against Lord George's wishes, in order to assert her independence, but she learns to abolish her own "Disabilities" by freely choosing married life and motherhood under conditions that she considers fair. Hers is a compromise, a limited freedom, but that is Trollope's solution. Men must obey the conventions of society; women must do the same, and for them the conventions usually include marriage and some public deference to their husbands' wishes. Mary understands these conventions and decides to accept them. It is not a romantic decision, but to Trollope it is inevitable that a woman of good sense will act as she does.

Mary grows into a mature and attractive woman. Her efforts and aspirations are rewarded. But is this what the book is about? Are all the schemes and excitements simply a backdrop to the story of one girl's growth? It seems hardly enough. Mary is an important character, and in the book order depends on the survival of her marriage, but Trollope seems more interested in the character of Lord George. Complex, and continually baffled by complexities, he is a

---

Congress or Parliament make the woman's arm as strong as the man's or deprive her of her position as the bearer of children. We may trouble ourselves much by debating a question which superior power has settled for us, but we cannot alter the law. . . . The necessity of the supremacy of man is as certain to me as the eternity of the soul. There are other matters on which one fights as on subjects which are in doubt,—universal suffrage, ballot, public education, and the like—but not, as I think, on these two." See also Sadleir, *Trollope: A Commentary*, pp. 384-385.

full-length portrait of a very ordinary man, foolish and rather dull, who is given only qualified approval.

When the story begins, George, like Mary, is an innocent. Trollope has opened with a traditional situation, the loveless marriage for rank and money between an innocent girl and an elderly husband, but he has turned the situation inside out. This time the innocent victim is not the girl but the elderly nobleman. Lord George's problems arise because he is by nature a dependent. He cannot dominate or command. "Had his elder brother been a man of whom he could have been proud, I almost think he would have been more contented as a younger brother,"[22] Trollope comments at his accession. Throughout the book he passes from dependence to dependence, for some stronger will is always taking over the direction of his actions. First his sisters carefully arrange his proposal. "They fooled Lord George to the top of his bent, smoothing him down softly . . . not suggesting Mary Lovelace at first, but still in all things acting in that direction." When George speaks to the Dean, another will takes over, for "the first appeal to Mary was made by her father himself, . . . in conformity with his own advice. Lord George . . . had thus arranged it, but had been hardly conscious that the Dean had advised such an arrangement."[23]

Not long after the marriage his old love, now Mrs. Houghton, appears at a party, and she too is quick to assert her power over him. He finds himself seated next to her. "How it had come to pass that he was sitting there he did not know, but he was quite sure that it had come to pass by no arrangement contrived by himself."[24] A hunting accident leaves Mrs. Houghton at Manor Cross, and she begins further manipulations. "I wasn't quite clever enough to contrive [the accident]," she tells George frankly, and Trollope adds, "She had formed no plot against the happiness of the husband and wife . . . but the plot made itself, and she

22. 2:62:289.   23. 1:1-2:10-11.   24. 1:4:36.

liked the excitement."[25] She deliberately throws Mary together with Jack De Baron, and stage-manages situations
that make Lord George doubt his wife. At the same time,
she tries to make George fall in love with her to destroy his
marriage.

The Marquis also exploits George's suggestibility. He insists to him that Popenjoy is legitimate, and accuses George
of greed and a desire for the title. His allusions to Mary's
low birth strike at a sensitive spot and later, getting wind of
Mary's innocent friendship for De Baron, he insists that she
is unfaithful. The combined machinations of the Marquis
and Mrs. Houghton soon bring George's marriage close to
disaster. At the same time, George is unwillingly investigating Popenjoy's status, this time under the orders of the
Dean. George is manipulated until he is estranged from
everyone—from Mary, the Dean, Mrs. Houghton, the
Marquis, his mother, and his sisters.

Lord George is easily led and easily fooled. He is not very
assertive or enterprising, and he does not develop in the
course of the novel, as Mary does. His final victory is only a
material one, accidentally attained, and his change in social
status is not accompanied by any inner growth. It is the
chance fact that Mary is about to bear a child, who will one
day inherit the family title, that brings him to resume their
marriage. At no time does Trollope allow George to make a
decision himself. He is presented as a man without will or
authority. Mary looks to him for direction but he is not
strong enough to provide it, and even in a literal sense he is
not lord in his own home. At Manor Cross he lives on his
brother's sufferance. The little town house which he and
Mary take for the London season is partly paid for by the
Dean, who consequently exercises some rights there.

We begin to understand George's role when we realize
that his lack of will is shared by the Marquis and Jack De
Baron. We have seen the Marquis's lack of will, perhaps the

25. 1:9:90.

only trait that the two brothers have in common. Despite Brotherton's attempt to live according to his own will, he is easily manipulated by his Italian wife. ("I hardly know whether she had been married or not," he admits to old Mr. De Baron. "I never could quite find out.")[26] As for the handsome and dashing Jack De Baron, he also turns out to be without a will of his own. Lord George sees him as an unprincipled rake, while to Mary he seems glamorous. But Mrs. Houghton controls him as easily as she controls Lord George. At the end of the novel he is pushed into marriage with one of Trollope's least attractive husband-hunters. Three people manipulate him to bring about this marriage. He has refused to marry Miss Mildmay because he is afraid of marriage, because he is too poor, and because he dislikes her, but she forces him to promise that he will marry her if he ever obtains a fortune. Then the Marquis leaves him a fortune in hopes that he will run off with Mary. A third schemer, Mrs. Jones, able at arranging marriages, completes the work, and De Baron finds himself caught. "He is a much altered man, and is growing fat, and has taken to playing whist at his club before dinner for shilling points," Trollope tells us at the end of the book. "I have always thought that in his heart of hearts he regrets the legacy."[27]

Lord George, then, is like those apparently determined characters who are his rivals. They are also manipulated; he differs only in that he is luckier. He inherits from his brother, his son does not die, his inheritance is more palatable than Jack De Baron's. But this is not enough to justify our regarding him as the hero of the novel. There is, in fact, an important positive quality that sets him off from his rivals, while his innocence and unworldliness are an ironic contrast to the Dean's worldly wisdom and worldly interests. Lord George's positive qualities are his devotion to work and to his duty as he understands it. "Work is a grand thing,—the grandest thing we have," Trollope once wrote, "but work is not picturesque, graceful, and in itself alluring."[28] It can give a life some sense of purpose. George finds his purpose in running his family's estate and protecting the family's greatness and continuity. The object may not be worthy of his devotion, but he believes that it is. The chief thing is to have some reason for going on. In these terms, George's life is valid.

In what he calls a "boiled mutton" introductory chapter, Trollope speaks of Lord George as "so grim, so gaunt, so sombre, and so old," and sums up his character briefly:

> He was a tall, handsome, dark-browed man, silent generally, and almost gloomy, looking, as such men do, as though he were always revolving deep things in his mind, but revolving in truth things not very deep—how far the money would go, and whether it would be possible to get a new pair of carriage-horses for his mother. Birth and culture had given to him a look of intellect greater than he possessed; but I would not have it thought that he traded on this, or endeavoured to seem other than he was. He was simple, conscientious, absolutely truthful, full of prejudices, and weak-minded. Early in life he had been taught to entertain certain ideas as to religion by those with whom he had lived at college, and had therefore refused to become a clergyman . . . though weak, he was obstinate . . . he knew himself to be a backward, slow, unappreciative man. He was one who could bear reproach from no one else, but who never praised himself even to himself.[29]

Dull, weak-willed, touchy, and without self-confidence—it is not a very promising catalogue, even when we add his devotion to the family, for this final trait takes curious forms, as when the Marquis's cruelty cannot shake "the belief which Lord George still held in the position of an elder brother."[30]

Throughout the book Lord George struggles to uphold the family by being a dutiful brother. After he comes into

28. Antony Trollope, *North America* 17:263.
29. 1:1:6-7.   30. 2:57:245.

the title, his only wish is to live up to his station and to be the father of a future marquis. Even his marriage is undertaken primarily to keep the family going. He does not love Mary, or care very much about her as a person, but at the end of the book the question of love seems irrelevant, just as the question of Popenjoy's legitimacy becomes irrelevant. Lord George must love a Marchioness of Brotherton, the mother of a race of titled Germains, and the question of love vanishes into his ideal of duty. It is significant that almost his first act after his accession is to open the family's town house in St. James's Square. Throughout the book he has considered London dangerous, a place where his wife can be tempted into indiscretions. Now he considers the London season a duty. Mary hates the town house, but he rebukes her: "My love, you should not talk of hating things that are necessary . . . it is the town residence belonging to the family. . . . There is a dignity to be borne which, though it may be onerous, must be supported." "I hate dignity," Mary replies, and he explains his creed to her:

"You would not say that if you knew how it vexed me. Could I have chosen for myself personally, perhaps, neither would I have taken this position. I do not think that I am by nature ambitious. But a man is bound to do his duty in that position in which he finds himself placed—and so is a woman."

"And it will be my duty to live in an ugly house?"

"Perhaps the house may be made less ugly; but to live in it will certainly be a part of your duty. . . . But, loving me as I know you do, I am sure you will not neglect your duty. Do not say again that you hate your dignity. You must never forget now that you are Marchioness of Brotherton."

. . . This lecture . . . she turned to wholesome food and digested, obtaining from it some strength and throwing off the bombast by which a weaker mind might have been inflated.[31]

31. 2:62:292-294.

Duty takes over, even after triumph. Lord George will not change, nor will he enjoy his new dignity. He looks upon it as one more duty to the family. He is at heart a kind of curator, but he cannot enjoy the things he guards so carefully, and only partially understands them. Trollope has scored a victory over his unpromising material by making George believable though very limited. He is temperamentally a celibate, as are his brother and sisters. "I hope he is not going to become ascetic,"[32] the Dean remarks, when George has been stiff about a ball that Mary and her father plan to attend. But George finds that the only career the world can offer him is that of a son, brother, husband, and father, and the role of family guardian. All his ascetic instincts are bent to this end, and if there is any heroism in *Is He Popenjoy?* it consists in the dogged way in which George tries to discern his duty. Trollope's portrait of him is a delicate blend of irony and compassion.

In *Is He Popenjoy?* Trollope lets us speculate about the worth of that social system which possesses unquestioned value elsewhere in his work. He shows us a group of people, allows us to decide which of them should be favored, then brings the bad to their downfall and the good to their triumph, only to suggest at last that there may be little meaning to that triumph. Objectively, he seems to say, it is meaningless, but a subjective faith in it can give form to life and can make sense out of existence. The man who deliberately alienates himself from the system finds that he has nothing, and by cutting himself off has become nothing himself.

The Marquis's plight is symbolized in little Popenjoy, for legally, socially, and even physically, the child cannot exist. The question about his identity is an attempt to define his place in the social order, to discover where he belongs. The answer is—nowhere. Only an acknowledged social position can confer identity. By refusing to fulfill the requirements

32. 2:37:50.

of his position, the Marquis has excluded himself, and his son, from society. The child embodies that disengagement which the father has sought. Lord George, however dull and foolish, does act out of a commitment to society and his place in it. The new order that comes with his accession is not perfect, but it is an order. George will not be guided by whims. The victory may be hollow—Trollope does not decide—but the victors are sustained. They have found a reason for living. The alternative is a life without meaning, and the other name for this is death.

❊ VII ❊

A NARROWING OF FOCUS
The American Senator, *John Caldigate*, and *Ayala's Angel*

> Such is the glory of a blameless king who reverences God and rules a people numerous and mighty, upholding justice. For him the dark-soiled earth produces wheat and barley, trees bend low with fruit, the flock has constant issue, and the sea yields fish, under his righteous sway. Because of him his people prosper.
> —*Odyssey* 19: 109-115 (trans. George Herbert Palmer)

IN *The American Senator* and *John Caldigate*, Trollope returns to a social theme already partially explored in *Is He Popenjoy?*: the political, social, and moral disruption created when a country gentleman does not perform his duty by living on his estate, where he can maintain the miniature society that depends upon him. In *Is He Popenjoy?* the Marquis abandoned his duties to live abroad, in aesthetic self-indulgence. John Morton, in *The American Senator*, prefers a diplomatic career to acting as Squire of Bragton; John Caldigate sells his right to inherit the family estate and uses the money to prospect for gold in Australia. *Ayala's Angel* has little thematic relationship with its two predecessors.

While two of these novels share a theme of duty evaded, they are otherwise different in themes and techniques. *The American Senator* is a novel of multiple plot, which deals with involuntary isolation, with husband-hunting, with the society of a country town, and with the titular character's misunderstandings about English life. In *John Caldigate*, Trollope is interested in deliberate self-isolation, in religious fanaticism, but the structure is simple; although the action

209

ranges from Cambridge to New South Wales and back, the book is concerned almost entirely with the Caldigate family and its fortunes. Trollope, in fact, abandoned the multiple plot after *The American Senator* and worked back toward a narrower form in *John Caldigate* and the even more simply constructed *Ayala's Angel*. To read his novels in order from *The Way We Live Now* to *Cousin Henry* (written 1878) is to become aware of a progressive narrowing of the social and psychological area depicted, and a corresponding simplification of technique. On this journey, *The American Senator* and *John Caldigate* mark important stages, while *Ayala's Angel* is an engaging byway.

I. *The American Senator*

"They must be queer people over there," said Larry.

"Brutes!" said Glomax. "They once tried a pack of hounds somewhere in one of the States, but they never could run a yard."

—*The American Senator*,
Chapter 48

Trollope began *The American Senator* on 4 June 1875, soon after arriving in Australia for his second visit; he finished it during his homeward journey, less than four months later. George Bentley published it in *Temple Bar* (May 1876 to July 1877), and the book appeared in July 1877.

The central issue in *The American Senator* appears under several different guises, in such variety that this novel has been charged with being "mere confusion."[1] This central issue is man's need for a place in the traditional social order, a place based upon ownership of land, and the rapid decay that can take place in a society when traditional order is weakened. The Senator stands outside the English order entirely and calls all its basic assumptions into question. He is a reformer who would reform by abstract principles while

1. John Hagan, "The Divided Mind of Anthony Trollope," p. 18.

ignoring sentiment and tradition. Arabella Trefoil, who hunts a landed and titled husband, is a duke's niece, but she is also as much of an outlaw as Lopez or Melmotte, and as ruthless, as she tries to gain a position. The theme of restlessness that she embodies is matched with a supplementary theme which emphasizes the social and political role of the landed gentleman and the vital part he plays in maintaining that local social fabric which sustains the national social fabric. In *The Way We Live Now* Trollope used Roger Carbury to embody the plain virtues that ought to accompany the traditional ownership of land. In *Is He Popenjoy?* he showed a neglected great house whose master was perpetually absent, and portrayed the emptiness that was the Marquis of Brotherton's lot after he had cut himself off from his own proper place. *The American Senator* examines the effects of a squire's absence on the little society that depends on his presence.

Dillsborough, the locale of most of the story, and Bragton Park, its great house, are a town and estate whose squire has abandoned them. The town is gloomy and dying. Although this depression is caused by external economic shifts rather than by the absence of the squire, the townspeople feel that there is at least a symbolic connection between the town's moribund state and the empty house at Bragton Park:

> The land around Dillsborough is chiefly owned by two landlords, of whom the greatest and richest is Lord Rufford. He, however, does not live near the town, but away at the other side of the county, and is not much seen in these parts. . . . He is much liked by all sporting men, but is not otherwise very popular with the people round Dillsborough. A landlord if he wishes to be popular should be seen frequently. If he lives among his farmers they will swear by him, even though he raises his rental every ten or twelve years and never puts a new roof to a barn for them. Lord Rufford . . . though he is lenient in all his dealings, is not much thought of in the Dillsborough side of the county. . . . At Rufford, where he generally has a full house for three months in the year

and spends a vast amount of money, he is more highly considered.

The other extensive landlord is Mr. John Morton . . . squire of Bragton. . . . As he had been an absentee since he came of age. . . he had been almost less liked in the neighborhood than the lord . . . there had been no continuous residence at Bragton since the death of old Reginald Morton, who had been the best known and the best loved of all the squires in Rufford. . . . He was the man of whom the older inhabitants of Dillsborough and the neighbourhood still thought and still spoke when they gave vent to their feelings in favour of gentlemen. And yet the old squire in his latter days had been able to do little or nothing for them. . . . But he had lived all his days at Bragton Park, and his figure had been familiar to all eyes in the High Street of Dillsborough and at the front entrance of the Bush. People still spoke of old Mr. Reginald Morton as though his death [twenty years before] had been a sore loss to the neighbourhood.[2]

At the end of the novel, when a new Reginald Morton takes up residence at Bragton Park, the restoration seems to promise better days to Dillsborough.

As the novel progresses, the titular hero, Senator Elias Gotobed of Mickewa, is loud in his denunciation of gentlemen as a parasitic class whose privileged existence is contrary to reason. His arguments are good ones, and they come from a man dedicated to truth and logic, but Trollope suggests that perhaps logic is not entirely trustworthy. A social institution that cannot be defended logically can still perform valuable functions, even though it is not easy to define them precisely. Instead of providing an English spokesman to defend landed gentry and tradition, Trollope refutes the Senator by the events of the story itself. In Dillsborough only the presence of the squire gives any meaning to life and to society, any sense of purpose. The place must have its resident gentleman and is nothing with-

2. *The American Senator* 1:4-6.

out him, even as Arabella Trefoil, who is well born but
homeless, must have a place, a local habitation to give her a
name. She schemes to become Lady Rufford, mistress of
Rufford Hall, and the book's only intense love scenes are
those in which she contemplates the estate. Her plight is
pointed up by her acute sense of what she lacks—a permanent address. Hers is a gypsy life of hotels and friends'
houses; she writes on borrowed stationery; during her campaign she begs the use of her ducal uncle's house as a temporary base. Without this pretense of belonging somewhere
she can do nothing, and the peripatetic nature of her
courtship—on horseback, in hired carriages, in other
people's houses—symbolizes and epitomizes her lack of any
fixed place.

Arabella is at the center of one of the novel's two plots,
that concerned with her hunt for a home and a husband.
Engaged to John Morton, the absentee squire of Bragton,
she jilts him to pursue Lord Rufford; at the end of the book
she has lost both men and prepares to go into exile as the
wife of a minor diplomat. The Arabella plot is loosely connected to the Dillsborough plot, which revolves around the
ownership of Bragton and the love of Reginald Morton,
John Morton's cousin and heir, for Mary Masters. They
finally marry and take up residence at Bragton Park, where
Reginald is prepared to perform the duties of a country
gentleman. Despite the apparently slight connection between the two plots, their themes supplement each other.
Trollope sets Arabella's nomadic life, and her desperate
need to settle, beside Dillsborough's need for a squire settled at Bragton, and Reginald Morton's willingness to fulfill
this need. As for the Senator, he is really external to both
plots. He performs a choric function by questioning, by
commenting, and by attempting to relate events to abstract
principles—a dangerous habit, Trollope continually reminds us, for the Senator's nationality and his rationality
alike prevent him from really understanding what he sees

and hears. As a result, he is mistaken about aspects of English life that Trollope implicitly justifies.[3]

The American Senator's concern with social themes is emphasized in the opening chapter, which Michael Sadleir admired because it so expertly places "before the reader in a few pages the whole geographical and social pattern of an English county."[4] The passage is one of Trollope's set pieces of social analysis, as well as a marvelously compressed introduction to his scene and characters and to the peculiarly characterless town of Dillsborough. "I never could understand why anybody should ever have begun to live at Dillsborough," Trollope begins:

> The town has no attractions, and never had any. It does not stand on a bed of coal and has no connection with iron. It has no water peculiarly adapted for beer, or for dyeing, or for the cure of maladies. It is not surrounded by beauty of scenery strong enough to bring tourists and holiday travellers. There is no cathedral there to form, with its bishop, prebendaries, and minor canons, the nucleus of a clerical circle. It manufactures nothing specially. It has no great horse fair, or cattle fair, or even pig market of special notoriety . . . no character of its own,

3. John Hazard Wildman, in "Trollope Illustrates the Distinction," *Nineteenth-Century Fiction* 4 (1949): 101-110, says that the Senator illustrates "the American's proneness to draw broad conclusions from isolated (and usually small) facts, the Englishman's contentment with the things that work, apart from their immediate logic, and his frequent attempts to compensate with sentimentality for the missing logic" (p. 104); Edgar F. Harden, in "The Alien Voice: Trollope's Western Senator," *Texas Studies in Literature and Language* 8 (1966): 219-234, agrees: "The Senator always argues the general principle, while the Englishmen, bound to their society by a hundred roots, are aware mostly of the inescapable particularities of their existence" (p. 225); apRoberts, in *The Moral Trollope*, describes the Senator as "not stupid . . . only somewhat too inclined to expect pure rationality from the human race. Trollope suggests by his title that we watch the Arabella Trefoil–Morton–Rufford story two ways: as the Senator might see it, and as we know it to be, in all its involvement and subtlety and complication . . . we . . . remember the double view: the superficial, rationalistic one, and the deep, detailed, circumstantial one and we are obliged to make some correlation. Both views seem 'true' " (pp. 177-178).

4. Michael Sadleir, *Trollope: A Commentary*, p. 397.

even as a market town . . . its parish church, though remarkable, is hardly celebrated.[5]

Trollope's carefully selected details create a town fallen into desuetude, a place without qualities and without purpose. Trade is vanishing, at each census the population is a little smaller, and the Bush, once a prosperous coaching inn, "has fallen from its past greatness." Even the landlord cannot remember why the inn sign is a bush. The petty aristocracy of tradesmen, professional men, and independent farmers have no natural social leader. As Trollope catalogues this little group he is careful to suggest the currents and allegiances that motivate them, and that generally motivate English county society. It is central to the novel's social themes that there is a traditional aristocracy at Dillsborough, that this aristocracy gives point to life and determines social standing, and that contact with it is to be sought and prized. In Dillsborough it is accepted that there is no personage more necessary than a landed gentleman, a central social fact that the Senator, Arabella Trefoil, and Mary Masters all come to realize in different ways. Old Mr. Masters, the Dillsborough attorney, has lived his life, like his father and grandfather before him, in devotion to the Morton family and to Bragton Park. The tradesmen are dependent upon the gentry for patronage. And it is the gentry who decide social status by conferring their recognition, a function that Trollope had earlier explored when he described the Ullathorne fête in *Barchester Towers*.[6] In *The American Senator*, Larry Twentyman, who calls himself a gentleman-farmer,[7] is raised to higher status by a gesture from Lord Rufford:

5. 1:1. The reference to the "past greatness" of the Bush is on p. 3.
6. *Barchester Towers* 36-40. The placement of guests at Ullathorne becomes a social precedent for future treatment.
7. Trollope sneers at this as a newly fashionable term, but in *Emma* Mr. Knightley calls Robert Martin "a respectable, intelligent gentleman-farmer" (Chapter 8).

It was the foible of [Larry's] life to be esteemed a gentleman, and his poor ambition to be allowed to live among
men of higher social standing than himself. Those din-
ners of Lord Rufford's at the Bush had been a special
grief to him. . . . Fred Botsey had dined at the Bush with
Lord Rufford, and Larry looked on Fred as in no way
better than himself.

Now at last the invitation had come. . . . Perhaps
Larry's happiest moment in the evening was when Run-
ciman himself [the landlord of the Bush] brought in the
soup, for at that moment Lord Rufford put his hand on
his shoulder and desired him to sit down, —and Runci-
man both heard and saw it.[8]

Mr. Masters's long devotion to gentlemen is rewarded when
his own daughter is raised to the gentry by marriage with
Reginald Morton. Though Arabella Trefoil is the daughter
of a duke's brother, she fails to obtain similar recognition to
regularize her uncertain status. Sociological analysis becomes a thematic device.

The isolation of Dillsborough emphasizes another major
theme, for in *The American Senator* various kinds of isolation
and misunderstanding predominate. Mary Masters is isolated in her father's house by her birth (she is the daughter
of the attorney's first, more genteel wife) and by her ladylike
upbringing with Lady Ushant. Reginald Morton lives behind the walls of Hoppet Hall in scholarly seclusion. John
Morton has exiled himself for a diplomatic career; later,
unable to communicate with Arabella, their engagement at
an end, he volunteers for a post that even the Foreign Office
considers a form of exile. Lady Ushant lives alone, exiled
from Bragton by a family feud. Old Mrs. Morton has also
exiled herself from Bragton because of that feud and lives
only to nourish her resentment. In her mind she excludes
Reginald and Lady Ushant from the Morton family and she
tries to keep Reginald from his inheritance. The Trefoils are
another divided family. Arabella's parents, Lord and Lady

8. 48:328-331.

Augustus, have not lived together for many years. Lord Augustus avoids his brother, the duke, and dislikes his daughter. Lady Augustus is despised by the whole family as a parvenu, married for her money which is now spent. Arabella and her mother continually irritate each other. The Senator is isolated by his nationality. His conversations with individual Englishmen end in annoyance or misunderstanding; his public lecture, in which he tries to communicate his theories about English life to the English public, is stopped by an angry mob.

With all his eagerness to communicate, at times the Senator often isolates himself. Gently reminded by Lady Penwether that he is "in a certain degree a foreigner," he answers her sharply. "You see you speak our language, Mr. Gotobed," she tells him, "and we can't help thinking you are half-English." "We are two-thirds English, my lady," he replies, "but then we think the other third is an improvement."[9] Even the people of Dillsborough are "divided, some two thousand five hundred of them belonging to Rufford, and the remaining five hundred to the neighbouring county. This accident has given rise to not a few feuds."[10] This preoccupation with separation and noncommunication is emphasized in the structure of the book, for Trollope keeps his several plots separate, with little direct connection between them. The structure reiterates one of the book's important themes; the plots seem unrelated because the lives of the characters are separate from one another.

Trollope creates these analogical connections by paralleling events or characters. There are analogous events in which almost every character is deceived by appearances. Here the Senator is the most obvious example. He looks at England through transatlantic eyes. His judgments are based on misunderstandings, misinformation, and prejudice, which cause him to see England and English institutions not as they are but as he thinks they are. His mistaken ideas about the entire nation are epitomized in his attitude

9. 21:141.   10. 1:2.

toward Goarly, a surly farmer who sues Lord Rufford for alleged damage caused by hunting, and later poisons foxes in Dillsborough Wood. To the Senator, Goarly is a village Hampden. "I respect that man," he announces. "He's one against two hundred, and he insists upon his rights."[11] But in fact, Goarly is a blackguard and a coward. The Senator has mistakenly idealized the situation and the man.

He is not alone in altering reality. Scheming to make Lord Rufford propose to her, Arabella revises events in her mind until she convinces herself that he has certainly done so. Lord Rufford revises the same events to convince himself that he has not. At Dillsborough, Reginald Morton reshapes in his own mind the image of Larry Twentyman when he learns that Larry is in love with Mary Masters. Larry is ordinary, but Reginald sees him as "a beast"[12] and imposes coarseness and vulgarity upon him; ". . . it sickened him to think that a girl who had . . . been loved at Bragton . . . who looked so like a lady, should put herself on a par with such a wretch . . . to his eyes the smart young farmer with his billicock hat, not quite straight on his head, was an odious thing to behold. He exaggerated the swagger, and took no notice whatever of the well-made limbs."[13] As for Larry, "his awe for Morton's combined learning and age"[14] (Reginald is forty, Larry twenty-eight) makes him incapable of considering Reginald as a rival.

Trollope also uses analogy in creating parallel characters who relate one plot to another. Arabella's mother, Lady Augustus Trefoil, is paralleled by the Honourable Mrs. Morton. Both women live only to scheme, and their ultimate fate is the same—at the end both face an empty future alone, all their hopes defeated. These two women also serve as parallels for Arabella. They have married without love, in one case for money and in the other for rank, and their fates suggest a possible end for Arabella's story. Mary Masters's stepmother, Mrs. Masters, provides another minor parallel to Lady Augustus. Both women are vulgar, both are

11. 10:66.   12. 6:41.   13. 6:36.   14. 6:40.

social liabilities to their husbands and daughters, both try to force their daughters into prosperous but loveless marriages. Throughout the book Reginald's aunt, Lady Ushant, is contrasted to this unpleasant trio. She is generous where they are greedy, gentle where they are hard. Hated by Mrs. Morton because of the family feud, she is also hated by Mrs. Masters, who blames her for making Mary too fine to marry a farmer. But at the end of the novel Lady Ushant is justified when Reginald inherits Bragton Park and marries Mary; she returns to family life at Bragton while Lady Augustus and Mrs. Morton depart into isolation.

Trollope's deliberate contrasting or paralleling of characters from the different plots is even more marked in the case of the four men involved in love affairs. John Morton and Lord Rufford are an obvious and direct parallel. Both are involved with Arabella, and she deceives both. Trollope works out a more subtle analogy between John Morton and Larry Twentyman. They both love girls who reject them for lovers of higher rank and fortune, and they react in the same way: Morton volunteers as Minister to Patagonia, Larry plans to emigrate to New Zealand. The two men meet, each thinking of his sorrow and his exile, and Larry tells his story to Morton so that we are made aware of the differences as well as the similarities in their situations. Morton has been jilted because Arabella wants a husband with more money and higher rank, Larry has been courteously refused because Mary Masters must marry a gentleman. "There's more of Bragton than there is of Dillsborough about her," Larry tells the Squire. "That's just where it is. I know what I am and I know what she is, and I ain't good enough for her. It should be somebody that can talk books to her. . . . She's right, Mr. Morton. I'm not good enough."[15] As Morton walks home he meditates on the similarity between his own position and Larry's and on the difference between Mary's honesty and Arabella's duplicity.

15. 35:240.

His meditation makes explicit the contrast between the two heroines that Trollope invites the reader to make throughout *The American Senator*. Mary is dark, natural, sincere, and real; Arabella is false, insincere, artificial, "white and red;—white as pearl powder and red as paint."[16] Mary refuses to marry a rich man because she cannot love him, for she realizes that to do so would be spiritual suicide; Arabella, already spiritually dead, as she half-realizes, bends all her energies toward such a marriage. Mary is almost too diffident to admit her love to Reginald, while Lord Rufford remarks that "Saint Anthony would have had to kiss" Arabella "if she had made her attack upon him as she did on me."[17] The behavior of the two girls is contrasted in a number of significant details. When Mary refuses to ride in a hired carriage with Reginald,[18] the incident reminds us of how carefully Arabella plotted to find herself alone with Lord Rufford in another hired carriage. Rufford's avoidance of any clear proposal of marriage on that occasion, and Arabella's desperate attempts to read one into his vague words, contrast with the unequivocal statements that Reginald and Mary exact from one another. "Will you by my wife?" he asks her. "No true man," she muses, "ever ought to ask the question in any other form."[19] Her conduct, and this quiet remark, juxtapose the two girls and allow us to judge their behavior.

Arabella is not condemned just because she does not live up to the standards set by Mary Masters. Trollope treats his husband-hunter with compassion, for he looks at events from Arabella's point of view. He does not pardon Arabella, but he explains her, until we realize her desperate plight. She is more victim that villainess. It is true that she tries to make Lord Rufford propose. It is equally true that he behaves shabbily and that he escapes because he is even more untruthful and unscrupulous than she is. Arabella is trapped between her rank, which compels her to marry

16. 46:315.   17. 45:313.   18. 53:367.   19. 71:489.

well, and her lack of money, which makes such a marriage almost impossible. She is a victim of that dangerous combination from which Trollope himself suffered in childhood, "poverty and gentle standing."[20] She fights with such weapons as she has. She cannot afford sincerity or love. Her circumstances drive her into the shabby expedients that Trollope exposes and analyzes, not so that he can make a moral judgment but so that the reader can understand what such a woman is like and how she has been formed. "I've been at it till I'm nearly broken down," she exclaims to her mother. "I must settle somewhere;—or else die;—or else run away. . . . Talk of work,—men's work! What man ever has to work as I do?" Trollope adds his own comment. "I wonder which was the hardest part of that work, the hairdressing and painting and companionship of the lady's maid or the continual smiling upon unmarried men to whom she had nothing to say and for whom she did not in the least care!"[21] In a letter to a fellow novelist, Anna C. Steele, written while *The American Senator* was appearing in *Temple Bar*, Trollope explained his attitude toward Arabella:

> The critics . . . will tell me that she is unwomanly, unnatural, turgid,—the creation of a morbid imagination, striving after effect by laboured abominations. But I swear I have known the woman,—not one special woman, . . . but all the traits, all the cleverness, all the patience, all the courage, all the self-abnegation,—and all the failure. . . . Will such a one as Arabella Trefoil be damned, and if so why? Think of her virtues; how she works, how true she is to her vocation, how little there is of self-indulgence, or idleness. I think that she will go to a kind of third class heaven in which she will always be getting third class husbands.[22]

20. *An Autobiography* 1:2.   21. 13:85.

22. *Letters* (Trollope to Anna C. Steele, 17 February 1877), p. 364. The critics did not respond to Arabella in the negative way that Trollope predicted. See Donald Smalley, *Trollope: The Critical Heritage*, pp. 428-439.

The device of comparing Arabella to Mary Masters is obvious enough to need little commentary. The sophistication with which Trollope uses contrast in *The American Senator* indicates how far he has come since the comparatively simple contrasting of Lady Glencora and Alice Vavasor in *Can You Forgive Her?* In *The American Senator* the contrast is less obtrusive and more carefully sustained.

Of greater interest is the repeated comparison Trollope makes between the fox-hunting scenes in the novel and Arabella's hunting of Lord Rufford. She takes up fox-hunting so that she can literally pursue him.[23] Most of the events in their uncertain courtship take place in and around the hunting field, while her major attraction in his eyes is her suddenly assumed interest in the hunt. The hunting scenes are an elaborately extended and dramatized metaphor for the great husband hunt, the hunter of foxes pursued by the huntress of men. Arabella "had been taught to think that a man was a heartless, cruel, slippery animal,

---

Gotobed annoys Lord Rufford and his relatives by remarking, "Miss Trefoil always gave me the idea of being a good type of the English aristocracy" (68:469), just after Rufford has shamefacedly dismissed her, but the Senator is right about her typicality.

23. Trollope ironically reverses some literary conventions of the period, perhaps glancing at Coventry Patmore's *The Angel in the House* (1854-62), which presents the hero's wooing of Honoria as a "Chace":

> . . . At times she stops, and stands at bay;
> But he, in all more strong than she,
> Subdues her with his pale dismay,
> Or more admired audacity . . .
> But still she flies. Should she be won,
> It must not be believed or thought
> She yields; she's chased to death, undone,
> Surprised, and violently caught. . . .

The Angel in the House, Book I, canto xxi, in *The Poems of Coventry Patmore*, ed. Frederick Page (London: Oxford University Press, 1949), pp. 132-137. In *The Eustace Diamonds*, Lizzie Eustace pursues the timid Lord Fawn. David Aitken in " 'A Kind of Felicity': Some Notes About Trollope's Style," comments briefly on Trollope's use of hunting metaphors when his characters are pursuing husbands or wives.

made indeed to be caught occasionally, but in the catching of which infinite skill was wanted, and in which infinite skill might be thrown away."[24] Trollope remarks that "She must have known that she had hunted him as a fox is hunted;— and yet she believed that she was being cruelly ill-used,"[25] while Lord Rufford, himself an experienced sportsman, is aware that he is "being hunted and run down, and, with the instinct of all animals that are hunted, he prepared himself for escape."[26] Later, as she upbraids him, he is willing to justify her behavior: "As for hunting him,—that was a matter of course. He was as much born and bred to be hunted as a fox."[27]

Trollope sustains his metaphor by continually creating analogies between events of the courtship and events in the hunting field. The first fox that we see hunted is not caught but found dead, a victim of Goarly's poison. John Morton, the first husband Arabella hunts, is an onlooker. Soon he too evades the hunt by dying. The Senator wonders why the huntsmen should be unhappy, restless, and eager for more pursuit when they already have a dead fox in hand, and Lady Augustus is puzzled and angry when her daughter, already engaged to Morton, begins the pursuit of Lord Rufford. The Senator ridicules the meaningless exertions of the hunting field and the elaborate costumes required, and we are reminded of the meaningless social rituals Arabella must perform and of her desperate expedients with clothes, cosmetics, and money to keep herself presentable. In a later hunt, which begins at Rufford Hall, Arabella has begun to look upon Lord Rufford as her prey. She sticks to him in the field as closely as the huntsmen stick to the fox. Together they are almost in at the death, but the hunt is interrupted by the fall of Major Caneback. Caneback's fall helps the fox to escape but also helps Arabella in her pursuit. Though the Major dies, she uses their mutual proximity to the accident to further her intimacy with Rufford.

24. 75:517.   25. 49:336.   26. 45:307.   27. 67:464.

In a final episode, Arabella nears her quarry. She has brought Lord Rufford to Mistletoe and arranged matters so that she can have a day's hunting with him. He explains to her that frost in the ground will make hunting impossible, and on the morning of the hunt she awakens. "The coming of a frost now might ruin her," she realizes. "The absence of it might give her everything in life that she wanted."[28] A drizzle of rain reassures her that conditions are right to hunt both fox and Lord, but during the day the sport is only "fairly good." The first fox is killed, they find a second but "could not do anything with him,"[29] the third goes to ground after half an hour. Arabella manages to stay close to Rufford in the field, to be alone with him in a carriage for an eight-mile drive, to be kissed, and to be proposed to in a vaguely hinting sort of way. But she cannot make him repeat his proposal or admit it in public. She can do nothing with him, and he goes to ground by escaping from Mistletoe by night.

This central set of analogues is organized metaphorically around Arabella as hunter and Lord Rufford as fox. Trollope compares her in defeat to some predatory bird "with shortened pinions and blunted beak."[30] But Trollope recognizes the element of risk and excitement in her pursuit, and he occasionally mixes his hunting metaphors to stress this, making Arabella speak of herself as a horse and of Lord Rufford as "a sort of a five-barred gate." "Of course there is a little danger," she remarks lightly, "but who is going to be stopped by that?"[31] When Major Caneback tames the spirited mare Jemima, Trollope allows us to realize the parallel in Arabella's efforts to control Lord Rufford. The Major succeeds at great risk, but then Jemima kills him. Arabella succeeds for a moment in making Rufford do her will, only to have him repudiate her. In another metaphor, Arabella herself is the prey, for while she hunts Rufford, time and society and poverty hunt her down. She and her mother have "as many holes to run to . . . as a four-year-old

28. 39:261. 29. 39:265. 30. 75:518. 31. 37:252.

fox,—though with the same probability of finding them stopped"[32] as they travel from country house to country house.

Senator Gotobed does not change or develop at all, he has no real adventures, and critics have been puzzled because the novel is named for this apparently unimportant character.[33] In *An Autobiography*, Trollope tells us that he used the title "very much in opposition to my publisher,"[34] and in the novel itself he remarks that the book "might perhaps have been better called 'The Chronicle of a Winter at Dillsborough.' "[35] Yet the Senator does perform an important function. His lecture on the anomalies and contradictions of English life, though it is full of misunderstandings and is never fully communicated to his rowdy auditors, does serve as a commentary on the rest of the book, especially on those episodes of misunderstanding and faulty communication that plague both Arabella and Mary.

Trollope has avoided caricature. Gotobed is described as "a person of an imposing appearance, tall and thin, with a long nose and look of great acuteness, dressed in black from head to foot, but yet not looking quite like an English gentleman."[36] Although the long nose and the sharp look suggest the stage Yankee of nineteenth-century British and American comedy, Gotobed is not another boastful and uncouth "American cousin." He is a monologuist, but not really a braggart. He makes it clear that he prefers American institutions, but he is neither wearisome nor immoderate in his praise of them. He is favorably impressed by many aspects of English life, eager to learn and understand English ways. His occasional rudeness usually stems from ignorance or from enthusiasm in pursuing a forbidden topic, while many Englishmen are deliberately rude to him. Trollope encourages us to see him as a stage Yankee at the

32. 20:133.

33. See the contemporary reviews in *Trollope: The Critical Heritage*.

34. *An Autobiography* 20:362. See also *Letters* (Trollope to George Bentley, 7 December 1875), p. 347.

35. 80:552.   36. 16:105.

beginning of the book, perhaps to trick the reader into judging from preconceived notions, just as the Senator does himself. In the last chapter the novelist reminds us how easily such wrong judgments can be made when a clergyman, embarrassed by Gotobed's questions about church livings, declares "that of all the blackguards that had ever put their foot in Dillsborough, that vile Yankee was the worst." Trollope continues, "Mr. Gotobed was no more a Yankee than was the parson himself;—but of any distinction among the citizens of the United States Mr. Mainwaring knew very little."[37]

The Senator is only in part portrayed as the conventional American innocent abroad. He also retains traces of another literary type, that of the outsider whose reasonable questions about the life of the country he is visiting have the effect of making the familiar and accepted seem strange or unreasonable. Critics have compared him to the Persian visitor to France in Montesquieu's *Lettres persanes* and to Goldsmith's Chinese traveler (Trollope used a similar "outsider" persona to describe, for the *Pall Mall Gazette*, a missionary meeting in London as it might appear to a visiting Zulu).[38] Senator Gotobed continually annoys his English hosts because he cannot understand how their illogical system manages to work. But his function is not really satiric. His questions are Trollope's admission that some English institutions and behavior cannot be logically defended. Yet these logical questions are really irrelevant, just as the exact words of Lord Rufford's supposed proposal to Arabella are

37. 80:555.

38. L. and R. Stebbins call him "the Observer" in *The Trollopes: Chronicle of a Writing Family*, p. 290. Harden compares him to the Chinese traveler and Howells's Altrurian in "The Alien Voice," p. 219, and apRoberts compares him to Montesquieu's Persian in *The Moral Trollope*, pp. 173-175. Bradford A. Booth quotes the "Zulu" account in "Trollope and the *Pall Mall Gazette* (Part Two)" *Nineteenth-Century Fiction* 4 (1949): 140-141. David Stryker, in "The Significance of Trollope's *American Senator*," *Nineteenth-Century Fiction* 5 (1950); 141-149, suggests that the Senator is a self-caricature, Trollope's satiric view of his own activity in writing *North America*.

irrelevant. Certain aspects of English life are not logical, but Trollope does not endorse the Senator's recommendations for reform. Their illogic has nothing to do with their rightness. When Gotobed tries to apply his ideas of justice in the Goarly case, he finds the farmer is not a martyr to the selfish pleasures of the British aristocracy but a worthless liar. Occasionally right and often wrong, the Senator is no more a moral center than he is an object of ridicule. He simple points out certain unresolved anomalies in English life; Trollope is not interested in their resolution.

Senator Gotobed comes from the corrupt Washington of Grant's second term. The winter at Dillsborough is specified as the winter of 1874–75, when every dispatch from the United States described an orgy of bribery and theft. Schuyler Colfax, Grant's vice-president, and prominent members of the House, Senate, and Administration were involved in the Crédit Mobilier scandal; the collection of internal revenue was fraudulent; the Secretary of the Treasury resigned to avoid a vote of censure. In 1875, while Trollope was writing *The American Senator*, Grant's private secretary and a number of politicians were indicted as members of the notorious Whisky Ring.

> The Union Pacific, the nation's pride, had been financed by a group of crooked promoters who hired Congressmen to do their bidding; the Navy Department openly sold business to contractors; the Department of the Interior was a happy hunting ground for land thieves; the Indian Bureau sold post traderships to the highest bidders and neglected the welfare of its wards; the Treasury Department farmed out uncollected taxes to tax gatherers who made a good thing of it; the customhouses of New York and New Orleans were permeated with graft; a "whisky ring" in St. Louis defrauded the government of millions in excise taxes, and a gang of boodlers in the national capital vied with the carpetbag regimes of the South in extravagance and waste.[39]

39. Allan Nevins and Henry Steele Commager, *A Short History of the*

Trollope had noted American political corruption on his mission to Washington in 1868. He described it in *The Pall Mall Gazette*: "no professional politician dreams of trusting an adversary for the commonest honesty, and none who are not politicians will trust any politicians at all. . . . I heard one of the worthiest Americans I have ever known declare the other day that no man could touch politics and not become foul."[40]

The dishonest Congressman is almost a cliché in American novels of the seventies, the period described in *The Gilded Age* (1873) by Mark Twain and Charles Dudley Warner, John William De Forest's *Honest John Vane* (1875) and *Playing the Mischief* (1876), and Henry Adams's *Democracy* (1880). The title of Trollope's novel seems to suggest that it will be a similar exposure of American corruption. But Trollope disappoints this expectation, just as he disappoints any expectation that the Senator will turn into a comic Yankee or a device for satirizing English institutions.[41] Gotobed is fair-minded and scrupulous, a better Senator than one was apt to find in President Grant's America. When we last hear of him he is "thundering in the Senate against certain practices on the part of his own country which he thought to be unjust to other nations. Don Quixote was not more just than the Senator, or more philanthropic,—nor perhaps more apt to wage war against the windmills."[42]

United States (1942; rpt. New York: The Modern Library, 1945), pp. 277-278.

40. *Pall Mall Gazette*, 15 June 1868, p. 10; Trollope's letter is dated 27 May.

41. Harden, "The Alien Voice," suggests (p. 228) that the Senator is simultaneously a vehicle and an object of satire; he argues that the book is about "the enormity of the gulf between individuals, and especially between nations" (p. 232), "the gulfs of separateness between human beings . . ." (p. 234). In *The Moral Trollope*, apRoberts declares that in this novel, Trollope, by "refusing exclusive loyalty to either nation, . . . declares his own passionate loyalty to the whole of the human race" (p. 188).

42. 80:553.

The comparison to Don Quixote is a fair one, for the Senator is an idealist. Trollope's readers should have perceived a calculated irony in the discrepancy between his views and the actual conditions of American life. His criticisms of England are based on democratic theories, but these theories seemed to have little connection with the practices of American political life. The Senator attacks the purchase of clerical livings in England before an audience well aware of the purchase of high offices in the United States. He complains of the disenfranchisement of English laborers when Federal bayonets were unsuccessfully trying to enfranchise Black citizens in the South. He criticizes the influence that some lords wield in the election of members of Parliament while ruthless American financiers sent their own candidates to Congress. The Senator's whole indictment of English ways is a sustained irony in light of the contemporary American scene.

By presenting the Senator as better than the institution that has produced him, Trollope is able to ridicule reformers who think in terms of black and white, and who insist on reforming institutions in obedience to abstract principles instead of human realities. In *The Warden* he pitted the principled reformer, John Bold, against Mr. Harding, a good man whose tenure of his wardenship is probably unjust. In *The American Senator*, the Senator himself is such a reformer.[43] Yet the institutions he deplores may preserve England from certain aspects of American corruption. Lord Rufford and Mr. Mainwaring are foolish but they are not evil.

"Who can but love their personal generosity," asks Trollope, speaking of Americans in the *Autobiography*, "their active and far-seeking philanthropy, their love of education, their hatred of ignorance, the general conviction on the minds of all of them that a man should be enabled to walk upright, fearing no one and conscious that he is responsible

43. See apRoberts, p. 179.

for his own actions?" But he complains that an English admirer of these American traits is soon repelled at "their politics, . . . their municipal scandals, . . . their great ring-robberies, . . . the infinite baseness of their public life. There at the top of everything he finds the very men who are the least fit to occupy high places."[44] Senator Gotobed, however, is, as Trollope told Mary Holmes, "a thoroughly honest man wishing to do good, and is not himself half so absurd as the things which he criticises."[45] He is endowed with all the virtues Trollope admired in individual Americans, and none of their public vices. His very virtues lead him to make serious mistakes in judging English life, and these mistakes suggest that American idealism is too theoretical for England. Democracy does not seem to work in America, and is not needed in England. The Senator can find a few abuses in the mother country but his solutions lead only to confusion.

"Your views, Mr. Gotobed, are utilitarian rather than picturesque,"[46] an exasperated Englishman tells the Senator, and the Senator is not annoyed. He finds it impractical and unreasonable that a man can purchase the cure of souls as an investment, that men should chase a fox with horses and hounds when a gun or trap would do the job more efficiently, that a farmer should let his fields be trampled for the amusement of idle gentlemen, that a man must leave his estate to his eldest son and exclude his other children. And Trollope agrees. These things *are* unreasonable. They cannot be defended logically. The novelist admitted to being "heavy" on the sporting Lord Rufford and on the clergyman Mainwaring: "It is the part of the satirist to be heavy on the classes he satirises;—not to deal out impartial justice to the world; but to pick out the evil things. With the parson my idea was not to hold an individual up to scorn

44. *An Autobiography* 17:314-315.
45. *Letters* (Trollope to Mary Holmes, 27 December 1876), p. 359.
46. 68:472.

but to ridicule the modes of patronage in our church."[47] But a reformation of society along utilitarian lines would not bring perfect justice. Even the Senator begins to sense this when faced with the contradictions of a "rotten borough" whose proprietor uses his control over the voters to send great statesmen to Parliament. The democratic candidate at Quinborough is a rascal, the aristocratic candidate is a noble patriot, and the Senator realizes that his principles would sent the rascal to Parliament. Abstract principles, Trollope suggests, are of little use in such a situation. It is necessary to invoke Reginald Morton's doctrine of moderation or "tanti" and recognize that strict logic is not always practicable. Reginald's attack on one of Trollope's favorite targets, the opponents of fox-hunting, is really an attack on that utilitarian ethic which even the Senator begins to find inadequate: "The ladies and gentlemen [who], not looking very clearly into the systems of pains and pleasures in accordance with which we have to live, put their splay feet down now upon this ordinary operation and now upon that, and call upon the world to curse the cruelty of those who will not agree with them . . . these would-be philosophers do not or will not see that recreation is as necessary to the world as clothes or food."[48] Reginald is urging the indefinable value of institutions that cannot be defended logically as useful, but give shape and meaning to life. Fox-hunting, like squires and gentlemen, and like tradition generally, has a social value that cannot be fitted into the Senator's theoretical classifications. In his last letter to his correspondent in Washington, the Senator admits that gentlemen give life an adornment which it would otherwise lack. He realizes that his principles conflict with his experiences to involve him in a mass of contradictions. "Even with such a popinjay as Lord Rufford, he himself felt the lordship,"[49] inexplicable

47. *Letters*, p. 359.   48. 73:504-505.

49. 51:350. Cf. apRoberts, *The Moral Trollope*, p. 182: "The love story of Mary Masters depends in large part on delicate gradations in class structure

though this may be. Like President Neverbend in *The Fixed Period* (1880-81), the Senator is a caricature of a theorist driven mad by logic as Don Quixote was driven mad by romance. His confrontation with the illogicality of English life produces a triumphant assertion of that life. The Senator does not admit that he is in error and he is never refuted, point by point, though some of his experiences shake his certainty. But with Reginald's accession to Bragton, the marriage of Reginald and Mary, and Reginald's promise that he will even take up fox-hunting in a mild way to do his duty as a squire and declare his independence of those "philosophers" who oppose the sport, Trollope shows us that the English system is stronger than ever. Illogical and picturesque, it cannot be judged or improved by utilitarian theories. It can be judged only in accord with the theory of "tanti," that which is enough, sufficient unto itself.

II. *John Caldigate*

> There was gold being found at this moment among the mountains of New South Wales, in quantities which captivated his imagination. And this was being done in a most lovely spot, among circumstances which were in all respects romantic.
>
> —*John Caldigate* 1

After completing *The American Senator*, Trollope briefly abandoned novels to write his *Autobiography* (October 1875 to April 1876), a work in which his distrust of reformers and his preference for the doctrine of "tanti" are even more decidedly asserted. The *Autobiography* finished and put away

---

and the effect they have on Mary's rejection of Larry Twentyman and her acceptance of Reginald Morton. If anyone had tried to explain it to the Senator, he would have snapped his fingers at it. And yet we know these delicate gradations make agony for Mary. . . ."

for posthumous publication, he turned back to the Palliser cycle to write the final episodes in the life of his favorite hero in *The Duke's Children* (written May to October 1876, published 1879-80). After a brief pause, he began *John Caldigate* on February 3, 1877, and finished at sea off the West Coast of Africa in July. Landing at Capetown on July 21, he began "banging about"[50] and writing his *South Africa*, after mailing *John Caldigate* to his publisher. The novel appeared in *Blackwood's Magazine* from April 1878 to June 1879, and was then published by Chapman and Hall.

Trollope's correspondence with John Blackwood indicates that the publisher was not entirely satisfied with the plot and motivation of the novel. Trollope's own dissatisfaction can be inferred from his unwonted docility in listening to suggestions and even making a few changes. The modern reader is likely to share these dissatisfactions, for *John Caldigate* is less a novel than a series of responses to types and situations which Trollope had exploited in the past, and which were to serve him again. Perfunctory in plot, motivation, and structure, full of inexplicable leaps forward that avoid a number of essential events, I cannot see in *John Caldigate* that unity between plot, theme, and method which is so marked in the major novels of the mid-seventies. With the Palliser cycle completed at last, Trollope abandoned his experiment with multiple plot, and he stopped reading Elizabethan and Jacobean dramas at about the same time.[51] After *The American Senator*, Trollope began to turn away from any great complexity of plot or structure. He also started to incorporate a greater amount of explicit political or moral commentary into his novels, in the form of

50. "Old Trollope, after banging about the world so long, now treading in my footsteps, and, like an intellectual bluebottle, buzzing about at Cape Town." The speaker is James Anthony Froude, who was at work on his own book about South Africa and resented Trollope's appearance on the same mission. See James Pope Hennessy, *Anthony Trollope*, p. 354.

51. *Letters*, p. 360. He shifted to nondramatic verse. He read *The Faerie Queene* aloud in November and December 1876.

semidetachable essays, a device he had used at the beginning of his career in *The Macdermots of Ballycloran* and *The Warden*. Senator Gotobed's lecture is such an essay; there are briefer ones in *John Caldigate*, *Cousin Henry*, and *The Fixed Period*, and several long ones in the uncompleted *The Landleaguers*.

John Caldigate seems to be an experiment in search of a method to replace the multiple plot. Trollope apparently hoped to combine a tight linear plot, of the type used in *An Eye for an Eye* and *Lady Anna*, with a broad statement about the essential rightness of the English system. He failed, partly because of an unaccustomed carelessness in structure, partly because the situation he had chosen was full of ambiguities that he was unable to resolve, partly because he was writing too much too rapidly.

The plot of *John Caldigate* is not very complicated. Caldigate is frivolous, in debt, bored with English life and his position as heir to a small Cambridgeshire estate, Folking. Relinquishing his heirship, he goes to Australia in search of gold, makes a fortune, then returns ready to settle at Folking and take up his duties. He marries Hester Bolton despite the opposition of her mother, a stern possessive Puritan who considers him unworthy of Hester and wishes to keep the girl to herself. Soon after their son is born, a woman from Australia turns up claiming to be Caldigate's lawful wife. Caldigate is tried for bigamy and convicted on her testimony and that of her associates, and on the evidence of a postmarked envelope addressed to her in his hand as "Mrs. John Caldigate." He goes to prison while Hester remains at Folking, convinced of his innocence, until a postal clerk proves the postmark a forgery. Caldigate is released, and the conspiracy exposed.

The basic pattern is one of withdrawal and return. Like Odysseus, John Caldigate goes on a long voyage in search of adventure and acquires great riches.[52] He also acquires wisdom and experience, for he learns that he really belongs at

52. Trollope was well enough acquainted with the *Odyssey* to advise

home in his native place. His greatest danger comes from his own weakness for the beautiful and licentious woman he meets on his voyage. Returning home he is greeted by his father and takes a chaste wife, but is prevented for a time from a full homecoming by his ordeal of imprisonment. His enemies try to break up his home and take his wife away from him. His protector—in this case not a goddess, but a clerk from Trollope's own Post Office—must intervene to save him and bring about his final triumphant homecoming.

But Trollope does not completely succeed with *John Caldigate*. He seems to have planned a more ambitious novel than he wrote, and the traces of this plan are evident in characters and episodes introduced as if destined to be important, then quietly dropped. He introduces in old Squire Caldigate and John Caldigate a father and son who cannot communicate their exasperated affection for one another. They can only make violent gestures of repudiation until they are separated. But he abandons any further attempt to work out this relationship after Caldigate's return from Australia, vaguely suggesting that it was all a misunderstanding. There is a promising mystery about Mrs. Smith, the Circe-Calypso of the voyage, but we never learn what it is. Later her character changes without any real explanation. She is introduced as a gallant, beautiful, and intelligent woman. Then she is transformed into a sordid adventuress behind the scenes, her disintegration neither described nor documented. Such characters seem to have been destined for larger roles and fuller analysis.

In the novel as we have it, Trollope constructs his plot around two problems which are only tenuously related, and their tenuous relationship dissipates the novel's force. The first is the validity of the English social structure itself, which John Caldigate rejects, regains, and then loses, only to be restored to his place by the careful work of one of

Blackwood about publishing Sir Charles Du Cane's translation of the poem; he performed this task about a year after completing *John Caldigate*. See *Letters* (Trollope to George Eliot, 13 August 1878), p. 399.

society's official agents. The Australian episodes are an aspect of this problem, for in Australia, as Trollope depicts it here, there is a general breakdown of society and of morality. The second problem is that of human isolation, which Trollope studies in the character of Mrs. Bolton, whose religious fanaticism separates her from all society and eventually leads her to repudiate her beloved daughter.

John Caldigate begins as a foolish and alienated young man, careless with money, careless with his affection, and careless with the most sacred thing of all, the entail to his paternal estate, which he sells to his father to go to Australia. He rejects his birthright and announces his disdain for the settled life of England, for Folking, and for the duties of a country gentleman. Trollope reminds us of the evil that can come from leaving one's own place and following a romantic quest for adventure and great wealth. But Folking, like Dillsborough in *The American Senator*, is not made to sound very inviting. "Folking is not a place having many attractions of its own, beyond the rats," he begins. "It lies in the middle of the Cambridgeshire fens . . . there is no rise of ground which can by any stretch of complaisance be called a hill. The property is bisected by an immense straight dyke, which is called the Middle Wash, and which is so sluggish, so straight, so ugly, and so deep, as to impress the mind of a stranger with the ideas of suicide. And there are straight roads and straight dykes, with ugly names on all sides, and passages through the country called droves, also with ugly appellations of their own, which certainly are not worthy of the name of roads." The house is uncomfortable, and just behind it "a great cross ditch, called Foulwater Drain, runs, or rather creeps, down to the Wash."[53]

There is an even-handed ambiguity in this partial admission that Caldigate might be justified in his desire to get away from Folking, and irony when he returns after experiencing the bleakness of life at the mining camps of Nobble and Ahalala in New South Wales.

53. *John Caldigate* 1:3-4.

Trollope is equally ambiguous in his treatment of the whole Australian episode. When the gold fields are described, it is clear that their rough way of life is demoralizing. Their promise of sudden riches through luck rather than industry is even more demoralizing. Dick Shand, Caldigate's companion, is quickly ruined—too weak to persevere in the business of getting rich, not stable enough to react calmly to a little prosperity, he becomes a penniless drunkard. But Caldigate is not ruined. Although he had wasted his time and money in England, he now works hard and becomes rich. Although he is weak enough to talk about marriage with Mrs. Smith, and to live openly with her, he avoids other pitfalls. Trollope never quite explains his hero. At one point he allows Caldigate to imply that the vision of Hester Bolton had become for him a kind of safeguard and goal. She causes him to bend his efforts to return and take up that family estate which he had repudiated, marry her, and become a country squire. Hester is a kind of enchanted Puritan princess. She causes her admirer to work hard, make money, and desire conformity but does not prevent his relationship with the more vivacious Mrs. Smith. Trollope also suggests another reason why Caldigate should triumph where so many others had failed. Contrasting him with Shand, he tells us that "There had not been hitherto much of veneration in Caldigate's character, but even he had, on occasions, been almost shocked at the want of respect evinced by his friend for conventional rules . . . he did not altogether approve of him."[54] It is perhaps the growth of this instinct toward conventional ways that saves him from Australian anarchy and sends him home rich, respectable, and ready to settle down.

Australian life stabilizes John Caldigate, but it completely destroys Mrs. Smith, Shand, and most of the miners we see. There are no traits in Caldigate's character that fully explain his survival. Trollope's failure to explain perhaps reflects his own uncertainties about a problem that was

54. 4:29.

bothering Englishmen as he wrote, that of defining the colonial adventure on which they found themselves embarked.[55] The problem had to do with the nature of colonies and the quality of colonial life. Could English social and moral attitudes be transplanted to the colonies? Could life in the colonies be organized along English lines? Or were the conditions of life so exotic in places like Australia and South Africa that English habits would be corrupted, or even improved? Trollope was caught between his personal dislike of Disraeli's expansionism, and his belief in the future of the colonies as places where England's race, language, and customs would increase in power and importance. "The blood and the language of Englishmen will be the blood and the language of the dominant race of mankind. . ." he wrote in *The New Zealander*. "Though the throne of our Kings and Queens may not prove itself to be less perishable than the seats of other monarchs, the language in which we speak and the mixed blood which is in our veins are destined to transfer themselves to other countries, which in their turn will become dominant, and will again in their turn fall away and decay."[56] These ideas engaged Trollope in his travel books, especially in *Australia and New Zealand* (written 1871-72) and in *South Africa*, his immediate task after finishing *John Caldigate*. As we have seen, related themes appear in *The American Senator*, and even earlier in *Harry Heathcote of Gangoil*.

Australia, as Trollope depicts it, is dangerous and lawless. The traditional English social and moral order does not seem to flourish there. Good can apparently come out of this wild place: Australia makes a good Englishman out of John Caldigate and restores him to his proper role. But Australian lawlessness also sends Mrs. Smith to destroy order at Folking. Caldigate is imprisoned. His son becomes

---

55. The debate took various forms, and became more vociferous during the eighties and nineties. Sir John Seeley's *Expansion of England* (1883) is the fullest argument justifying the colonies.
56. *The New Zealander* 1:11.

a bastard, his wife is robbed of her name, and the Caldigate and Bolton families disintegrate. The English social and moral system, embodied in a Cambridge judge and jury, takes a harsh view of the informality of Australian conditions. The prodigal son has returned, but he is punished when embarrassing revelations come out about his life among the swine.

The discrepancies between Australian disorder and the placid order of English life is personified when two miners invade the village church at Folking while John Caldigate's son is christened. The two miners, who conspire with Mrs. Smith, are "clean, but rough, not quite at home in their clothes . . . with rough, ignoble faces,—faces which you would suspect, but faces, nevertheless, which had in them something of courage."[57] They cannot be fitted properly into the christening party or into English life, and their rough courage, which enables them to survive in New South Wales, threatens the peace and order of Folking and of England.

By speaking of their roughness and their courage in the same breath, Trollope honestly presents his own unresolved attitudes about the colonies and their different standards. This ambiguity pervades the entire novel. The colonies and their anarchy can produce good and evil, Caldigate's wealth and his liaison with Mrs. Smith. Trollope is not even sure that conventional morality ought to be expected from a dweller in the antipodes. He avoids any close examination of Caldigate's behavior there, and neither condemns nor defends his affair with Mrs. Smith. Mrs. Bolton's argument, that moral laws are universal, that moral behavior unacceptable in England cannot be condoned because of a mere accident of geography, is never answered. She is condemned as a Puritan, and Trollope does not distinguish between her valid objections to Caldigate and his conduct and her hysterical fanaticism.

57. 27:255-256.

239

The book's moral issue, such as it is, is evaded. Trollope's ambiguous attitude toward some of the social questions he raises is repeated when Caldigate is rescued from the prison where the English social system, operating through its official agencies as well as through public opinion, has placed him. Mr. Bagwax of the Post Office, representative of another official agency, rescues him by proving that the stamp on the incriminating letter was not printed until after the letter was supposed to have been sent. Public opinion turns in Caldigate's favor, and he is pardoned by the Queen, while the newspapers rejoice. "The case became really public," Trollope remarks sardonically, "and the newspapers were bought and read with the avidity which marks those festive periods in which some popular criminal is being discussed at every breakfast-table."[58] An efficient public employee sets the whole system in motion and an innocent man is saved and restored to his place.

Because it can detect and redress injustice the system itself is justified. Trollope's assurance that the social system can act justly is a sharp contrast to Dickens—Trollope invites this comparison by reminding the reader of the Circumlocution Office in *Little Dorrit* and denying the truth of the picture there presented: "The popular newspaper, the popular member of Parliament, and the popular novelist,—the name of Charles Dickens will of course present itself to the reader . . . have endeavoured to impress the . . . idea on the minds of the public generally,—that the normal Government clerk is quite indifferent to his work. No greater mistake was ever made. . . ."[59] Old Squire Caldigate, who is something of a radical, believes all government offices and officials are slow, lazy, unnecessary, and indifferent to justice, but the exertions of the Home Secretary and other officers of state in Caldigate's behalf prove that he is wrong.

There is some connection between this concern with the

58. 55:529.   59. 47:452.

problem of order and society and the book's other main problem, that of human isolation created by fanaticism. In her way, Mrs. Bolton is a greater anarchist than the most lawless of Australian miners. She disdains society and is self-isolated even from her own family. She refuses to believe in Bagwax's evidence, and she is furious at Queen Victoria when Caldigate is pardoned. "The Queen!" she exclaims. "As though she could know whether he be guilty or innocent. What can the Queen know of the manner of his life in foreign parts,—before he had taken my girl away from me?"[60] In Mrs. Bolton, Trollope attempted a portrait of the Puritan temperament and its spiritual arrogance. She is convinced that her wishes echo the divine will. Because she disapproves of the marriage of Caldigate and Hester she does not hesitate to call him an infidel. When he is accused of bigamy, Mrs. Bolton tries to imprison Hester at Puritan Grange; later she tries to persuade her to leave Folking. When Hester insists that she herself is acting under divine guidance in remaining faithful to Caldigate, Mrs. Bolton is convinced that this "counsel had not come from the Lord,—had come only from Hester's own polluted heart."[61] Even her language has an echo of Cromwell or Prynne about it. "Ask yourself whether you have stood upright or have fallen, since you left your father's house," she writes to Hester, when it is clear that Caldigate has been wrongfully accused and will soon be pardoned:

> whether you have trusted in the Lord your God, or in horses and chariots,—that is, in the vain comforts of an easy life? If it be so, can it be for your good that you have left your father's house? And should you not accept this scourge that has fallen upon you as a healing balm from the hands of the Lord?
>
> My child, I have no other answer to send you. That I love you till my very bowels yearn after you is most true.

60. 61:590.   61. 46:444.

But I cannot profess to believe a lie, or declare that to be good which I know to be evil.

May the Lord bless you, and turn your feet aright, and restore you to your loving mother.[62]

Mrs. Bolton's moral confusion is summed up in the delicate ambiguity that lurks around the phrase "your father's house" in this letter, and in her confidence that the Lord's blessing will take the form of restoring Hester to her mother's exclusive possession. "Love on the part of a mother may be as injurious as cruelty, if the mother be both tyrannical and superstitious,"[63] Trollope observes, and with Mrs. Bolton "Superstition was as strong . . . as with any self-flagellated nun."[64] She masks her own selfish possessiveness in religion and is thoroughly confused about her own motives, unwilling to admit that she wishes to dominate her daughter with divine authority, hoping for her daughter's disgrace and humiliation so that she alone can offer her aid and redemption, dreaming of an arid and impossible isolation in which she, Hester, and her "nameless grandson . . . should live together a stern, dark, but still sympathetic life, secluded within the high walls of that lonely abode . . . she should thus be able to prove how right she had been, how wicked and calamitous their interference with her child, — that had been the scheme of her life."[65]

The character of Mrs. Bolton is more powerful than anything else in the novel, but in creating her, Trollope weakened *John Caldigate*. She does not really exert any influence on events, her justified doubts about Caldigate are never really given a hearing, and her relation to the Australian episodes is not clear. Striking as her character is, Trollope never uses her with the fullest possible effect.

If *John Caldigate* is worth studying at all, it is because we find a few of Trollope's favorite themes more carefully de-

---

62. 56:543. See Cockshut's discussion of Mrs. Bolton as an "analysis of the evangelical mentality at its most forbidding" in *Anthony Trollope*, pp. 73-75.

63. 19:174.   64. 18:172.   65. 60:581-582.

lineated here than elsewhere, even though these themes are imperfectly related to one another. His distrust of fanaticism, especially of the evangelical type, his fear of isolation and disorder, and his belief that the English social system could protect its members from outsiders are all presented clearly and directly. This novel also indicates some of the ways in which Trollope's powers were limited. He could maintain a mystery only by concealing episodes and facts that should be revealed to the reader. Here he conceals the Australian liaison until very late in the book. The original title, *Mrs. John Caldigate*, and an alternate, *John Caldigate's Wife*, suggest that he hoped to tantalize the reader about Caldigate's guilt. He tries to combine length and an expanded setting, England, Australia, and the steamer *Goldfinder*, with a narrowly focused plot. But by introducing Mrs. Bolton's fanaticism and Bagwax's postal enthusiasm he diffuses that plot. Trollope's complex method and his plain style were not well adapted to the task he had set himself. He could accurately depict the multiplicity of the social structure in a long novel of multiple plot, but without a multiple plot, his control was uncertain when he attempted a long novel, and his beliefs were too baldly stated. Nor could he, without a multiple plot, give any real sense of the strength and variety of that English society he was so anxious to justify. In *John Caldigate* it is also clear that, while Trollope had mastered the short novel that deals intensely with a case of individual conscience, he could not spin such a situation into a long novel without digressions, and a general blurring in the whole depiction of moral crisis. *John Caldigate* is one of Trollope's failures, but a failure from which he learned. Its obvious faults are never repeated.

243

III. *Ayala's Angel*

Her angels face,
As the great eye of heaven, shynèd bright,
And made a sunshine in the shady place;
Did ever mortall eye behold such heavenly grace?
—Spenser, *The Faerie Queene* 1:3:4

Trollope toured South Africa and described what he saw in two large volumes before he began another novel. His five months (25 April to 24 September 1878) of work on *Ayala's Angel* were interrupted by a trip to Iceland in John Burns's yacht *Mastiff*, and by his description of that tour in a little book, *How the "Mastiffs" went to Iceland*, published privately in 1878. The new novel, which does not fit easily into the general canon of Trollope's work, was never published serially, and remained in manuscript until its appearance in book form in June 1881.

At first glance, *Ayala's Angel* appears to be another of Trollope's attacks on romanticism. The initial description of the Dormer sisters, Ayala and the more practical Lucy, prepares us for one of those confrontations between Mary and Martha that Trollope so often resolves in Martha's favor, as when he contrasts Arabella Trefoil and Mary Masters in *The American Senator*, or Lizzie Eustace and Lucy Morris in *The Eustace Diamonds*. But Trollope is in a self-mocking mood in *Ayala's Angel*. Ayala is foolish, perverse, and obsessed with the romantic dream of an "Angel of Light," the ideal suitor for whom she rejects all others. Yet she is neither ridiculed nor condemned. Instead, Trollope seems to find her foolishness and perversity charming. At the end of the novel her romantic dreams are fully satisfied.

In *Ayala's Angel*, Trollope reversed his usual anti-romantic attitudes to write a tongue-in-cheek defense of the romantic temperament. He teases his reader by turning his usual character-types, situations, and ideas inside out, at the same time reversing certain clichés of the contemporary novel. He provides Ayala with two lovers: one is long suffering and constant in the face of her indifference, slow, and unspectacular in every way, while the other is a genuine hero, conqueror of an Asiatic province, witty, frivolous, a favorite with the ladies. Trollope admits that, "if the matter be looked at aright," the long-suffering Tom Tringle "should be regarded as the hero of this little history," but Colonel Jonathan Stubbs, the more dashing lover, eventually marries Ayala. Constancy does not get its reward, though Trollope's defense of the less spectacular lover proclaims his moral superiority. "A very vulgar and foolish young man!" is his comment on Tom,

> But a young man capable of a persistent passion! Young men not foolish and not vulgar are, perhaps, common enough. But the young men of constant heart and capable of such persistency as Tom's are not to be found every day walking about the streets of the metropolis. Jonathan Stubbs was constant, too; but it may be doubted whether the Colonel ever really despaired. The merit is to despair and yet to be constant.[66]

Despite this, Trollope does not take Tom very seriously, and we are encouraged to laugh at the "lout" as he departs on a voyage to forget Ayala. "If the ship could be dashed against a rock I should prefer it!" he exclaims, attempting to strike the pose of the romantic lover. "That's nonsense," is his father's practical reply. "The Cunard ships never are dashed against rocks. By the time you've been three days at sea you'll be as hungry as a hunter." Later, when Tom is rebuked for threatening to drown himself by leaping into Niagara Falls, he promises, "I won't do it if I can help it,—but perhaps I had better not go there."[67]

Ayala's Angel is the most light-hearted of Trollope's later works. It is a social comedy revolving around that concept

---

66. *Ayala's Angel* 61:594.
67. 61:595-597. John Burns, Trollope's host on the *Mastiff* expedition, was chairman of the Cunard Steamship Company.

of the romantic hero he so frequently exposes as menda-
cious. This time he provides real heroes. Instead of plain
and dutiful heroines we have real beauties who are rewarded for headstrong behavior. Lucy and Ayala object to
the economies practiced in the home of a poor uncle when
he shelters them, and complain about the quiet life there. In
the home of their millionaire uncle, Sir Thomas Tringle,
they are self-assertive and rude. They are nevertheless ultimately justified. Trollope seems to be on vacation with them
in a world where romantic and perverse behavior is permitted. It may be that the man who attacks romanticism often
has a strong predisposition toward it.[68] There is some evidence that this was Trollope's case, in his careful and, at
times, sympathetic portrayal of such figures as Lady Glencora, Ferdinand Lopez, and Arabella Trefoil. But, predisposition or not, *Ayala's Angel* is Trollope's romantic comedy.

This reversal of customary attitudes is carried out all
through the book. Trollope's unexpected tolerance for
Ayala's romantic dreams is paralleled by his unexpected
satire at the genteel poverty of the sisters' poorer uncle, and
by his unexpected sympathy for the rich Sir Thomas. His
treatment of this self-made man of business is a far cry from
his portraits of Sir Roger Scatcherd or Mr. Melmotte, for
there is nothing of the pirate-financier about Sir Thomas.
Trollope depicts him as a kind man, though a little ponder-
ous in his habits and a little sharp of tongue. Sir Thomas
understands the complicated business of international finance and practices it with genuine zest. Given this deliberate avoidance of his usual attitudes, it is not surprising that
Trollope includes a degree of self-satire in *Ayala's Angel*, as
when he allows one of his characters to speak of "that fault
which is so prevalent in the novels of the present day. The
hero would be a very namby-mamby sort of a fellow,

68. See Donald D. Stone, "Trollope, Byron, and the Conventionalities," pp. 179-203. Cockshut, *Anthony Trollope*, p. 198, remarks that *Ayala's Angel* seems out of phase with the other novels of this period, and is
"similar in many ways to what Trollope had been writing in the early
sixties."

whereas the heroine would be too perfect for human nature." Thinking perhaps of Reginald Morton or Lord
George Germain, the speaker goes on to remark that,

> in novels the most indifferent hero comes out right at
> last. Some god comes out of a theatrical cloud and leaves
> the poor devil ten thousand a-year and a title. He isn't
> much of a hero when he does go right under such in-
> ducements, but he suffices for the plot, and everything is
> rose-coloured.[69]

To this self-satire Trollope adds a mockery of the Victorian novel's most cherished clichés. A lover in a novel was
expected to think of the woman of his heart as an angel, an
ethereal visitant from a higher plane of existence.[70] Here the
convention becomes absurd, for the "angel" is a man. This
angel is endowed with a heroic reputation, but also with an
unromantic name. Lucy falls in love with another unroman-
tically named figure of romance, the artist Isadore Hamel,
but he is hardly the glamorous Bohemian of fiction. Although he is the son of a father who rejects all convention,
Hamel wishes "to live in London, and after the manner of
Londoners," preferring

> the conventional mode of life. . . . A small house, very
> prettily furnished, somewhere near the Fulham Road, or
> perhaps verging a little towards South Kensington, with
> two maids, and perhaps an additional one as nurse in the
> process of some months, with a pleasant English break-
> fast and a pleasant English teapot in the evening . . . a
> very conventional aspect of life.[71]

Hamel believes in his own talent, and he bravely defends
his poverty to Sir Thomas, but he is extremely practical.

---

69. 38:363.

70. Trollope may again be thinking of Patmore's *The Angel in the House*.
Women—especially mothers—are described as angels in *Pendennis*, Tennyson's *The Princess* and *David Copperfield*. See Walter E. Houghton, *The Victorian Frame of Mind* (New Haven: Yale University Press, 1957) 3:13, esp.
p. 355.

71. 17:155-156.

His aim is to become rich and he has no romantic ideas about sacrificing profit for art. Instead, he dreams of doing portrait busts of the wealthy. Another favorite device of contemporary novelists, the romantic elopement to Ostend and the hasty marriage there, is deflated when Gertrude Tringle and one of her suitors make the journey. They discover that banns, licenses, and all the other impedimenta of conventional weddings are as necessary in Ostend as in London. Gertrude's letter to her mother does not enhance the glamor of the escapade:

> We mean to be married at Ostend, and then will come back as soon as you and papa say that you will receive us. In the meantime I wish you would send some of my clothes after me. Of course I had to come away with very little luggage, because I was obliged to have my things mixed up with Ben's. I did not dare to have my boxes brought down by the servants. Could you send me the green silk in which I went to church the last two Sundays, and my pink gauze, and the grey poplin? Please send two or three flannel petticoats, as I could not put them among his things, and as many cuffs and collars as you can cram in. I suppose I can get boots at Ostend, but I should like to have the hat with the little brown feather. There is my silk jacket with the fur trimming; I should like to have that. I suppose I shall have to be married without any regular dress, but I am sure papa will make up my trousseau to me afterwards. I lent a little lace fichu to Augusta; tell her I shall so like to have it.[72]

At the end of the book, the novelist is cheerfully nonchalant and self-mocking about the convention of closing with at least one wedding. Trollope closes with four after following eight different love affairs, with some doubling of personnel. "If marriage be the proper ending for a novel," he tells us, "the only ending, as this writer takes it to be, which is not discordant,—surely no tale was ever so properly ended, or with so full a concord. . . . Infinite trouble has been

72. 48:464-465.

taken not only in arranging these marriages but in joining like to like,—so that, if not happiness, at any rate sympathetic unhappiness, might be produced."[73]

Insofar as there is any hint of a serious subject in *Ayala's Angel*, it lies in the suggestion that too clearly developed an ideal, and too persistent an adherence to that ideal, can inhibit life, can prevent the necessary acceptance of the real world. Ayala's devotion to her imagined angel is so great that she twice refuses Stubbs because she cannot distinguish the angelic form lurking beneath his name, his ugly features, and his breezy manner. Trollope warns that it is possible to be so romantic as to miss life entirely, but he is not very serious about the warning. Ayala gets her third chance and accepts Stubbs. She comes to realize that she has loved him from the start, though Trollope himself is a little bit at sea with her perversity, for he cannot explain her state of mind and her reasons for rejecting the man earlier. He falls back on an indulgence of her perversity, admitting that her devotion to the unreal angel has created her charm in Stubbs's eyes. "That the dreams had been all idle she declared to herself,—not aware that the Ayala whom her lover had loved would not have been an Ayala to be loved by him, but for the dreams."[74]

Trollope's light-hearted approach is reflected in the book's casual structure, and in his frequent apologies for getting behind or ahead of his story as he follows one pair of lovers for a time, only to break off, go back, and retrieve some of the others. Ayala and Lucy are separated for long periods, and one of Gertrude Tringle's suitors, Frank Houston, pursues another unrelated love affair at intervals, so there are marked difficulties in narration. Trollope simply notes these difficulties. He makes little effort to solve them.

The number of couples at first seems to promise a complex and multiple structure, with some sort of analogical or contrasting relationship between the various heroes and

73. 64:624.   74. 51:493.

heroines. But there is no real effort to organize the book in this way. Lucy and Ayala both marry for love, but Lucy's part in the story is not very large. Their cousins, the Tringle sisters, both marry for money, but the Tringle marriages are happy enough, and Trollope develops most of the comedy around them.

Gertrude Tringle's abortive engagement to Frank Houston does lead to one of the few deliberately contrasted situations. Houston really loves his cousin, Imogene Docimer, and eventually they marry. She voices the customary attack on a marriage for money when she upbraids him for his designs on Gertrude; he provides the customary defense of such a marriage, urging his unfitness for work or for poverty, the need for wealth that his upbringing has imposed upon him. His practicality and his willingness to sacrifice love for money contrast with Ayala's excessive romanticism and her willingness to sacrifice everything to her ideal of love. The contrast is ironically worked out when Houston finally accepts poverty and marries for love, while Ayala finds that her romantic angel enjoys a comfortable income.

Ayala's obsession with her dream has a comic analogue in the infatuation of Tom Tringle for Ayala herself. His yearning for the ideal and the romantic is as great as her own. The difference is that she cannot discern her Angel of Light in any earthly shape, while Tom exalts Ayala into a goddess from the start. "If you had made no more than a woman of her it might have been better," his mother tells him mournfully. Trollope adds that, when a man "feels the goddess, he cannot carry himself before her as though she were a mere woman, and, as such, inferior to himself in her attributes. Poor Tom had felt the touch of something divine, and had fallen immediately prostrate before the shrine with his face to the ground."[75]

There does not seem to be any particular reason for Trollope's self-reversal in *Ayala's Angel*. The book seems to be an

75. 54:528-529.

essay in self-indulgence, suggesting Trollope's capacity for irony and his ability to manipulate an almost purely comic situation. Its openness and brightness contrast with the more oppressive atmosphere of *Cousin Henry, Kept in the Dark*, or *Mr. Scarborough's Family*, and Ayala's tolerantly described obsession contrasts with the darker obsessions of these novels. There is no reason to exalt *Ayala's Angel* to any place of special importance in the Trollope canon, but the reader who seeks only to be charmed can make no better choice.

✳ VIII ✳

GETTING AT A SECRET

Cousin Henry, Dr. Wortle's School, Marion Fay, and Kept in the Dark

Secret guilt by silence is betrayed.
—Dryden, *The Hind and the Panther* 3

IN HIS last years, Trollope once again worked almost exclusively in the form he had developed between 1868 and 1873, from *Sir Harry Hotspur* to *Harry Heathcote of Gangoil*, the short novel of single plot focussed on a single moral and social problem; and, as before, he explored each problem more fully by discussing it in several successive novels. *Cousin Henry, Dr. Wortle's School, Kept in the Dark*, and to some extent *Marion Fay* form such a group, sharing the theme of secrecy, and portraying the moral and social effects of keeping or revealing secrets. Trollope's last three completed novels, *The Fixed Period, Mr. Scarborough's Family*, and *An Old Man's Love*, form another thematically related group. In each of these novels, Trollope attempts an intensive treatment of a single theme; in most of them, there is also a single plot. Most of his protagonists are obsessed, and isolated in their obsessions. They may reflect the novelist's own growing sense of isolation as age and ill health worked to limit his participation in the social life that meant so much to him, both in itself and as proof that he had earned his rightful place.

In *Cousin Henry, Dr. Wortle's School*, and *Kept in the Dark*, the concealing of important facts is psychologically and socially destructive; in *Marion Fay*, facts are also concealed, but they are not very important, and their revelation does not have much effect. In each of these novels, Trollope is

252

not very interested in his secret. He is writing about the behavior of people in the presence of a secret, not about the secret itself.

I. *Cousin Henry*

See the corrupted use some make of books.
—Webster, *The White Devil* 3:2

Trollope wrote *Cousin Henry* in about six weeks, finishing on 8 December 1878. In a letter to Alexander Ireland, who was to publish the novel in his newspaper during the following year (it appeared as a two-volume book in November 1879), Trollope offered three titles: "Cousin Henry, Getting at a Secret, and Uncle Indefer's Will." He added that the second of these was "exactly apposite," but that Mrs. Trollope "says that it sounds clap trap."[1] Ireland apparently agreed with Mrs. Trollope, but "Getting at a Secret" is apposite in more ways than one.

The secret is the whereabouts of Indefer Jones's last will, which leaves his estate of Llanfeare to his niece, Isabel Brodrick, rather than to her cousin Henry. The reader soon learns that Indefer concealed the will in a volume of Jeremy Taylor's sermons, where Cousin Henry finds it. What Henry will do with this will becomes the book's central issue. Will he destroy it, and continue to enjoy the estate under an earlier will, which makes him heir? Or will he disinherit himself by producing it? The book becomes a study of guilt and vacillation. Henry is afraid to destroy the will and unwilling to reveal it. His awareness of it prevents him from enjoying the estate, and at the same time he is an object of general suspicion and hostility. His neighbors and servants had all hoped that Isabel would inherit, and they suspect that Indefer made a final will leaving the estate to her. They also suspect that Henry has found and destroyed that will. But all he does is sit, day after day, afraid to leave

1. *Letters* (Trollope to Alexander Ireland, 10 December 1878), pp. 408-409.

the room where the will is hidden, unable to decide what
to do.

Trollope has set a difficult problem by making his novel
depend on the crushing of a nonentity. Henry is shown
from the start as a miserable creature, even in childhood "a
sly boy, given to lying . . . unlike a Jones of Llanfeare."[2]
He has been expelled from Oxford "for some offence not
altogether trivial," run up large debts, and has settled down
as a London clerk when the novel opens. Trollope's description is deliberately indeterminate and negative, emphasizing
the lack of positive qualities:

> The man was not evil to the eye, a somewhat good-
> looking man rather than otherwise, tall with well-formed
> features, with light hair and blue-grey eyes, not subject
> to be spoken of as being unlike a gentleman, if not notice-
> able as being like one. That inability of his to look one in
> the face when he was speaking had not struck the Squire
> forcibly. . . .[3]

Henry is despised throughout. Isabel calls him odious and
his uncle dislikes him. When Henry takes possession of the

---

2. *Cousin Henry* 1:8.
3. 2:15. The first edition reads ". . . a somewhat cold-looking
man. . . ." Cockshut, noting the intensity with which Henry is loathed by
the other characters, comments that "From one point of view the book is an
exposure of the moral dangers of being repulsive to others . . ." (*Anthony
Trollope*, p. 34). Polhemus, in *The Changing World of Anthony Trollope*,
suggests that in Henry, Trollope is portraying his own boyhood situation
as an object of undeserved hostility (p. 235), and so indicting "intentionally
or not, organized morality and 'respectable' society as a conspiracy against
a weak single man." Polhemus argues that the reader must "sympathize
with the weak and disreputable side of human nature and distrust the
supposedly virtuous and respectable side" (p. 231). It seems to me that
Trollope is prepared to pity Henry, but not to sympathize with him.
Henry is, after all, not the rightful owner of the estate; he is a usurper, and
knows it. Polhemus is too charitable when he remarks that Henry fails to
reveal the will because "people bully him and frighten him so much" (p.
232), and that he is forced "to become the guilty sneak which everyone had
always thought him" (p. 233). Henry is well aware that he stands to lose a
valuable property if he reveals the missing will. Polhemus's comments first
appeared as "*Cousin Henry:* Trollope's Note from Underground,"
Nineteenth-Century Fiction 20(1966): 385-389.

estate, the servants give notice. The tenants threaten and insult him, a newspaper campaign against him begins, his own lawyer works against him, and on a visit to the county town he is advised not to use his own carriage lest he be mobbed by the populace, who are Isabel's partisans.

Henry is too cowardly to be a villain, too guilty to be pitied. He is a study in insignificance. Trollope shows us the vacillating of a man incapable of doing anything. He cannot make up his mind to destroy the will, to reveal it, or even to hide it more securely. He allows it to remain where his uncle had placed it, and broods about the situation until lawyer Apjohn deduces the will's whereabouts.

Trollope does not relieve his restricted little story with other characters and incidents. Old Uncle Indefer is conventionally crusty, and lawyer Apjohn has ingenuity and doggedness, but they are not developed enough to distract us from the sordid little drama in Henry's mind. There is little scenery and no society. We see only Henry's isolation and introspection. As for the love story between Isabel and the Reverend William Owen, Trollope rightly remarks that "any little interest which this tale may possess has come rather from the heroine's material interests than from her love."[4] Isabel is necessary to the plot as dispossessed heiress and wronged heroine. She has a few individual traits, notably generosity—except to Henry—and affection, and a strongly developed moral sense, but most of these traits exist to point up Henry's lack of them. He is timid, Isabel imperious, he is vacillating, she decisive. Isabel functions in part as a touchstone against which Henry's conduct can continually be tested. But the reader is not encouraged to be very interested in her.

"The intricacies of a weak man's mind,"[5] then, constitute the locale in which *Cousin Henry* takes place. His doubts, prayers, qualms, and half-formed resolutions are the real actors of the novel. The book is a remarkable example of concentration, focusing on a very narrow area of action: the

4. 24:280.   5. 21:235.

most important object is a piece of paper in a small room, the hero is confined to that room, the principal incidents are the half-formed thoughts in his mind. Nothing could be farther from the crowded panorama of *The Way We Live Now*. But what this novel necessarily lacks in scope, it makes up in intensity. Cousin Henry's sufferings are real, and the mind of the "poor, cringing, cowardly wretch" is fully explored. Every shift of his conscience, every foolish self-betraying act is laid bare.

At first Henry feels the cruelty of his position—promised an estate he had not sought, then suddenly denied that estate for no very good reason, then inheriting, then accidentally given the power to publish or to destroy the will that disinherits him. "He had not placed it" in the book where he finds it. "He had not hidden it. He had done nothing."[6] So he tries to justify himself to himself. He resolves to reveal the will, only to be deflected by trivial accidents. It is impossible for him to leave the estate, or even the book-room, lest the will be accidentally found. As time goes on (Henry's suspense lasts for about two months) he is tormented by dreams in which he is exposed. He tries to offer the use of the house to Isabel, hoping that she will discover the will. He plans to pretend that he has just discovered the will, but is afraid that no one will believe him, for he has no confidence in his own powers of dissimulation. At one moment he is ready to mail the document to his lawyer, at the next he is trying to summon up courage to destroy it. Visions of judges and prisons dance through his head, and finally fears of hell and eternal damnation. Libeled by the newspapers, who charge that he has destroyed the will, he

6. 7:79. In *The Moral Trollope*, apRoberts finds Henry guilty of *turpe* as defined by Cicero in *De Officiis*: "The sin is one of omission: he has failed in courage to take the positive action *bonestum* requires. And it would seem that the failure to take the right action, the 'leaving undone those things which we ought to have done,' is just about as base as overt crime" (p. 169). See also apRoberts's "*Cousin Henry*: Trollope's Note from Antiquity," *Nineteenth-Century Fiction* 24 (1969): 93-98, where she notes a possible source for Trollope's plot in *De Officiis*.

is forced into a suit against them in which he will be cross-examined by Mr. Cheekey, from whom no secrets can be kept. At times he is unable to avoid looking at the volume in which the will is concealed; on one occasion "His neck became absolutely stiff with the efforts necessary not to look at the book."[7] As the trial approaches he becomes more frantic, but still he cannot act. Finally Mr. Apjohn deduces the secret, invades the book-room, and easily locates the will. Henry resists feebly, and is knocked down, then sent ignominiously on his way.

The secret of the will's whereabouts is not the only secret in *Cousin Henry*, nor is the volume of Jeremy Taylor's sermons the only book with something concealed inside. The book of sermons is in fact a kind of analogue for the novel. "There is a pleasant game," Trollope tells us, "requiring much sagacity, in which, by a few answers, one is led closer and closer to a hidden word, till one is enabled to touch it. And as with such a word, so it was with [Henry's] secret."[8] For Henry and the other characters in the book the hidden object is the will, and Mr. Apjohn has the sagacity to find it. Trollope invites the reader to play the same game, seeking a pun on *will*. The action of the novel depends on a missing will—that is, on the final testament prepared by Uncle Indefer—and its discovery. The psychological action also depends on a missing will, Henry's inability to make up his mind.

"I have a conscience, my dear, on this matter,"[9] Indefer remarks as the book opens, and his struggle between conscience and inclination is a parallel to Henry's subsequent dilemma. Indefer wants to give the estate to Isabel, but believes that he should leave it to Henry, his only male heir. Since there is no entail, this difficult decision is Indefer's to make. In Trollope's novels, the disposition of an estate is always a dangerous decision. It can be damaging to the person who makes the decision, and to those whose lives will be shaped by the decision. Here indecision is equally

7. 10:110.   8. 9:103.   9. 1:1.

damaging. Indefer's uncertainty creates too many wills, and so brings about Henry's plight. Henry's knowledge of Indefer's final decision destroys his power to decide. A will and the lack of a will, in both meanings, are at the heart of the book. "A will . . . should be the outcome of a man's strength, and not of his weakness,"[10] meditates Isabel, when she realizes that her uncle has sacrificed duty to affection and left the estate to her.

Trollope's ingenuity has not stopped here, for he has added another ironic secret. There is patent irony in the hiding place of Uncle Indefer's will, a volume of sermons. A book concerned with spiritual matters contains a paper of great material importance, and Henry is corrupted rather than improved by the book's contents.

Trollope has carefully specified the book in which the will is found: Volume IV of a ten-volume set of Jeremy Taylor's works. When we turn to Bishop Heber's edition of 1822 (reissued 1847-54), the only edition available at the time Trollope was writing, we find in Volume IV a course of sermons written at Golden Grove, in Carmarthenshire, only a few miles from the imaginary estate of Llanfeare, and from its book-room where Henry broods for so long.

The sermons themselves have some bearing on the situations in *Cousin Henry*: Henry's lack of pleasure in his ill-gotten estate, the reward for his sin of omission, and his fear of punishment. One sermon, "Of godly fear," describes and warns against the kind of "servile fear" that afflicts him. "Apples of Sodom; or, the fruits of sin" is even more to the point, as is "The foolish exchange," in which the possession of the worldly goods for which men hazard their souls "is not mere and unmixed, but allayed with sorrow and uneasiness."[11] Taylor warns against men who "believe that the story of hell is but a bugbear to affright children and

---

10. 7:71.
11. Jeremy Taylor, *The Whole Works of the Right Rev. Jeremy Taylor, D.D.*, ed. Reginald Heber (London: Longman, Brown, Green, and Longman, 1850), 4, *A Course of Sermons for All the Sundays in the Year*, 18 "The Foolish Exchange," p. 556.

fools,"[12] and Henry tries hard to "bring himself to believe
that all that story of a soul tormented for its wickedness in
everlasting fire was but an old woman's tale."[13] Taylor
warns against dissembling and being "crafty to another's
injury, so much as by giving countenance to the wrong." In
"Apples of Sodom" he analyzes Henry's case: "the bondage
of a vicious person is . . . as a sick man in his bed . . . he
that is almost taken in a fault tells a lie to escape; and to
protect that lie forswears himself . . . a man . . . must have
his sin and his peace too, or else he can have neither
long . . . therefore they must make a fantastic peace by a
studied cozening of themselves, by false propositions, by
carelessness, by stupidity. . . ."[14] Nor can a sin be kept
secret, for "sin discovers itself; or else the injured person
will proclaim it . . . or curious people will enquire and discover, or the spirit of detraction shall be let loose upon
him. . . . Many persons have betrayed themselves by their
own fears."[15] One could continue to quote from Jeremy
Taylor, but it is hardly necessary. In the course of the book
Cousin Henry is never far from Volume IV of the sermons,
and Trollope's analysis of a sinner's discomfort suggests that
while writing his novel Trollope was never far from that
volume either. He has allowed the sagacious reader the
same "pleasant game" of "getting at a secret" that Mr.
Apjohn plays. Trollope invites the reader to understand the
secret connotations of *will*, and perhaps to seek a commentary on the book's moral concerns in the volume where
Uncle Indefer's will lay hidden.

In *Cousin Henry*, Trollope has created another of his isolated men. Henry cannot act, and cannot be loved, or even
tolerated. Trollope examines the moral and psychological
aspects of his situation—the permanent situation created by
his personality, and the specific and temporary situation
caused by his inheritance and his discovery of the will. He

12. Taylor, p. 570.
13. *Cousin Henry* 20:231.
14. Taylor, "Apples of Sodom," 4:20:258-259.
15. Taylor, pp. 264-265.

is prepared both to pity Henry and to condemn him. Trollope pities the isolated man, but he reminds us that Henry's personality and actions have social consequences. The inheritance is the rule of an estate, and society instinctively recognizes Henry's unfitness for this task. It is society's disapproval that brings about his ultimate exposure: because public opinion is critical, he is forced to initiate a libel suit. The threat of a trial, and Mr. Cheekey's cross-examination, terrify him. He is sure he will break down, and either reveal the existence of the will, or reveal that he has destroyed it. These fears so weaken him that he is an easy victim for Mr. Apjohn's *coup de grâce*. Even Uncle Indefer's final action and his indecisions are considered in their social aspect, as Mr. Apjohn and Isabel ride in triumph to Llanfeare. A squire shares his estate with the people around him, for "where land is concerned, feelings grow up which should not be treated rudely," and when Indefer

> induced by a theory which he did not himself quite understand [brought] . . . Henry down among these people, he outraged their best convictions. . . . He did not understand the root of that idea of a male heir. The object has been to keep the old family, and the old adherences, and the old acres together. England owes much to the manner in which this has been done, and the custom as to a male heir has availed much in the doing of it. But in this case, in sticking to the custom, he would have lost the spirit, and, as far as he was concerned, would have gone against the practice which he wished to perpetuate. There, my dear, is a sermon. . . .[16]

Trollope's basic concern is with a weak man, one unfit to be an English squire and to perform the duties of that position. He offers a psychological explanation for society's instinctive recognition of this unfitness, and the book studies Henry's morbid weakness in its material and social context. This juxtaposition of the psychological and the social is Trollope's achievement in *Cousin Henry*. The book falls into

16. *Cousin Henry* 24:273.

its place in the Trollope canon as a study "from the inside"
of isolation from the forces that demand and enforce social
conformity, and of the psychological wear and tear such
isolation can impose.

II. *Dr. Wortle's School*

> It would at first have seemed very improbable
> that Dr. Wortle should have taken into his
> school . . . a gentleman who had chosen the
> United States as a field for his classical labours.
> —Chapter 2

Trollope began *Marion Fay* at the end of 1878, but abandoned it to write his biography of Thackeray. Then, before
turning again to *Marion Fay*, he wrote *Dr. Wortle's School* in
the space of three weeks (April 1879). The book, serialized
in *Blackwood's Magazine* during the last six months of 1880,
appeared as a two-volume novel in January 1881.

Although parallels with *Cousin Henry* indicate that the
theme of isolation is still a basic concern, *Dr. Wortle's School*
is more cheerful and less introspective. Trollope wrote the
novel while staying at Lowick, in Northumberland, where
the rector had loaned him the parsonage for a month's vacation. The hero, Dr. Jeffrey Wortle, is Rector of Bowick and
Headmaster of Bowick School. T. H. S. Escott considered
him to be, especially in temperament, Trollope's self-
portrait.[17] He is a character completely antithetical to
Cousin Henry—Dr. Wortle is bold, wilful, large-hearted,
impulsive, generous, and eager to command all those
around him.

Trollope discarded two alternative titles, "Mr. and Mrs.
Peacocke," and "Bowick School," in favor of that the book
carries, which properly concentrates attention on the Doctor and emphasizes his control over the school. The novel is
not a school story in the ordinary sense. The schoolboys

17. T. H. S. Escott, *Anthony Trollope*, pp. 302-303.

rarely appear, though their presence—or potential absence—is an important element. In this book the teachers must be taught, and the masters learn that they must master themselves. Dr. Wortle keeps a school, but he himself must in a sense go to school, and he learns an important lesson from his neighbor, Mr. Puddicombe.

Dr. Wortle's problem, like Cousin Henry's, is that of maintaining the right relationship with the society of which he is a part, and of having a secret impede this relationship. The book suggests that to violate this relationship can lead to disaster, even if the violation is motivated by benevolence. Dr. Wortle is one more variation on Trollope's favorite subject, the man somehow at odds with society. He is not an outsider nor is he isolated because of morbidity. It is his insistence on creating his own moral code that puts him at odds with society, but the wilfulness that causes him to do this sustains him when society disapproves. In *Dr. Wortle's School*, Trollope presents the Doctor as sympathetic, and in every way possible justifies his defiance of public opinion. Those who speak for society are neither interesting nor attractive. Nevertheless, society and its laws must be placated. Public opinion can and will punish those who disregard its power.

Dr. Wortle is by nature unwilling to accept direction or advice from anyone. When the novel opens he has so far been successful. His life is happy, his school is prosperous, and the bishop of the diocese is afraid to interfere with him. His one enemy, a Mrs. Stantiloup, the dissatisfied mother of one of his pupils, is unable to harm him in any way, hard as she tries.

The novel's main plot, and its moral problem, revolve around a secret, and the inevitable repercussions which follow the existence of that secret. As in *Cousin Henry*, the secret itself is soon out, and we are invited to watch the behavior provoked by the revelation of certain facts about Dr. Wortle's assistant, Mr. Peacocke. Mr. Peacocke is an excellent teacher and a good man, but there is a mystery about him. He and his wife refuse all invitations, and Mrs. Peacocke—who handles the school's domestic arrangements—will not associate with anyone. As in *Is He Popenjoy?* and *Cousin Henry*, a mystery attracts attention. A man who isolates himself makes society wonder about him.

The Peacockes' secret is that they are not properly married. Mrs. Peacocke's first husband, Colonel Ferdinand Lefroy of New Orleans, was alive at the time of her second marriage, and may be alive still. Lefroy and his brother, Colonel Robert Lefroy, are familiar types in American literature, but Trollope is probably the first English novelist to deal with them. They are Southern gentlemen, ruined by the Civil War, who have lost their plantation and turned into drunken spongers and bullies. The Southern cavalier ruined by his own improvidence was a staple of Southern fiction even before 1865, created by such novelists as William Gilmore Simms, John Esten Cooke, and William Alexander Caruthers. The type was revived after the Civil War by Thomas Nelson Page and others, this time as the noble-hearted cavalier ruined by the grasping and puritanical Yankee. ("Kilbrack was the name of our plantation," says Robert Lefroy, "where we should be living now as gentlemen ought, with three hundred niggers of our own, but for these accursed Northern hypocrites.")[18] Even non-Southern writers like Henry Adams and Henry James presented idealized Southern cavaliers, in *Democracy* (1880) and *The Bostonians* (1886), but Trollope refused to glamorize the type. He portrays the Lefroys as men whose social role has vanished, but he does not justify their actions because of this. The ideal of the Southern gentleman receives a debunking at his hands.

The Peacockes met in St. Louis, where Mr. Peacocke had gone to act as vice-president of a university.[19] He helps

18. *Dr. Wortle's School*, Part 5:6:204.

19. Trollope is presumably thinking of Washington University, where Mr. Peacocke would have assisted the first chancellor, Dr. William Eliot, Trollope's friend (Trollope to Kate Field, 4 February 1862, *Letters*, p. 108) and T. S. Eliot's grandfather.

Mrs. Lefroy when she is mistreated and then abandoned by her husband. Later word comes that Lefroy is dead. Mr. Peacocke, already in love, undertakes a long journey to make sure that she is free to marry. He finds Robert Lefroy, who confirms the death of his brother, and the marriage takes place. But Ferdinand Lefroy is not dead. He reappears briefly in St. Louis, then vanishes again.

The Peacockes realize that, although they married in good faith, their marriage is not valid. But they decide to remain together. They love each other, and he cannot bring himself to abandon her to poverty and loneliness. Since their plight is known in St. Louis, they return to England and settle at Bowick School. Peacocke is conscious of the harm they could do to the school's reputation, so he decides to admit everything to Dr. Wortle, and at this point the novel begins. Before he can act, Robert Lefroy turns up, tells the Doctor of the Peacockes' crime, and then spreads the information throughout the country. Because his story is slightly awry, the Doctor shrewdly guesses that now Ferdinand Lefroy is dead. He sends Peacocke and Lefroy to the United States to investigate, and Peacocke is able to find proof that his predecessor is really dead. The center of interest, however, remains at Bowick. The Doctor has bravely allowed Mrs. Peacocke to remain there during the American trip, and the presence of this scarlet woman makes him vulnerable. Rumors circulate and find their way into *Everybody's Business*, a cheap newspaper. The bishop rebukes him, pupils are withdrawn from the school, Mrs. Wortle is unhappy, and because of his impulsive charity Dr. Wortle is sorely tried. When Mr. Peacocke returns, all ends happily, with the Peacockes properly married, the school flourishing again, and Mary Wortle about to marry the heir to an earldom.

Trollope's concern is not the bizarre misadventures of the Peacockes and their great secret, which he reveals in the third chapter. "It is my purpose," he warns the reader, "to disclose the mystery at once, and to ask you to look for your interest,—should you choose to go on with my chronicle,—simply in the conduct of my persons, during this disclosure, to others."[20] The statement is an accurate summary of the book. Trollope's deliberate avoidance of suspense is coupled with an equally deliberate refusal to dwell at length on the morality of the Peacockes' conduct. ("I think I have managed the question as to the marriage so as to give no offence,"[21] he wrote his publisher in April 1880.) Were they justified in remaining together, as Dr. Wortle enthusiastically declares, or is public opinion right in insisting that they should have parted as soon as Ferdinand Lefroy's resurrection became known to them? Should they be condemned or condoned? The question of justification is not finally answered. Every possible excuse is made for the Peacockes, but we are firmly reminded of the fact that they are, after all, living in adultery. Dr. Wortle forcibly argues the rightness of their conduct, but Mr. Puddicombe, Mrs. Wortle, and others argue its wrongness with equal force.

The reader is turned away from this interesting debate to consider, not the conduct of the Peacockes, but the conduct of Dr. Wortle. We are not asked to speculate whether adultery can, under certain conditions, be right, but to speculate instead whether it can ever be right to defend publicly a confessed and unrepentant adulterer against society's judgment. Even this question is of less interest to Trollope than the larger question of the individual's relation to society. Is Dr. Wortle right to disregard convention? The only answer comes from the Reverend Mr. Puddicombe, who stands for plain objective truth in the novel. "You condoned [the Peacockes' action]," he reminds the Doctor. "I am not condemning you. . . . There will be those, like myself, who, though they could not dare to say that in morals you were strictly correct, will love you the better for what you did."[22] Here, as elsewhere, Trollope declines to present an absolute

20. 1:3:27.
21. *Letters* (Trollope to William Blackwood, 8 April 1880), p. 433.
22. Conclusion 11:257-258.

moral judgment. The question of the rightness of the Peacockes' conduct, and even of Dr. Wortle's conduct, is made irrelevant at the end. Mary Wortle's engagement distracts the reader—and the characters—from moral questions.

After the fuss is over, a parent who had withdrawn his children writes to Dr. Wortle to say that he had "heard a story told two ways . . . he declared that he had believed both the stories."[23] The Doctor—and the reader—must be content with this simultaneous praise and blame. With Lefroy proven dead and the Peacockes legally married, society indicates approval of the Peacockes and of the Doctor. It does not approve their past conduct, but it is willing to accept them in the future at face value, now that Mr. Peacocke has made his position publicly and socially right. Mr. Puddicombe, who is unsparing in his condemnation of the Peacockes' sin throughout the book, volunteers to attend their second wedding so that Peacocke will feel that now "the clergymen from his neighbourhood are standing with him."[24] Society, which can condemn unsparingly, can also pardon, once its minimal requirements are met. The man or woman who flouts the social order by sinning, or by condoning sin, is punished, but conformity earns forgiveness. The title of the cheap little newspaper *Everybody's Business*, which impugns the Peacockes and the Doctor, is a reminder of the truism Trollope illustrates: any mystery or scandal or excessively self-willed conduct becomes "everybody's business," because all men are a part of society and society judges individual conduct.

Because the action of the book depends on the defense and assistance Dr. Wortle offers to the Peacockes, it is the Doctor's impulsive refusal to conform that provides the main interest—his generous stubbornness, his foolish pride. The Doctor tries to live without recourse to others. He was, Trollope tells us in the first sentence of the book, "a man much esteemed by others,—and by himself." As he is introduced, we learn that

23. Conclusion 12:271.   24. Conclusion 11:259.

he recommended all those who gave him advice to mind their own business. . . . He liked to be master, and always was . . . a man who would bear censure from no human being. He had left his position at Eton because the Head-master had required from him some slight change of practice. . . . There can be no doubt that he made himself wilfully distasteful to many of his stricter brethren.[25]

This deliberate and consistent disregard of public opinion long before the Peacocke case explains his conduct throughout the crisis. It may even be that the Peacockes' refusal to conform finds a sympathetic chord in Dr. Wortle, for they too have chosen to disregard convention and go their own way. Aware of their transgression, they make up their own law, and in defending them the Doctor does the same.

Trollope does not defend social rebellion, as Hugh Walpole and Robert Polhemus seem to think, nor does he condemn it, as A. O. J. Cockshut argues.[26] He simply portrays the consequences of a disregard for convention. A great deal can be argued in favor of this rebellion: the Doctor's sturdiness and benevolence, Peacocke's manliness, the rascality of the Lefroys. Those who argue against rebellion are not benevolent or noble. The timid bishop, the chilly Mr. Puddicombe who is dry and "hard-looking,"[27] the libelous newspapers, the lupine Mrs. Stantiloup—these represent society and its reaction, which is to condemn imprudence. Dr. Wortle realizes that "according to my way of thinking I did my duty," but that the result is "a grand opportunity for slander."[28]

Mr. Peacocke's journey to the United States is another device Trollope uses to present the rebellion as favorably as possible. His trip is a kind of quest, which a hero traditionally must carry out before he can win his lady. It provides

25. 1:1:2-5.
26. Hugh Walpole, *Anthony Trollope* (London: Macmillan and Co., 1928), pp. 163-164. Polhemus, *The Changing World of Anthony Trollope*, p. 238. Cockshut, *Anthony Trollope*, pp. 220-223.
27. Conclusion 11:258.
28. 5:7:215.

Peacocke a chance to show courage and manliness equal to the Doctor's (Robert Lefroy twice threatens to kill him, and the clergyman-scholar has to brandish a gun). The trip also shows the twisted character of Robert Lefroy and by implication develops the personality of Mrs. Peacocke's first husband, to add one more justification for her conduct. Peacocke is brave and behaves admirably. The Lefroy brothers are despicable. The goodness of the Peacocke defenders and the badness of their enemies are Trollope's method of making the case for the Peacockes' conduct and Dr. Wortle's defense of it as strong as possible, even while he describes the "grand opportunity for slander" that such conduct provides, and society's violent reaction to even an apparently justified violation of its norms.

For society, in Trollope's opinion, is based on a code, and cannot recognize emotions or states of mind. Peacocke's journey is a search for the fact that will help him to satisfy the social code, proof of Ferdinand Lefroy's death. Only when that fact has been fully established can the Peacockes marry and look forward to happiness. Until then Dr. Wortle and the Peacockes are vulnerable. They have concocted their own moral code in response to pressing human needs. As a clergyman, Peacocke knows that he is breaking moral and social law by remaining with Mrs. Peacocke after her husband's unexpected reappearance:

> If it were a crime, then he would be a criminal. . . . She had felt herself more at liberty to proclaim to herself a gospel of her own for the guidance of her own soul. To herself she had never seemed to be vicious or impure, but she understood well that he was not equally free from the bonds which religion had imposed. . . .[29]

Later, Mr. Peacocke admits that they have been living a lie, deceiving Dr. Wortle and

> all the world. . . . No doubt it is a lie,—but there are circumstances in which a lie can hardly be a sin. I would

29. 2:4:43.

have been the last to say so before all this had come upon
me, but I feel it to be so now. . . . I have found, since
this came upon us, that it may be well to choose one sin
in order that another may be shunned.[30]

On hearing the Peacockes' story, Dr. Wortle makes the
same choice, for a subjective moral code rather than an
objective social one. "I would have clung to her, let the law
say what it might," he exclaims, "and I think that I could
have reconciled it to my God. But I might have been wrong.
. . . I might have been wrong. . . . We are both sinners.
Both might have been wrong."[31] Objective morality and
objective truth are left to the "dry, thin, apparently unsym-
pathetic . . . but just" Mr. Puddicombe, who is "by no
means given to harshness," but "would not be driven by
impulses and softness of heart to save the faulty one."[32] He
refuses to quibble. He points out that "no reference in our
own minds to the pity of the thing, to the softness of the
moment,—should make us doubt"[33] the objective fact of the
Peacockes' sin and their obligation to conform to conventional morality.

"No man," Dr. Wortle realizes, "had a right to regard his
own moral life as isolated from the lives of others around
him."[34] Later Peacocke repeats this lesson to his wife. The
impossibility of moral and social isolation is the subject of
the book, the very difficulty of reconciling conscience and
inclination, public judgment and private judgment. Men
live together, and their actions must be capable of general
and dispassionate scrutiny. The end of the book affirms that
moral and social law are one. Trollope suggests the
difficulties—perhaps impossibilities—of objective judgment
for those involved in a case of conscience, and his own
refusal to make such a judgment gives to these difficulties an
extra emphasis. But his eye is fixed not on moral conduct
but on the social reactions to a moral question.

30. 2:6:63-64.   31. 3:8:88.   32. 3:9:97.   33. 3:9:99.
34. 3:8:84.

The story is occasioned by a secret which, in the nature of things, comes out. The novel is one more in Trollope's series of studies in the conflict between the individual and society. He narrows his stage progressively. Melmotte and Lopez, individual outlaws, agitate all society; Arabella Trefoil and the Marquis of Brotherton agitate small sections of society. In *Cousin Henry* and *Dr. Wortle's School* it is society that is active and aggressive, and refuses to leave the self-isolated alone. In these books, Trollope consistently portrays the power the social order has to enforce its standards, and dramatizes his theme by focusing on an individual who is undergoing a kind of social siege.

III. *Marion Fay*

FAY, obs. var. of Fey *a.*, fated to die.
—*Oxford English Dictionary*

Trollope began *Marion Fay* in December 1878, just after completing *Cousin Henry*. At the end of January 1879 he abandoned the book, and wrote *Thackeray* and *Dr. Wortle's School* before returning to *Marion Fay* in August. Despite these interruptions, the tale was written in a little over four months. He finished in November 1879. Serialized in *The Graphic* from December 1881 to June 1882, *Marion Fay* was published by Chapman and Hall in May 1882.

In *Marion Fay* the theme of secrecy and exposure is less important than in *Cousin Henry*, *Dr. Wortle's School*, and *Kept in the Dark*. There are secrets—the secret of George Roden's birth, which raises his social status when it is revealed; Lady Kingsbury's secret desire for her stepson's death so that her own son can succeed to the family titles and estates; and her friend Mr. Greenwood's secret project for causing that stepson's death. But in *Marion Fay* Trollope is not really interested in the psychological or social consequences of secret-keeping. Perhaps as a relief from the other three novels of this period, Trollope seems to have set out in *Marion Fay* to write a novel full of secrets and mysteries which are of no importance at all when they are revealed. They provoke neither guilt nor any important consequences.

In this novel Trollope himself displays a curious reticence. He creates three situations which are inherently dramatic: Marion Fay dies, to the despair of her lover, Lord Hampstead; Hampstead's stepmother and the family chaplain meditate his murder; and George Roden, a penniless young Post Office clerk, loves Hampstead's sister, overcoming the opposition of her family when he turns out to be an Italian duke. But Trollope deliberately avoids the dramatic possibilities of these situations. Although Marion suffers from the lingering illness that destroys so many nineteenth-century literary heroines, there is no attempt at a pathetic deathbed scene. There is instead a dignified interview in which Trollope stresses Lord Hampstead's sorrow and future loneliness rather than the pathos of Marion's death. Mr. Greenwood, the murderous chaplain, is a pale reflection of the sinister priests of Gothic romance. He contemplates but never attempts his crime. We see him preparing for it, we learn that Lord Hampstead will cross a deserted portion of the estate alone at 4:30 in the morning, and then the occasion is past and Mr. Greenwood is thinking about what might have happened. There is no crime, nor even a scene in which Greenwood wrestles with his conscience or his fears until he is prevented from crime. As for Roden's Italian title, he refuses to assume it because he despises hereditary honors, and because he has no money to support it. Even the great revelation that he is a duke is treated without drama or excitement. The facts are communicated to him off stage, nothing much is made of his reaction, and the reader is given only a brief circumstantial account of Mrs. Roden's early life. George has never been interested in his paternity because as a Radical he has no interest in the past—Trollope's rather transparent device for making it plausible that the young clerk should know nothing about his father, and for explaining his refusal to be impressed when he finds that he has noble and even royal blood. Trollope introduces the clichés of the melodramatic novel into *Marion Fay* but makes no use of them.

The book is muted in every way, like the beautiful Quaker maiden who is its titular heroine. "I think it was my Quaker dress," she remarks, when she is trying to explain why Lord Hampstead finds her attractive. "His eye, perhaps, likes things all of a colour."[35] The remark could serve as a description of Trollope's deliberately anti-dramatic method. In *Marion Fay* he seems to enjoy tantalizing the reader by holding out promises of dramatic happenings, bringing them nearer and nearer, and then not letting them occur.

Trollope combines lack of drama with a pattern that is obtrusive. Because the old Marquis of Kingsbury was a Radical in his youth, he married beneath his rank. There are two children of this marriage: Lord Hampstead, the Marquis's heir, and Lady Frances Trafford (the family name is Trafford). Both children inherit their father's radicalism, while the old Marquis becomes more conservative as he grows older. When he marries again, the second Lady Kingsbury comes from "among the dukes,"[36] but his two elder children decide to marry out of their order. Hampstead chooses Marion Fay, the daughter of a clerk. Lady Frances chooses George Roden, himself a clerk. This deliberate repetition of the father's acts by the children offers Trollope a chance to satirize the zealous reformer who is personally inconvenienced by his longed-for reforms—one of his favorite devices for ridiculing doctrinaires and the panaceas they advocate. The pattern is equally obtrusive when we learn that Marion Fay's mother died just as her daughter does, and that Mr. Fay thereafter lived alone, as Lord Hampstead vows to do. Mrs. Roden's noble marriage was unhappy, and so she warns Marion against marrying Hampstead.

35. *Marion Fay* (London: Chapman and Hall, 1882), 3 volumes, 2:3:41.
36. 1:1:5. Cockshut, *Anthony Trollope*, p. 58, remarks on the hereditary likeness between Lord Kingsbury and his son.

Most of the events in the book are connected with the issue of social inequality. Lady Kingsbury believes that a whole family can be tainted if one of its members marries someone of lower rank, and therefore sees her own children as threatened by her stepchildren's plans. Because Lord Hampstead's inherited radicalism impels him to find friends who are not his social equals, George Roden and Lady Frances meet. In this way, every episode and character is connected to the book's main themes.

There is nothing new in the conflict between love and class, and in *Marion Fay* important elements of plot as well as theme are taken from some of Trollope's other novels. A nobly born brother and sister each choosing to love a social inferior occurs in *The Duke's Children*; there are dubious Italian marriages in *Is He Popenjoy?* and *Lady Anna*. In the latter novel, we also find a commoner who is miserable after a noble marriage, and most of the arguments with which society urges George Roden to assume his title are rehearsed in *Lady Anna*, when Sir William Patterson argues with Daniel Thwaite.

Trollope is at his most ironic when he depicts the excited activity after Roden is known to be heir to an Italian title. The young clerk sticks to his principles and refuses to call himself Duca di Crinola, but society will not permit this. Everyone urges the title upon him, from the landlady at the "Duchess of Edinburgh"[37] to Sir Boreas Bodkin, Trollope's self-portrait as a Post Office official, and Lady Frances's noble relatives; he is even threatened with the intervention of Queen Victoria. It is a reversal of one of Trollope's favorite themes. This time the low-born outsider, foreign and even Latin, suddenly becomes an insider with his foreign

---

37. Trollope houses the Rodens, the Fays, and the Demijohns in Paradise Row, Holloway, at that time a newly developed middle-class London suburb. He emphasizes the newness by naming his public house: it would have been named no earlier than January 1874, when Queen Victoria's second son, the Duke of Edinburgh, married Grand Duchess Marie of Russia. All the Trafford family titles—Kingsbury, Hampstead, and Highgate—are taken from middle-class London suburbs.

origin an advantage. He finds more difficulty in retaining his old name and status than many of Trollope's outsiders find when they try to penetrate society. Society, which repels invaders with such vigorous decision, is equally vigorous at including those whose birth makes them worthy of membership. "I think . . . that the good sense of the world will prevail against you," Sir Boreas tells George. ". . . The world never insists on calling a man a Lord or a Count for nothing. There's too much jealousy for that. But when a thing is so, people choose that it shall be so."[38] Society can insist on status as well as deny it. The "good sense of the world" admits George, finds him an income, and transfers him to the more aristocratic Foreign Office. At the end of the book we are told that George is still Mr. Roden, but that he will probably soon begin to use his title.

The situation allows Trollope to argue once again some of his favorite theories about rank and gentlemen. "It is well to be a gentleman," George Roden admits, before his own rank is made known to him, "and if the good things which are generally attendant on high birth will help a man in reaching noble feelings and grand resolves, so it may be that to have been well born will be an assistance. But if a man derogates from his birth,—as so many do,—then it is a crime."[39] He is echoed by Lord Hampstead: "Nobility, whatever may be its nature, imposes bonds on us. And if these bonds be not obeyed, then nobility ceases. . . . I do acknowledge that as very much has been given to me in the way of education, of social advantages, and even of money, a higher line of conduct is justly demanded from me than from those who have been less gifted. So far, *noblesse oblige*."[40] Later, when Roden has been recognized as a duke, he argues that he should not be promoted or treated differently because of his birth, but he is told that this is the way of the world. "I will not dispute it with you,—whether it ought to be so;—but, if it be probable, there is no reason

38. 3:10:113.   39. 1:20:264-265.
40. 1:10:134. See apRoberts, *The Moral Trollope*, p. 153.

why you should not take advantage of your good fortune, if you have capacity and courage enough to act up to it. Of course what we all want in life is success. If a chance comes in your way I don't see why you should fling it away."[41]

But it is not possible to assign to *Marion Fay* any high place among Trollope's novels. The book is desultory, and even the parallel plots are awkward, for the comic plot undercuts some of the more serious elements. Lord Hampstead's resolution never to marry if he cannot have Marion, and his sincere conviction that the world will mean nothing to him after her death, is comically parodied in a clerk named Tribbledale, who mourns in alcoholic despair when he is jilted and threatens to leap from the Whispering Gallery of St. Paul's: "You'd be more talked of that way, and the vergers would be sure to show the stains made on the stones below. 'It was here young Tribbledale fell, —a clerk at Pogson and Littlebird's, who dashed out his brains for love on the very day as Clara Demijohn got herself married.' "[42] Tribbledale's grotesque project jars with Lord Hampstead's real grief, and later the parallel between Tribbledale's marriage to his Clara and Roden's marriage to Lady Frances (both take place on the same day) seems irrelevant. Mr. Crocker is one of Trollope's memorable cads, and there is potential interest in the characters of the murderous clergyman and the archetypal evil stepmother, but these characters are not really explored. Lady Kingsbury's moral descent is barely charted, though she moves from a snobbery that sees her stepchildren's low marriages threatening the social standing of her own children, to a readiness to welcome the death of her stepson. She herself has almost no moral awareness of her own conduct, and Mr. Greenwood has none at all. Hugh Walpole hardly states the case too strongly when he remarks that *Marion Fay* "is the exact negation of every virtue Trollope possessed." He classes it among "novels of Trollope's that may be eternally and remorselessly forgotten as though they had never been

41. 3:6:65.   42. 2:8:101-102.

born."[43] Though the reviewers of 1882 united in rather perfunctory praise for the book, the New York *Critic* anticipated Walpole by calling *Marion Fay* "very, very tiresome and unnatural."[44] Trollope's heroes are merely stubborn, the villainess is foolish and snobbish rather than bad, the angry old Marquis is not in fact very angry. Lord Hampstead's fatal accident in the hunting field is merely a rumor, his murder is merely planned, the Post Office clerk is not a mere clerk. The social barriers that loom so high at the beginning of the book become irrelevant, and it requires an act of God for something to happen, the death of Marion Fay. Trollope's delight in the nondramatic, which elsewhere leads to effective understatement, has fatally weakened this novel.

IV. *Kept in the Dark*

> This jealousy
> Is for a precious creature: as she's rare
> Must it be great; and, as his person's mighty,
> Must it be violent.
> —*The Winter's Tale*, 1:2:449-452.

Trollope completed *Marion Fay* and moved from London to his last home at Harting Grange before he settled to the four-month task of writing *Kept in the Dark* (18 August to 15 December 1880). Published in *Good Words* from May to December 1882, the novel appeared in book form in late August or early September of that year, the last of Trollope's novels to be published as a book in his lifetime. With *Kept in the Dark* Trollope is concerned with a secret once again, as the title implies, and with the effect secrets can have on society when they inevitably cease to be secrets.

As in *Cousin Henry* and *Dr. Wortle's School*, the tale combines secrecy with isolation. The chief interest lies in the

43. Hugh Walpole, *Anthony Trollope*, p. 122.
44. *Critic* (New York), 2 (29 July 1882), p. 201, reprinted in Donald Smalley, *Trollope: The Critical Heritage*, p. 495.

growth of a sense of injury in the minds of two morbid people, Cecilia Holt Western and her husband. The secret—revealed to the reader in a kind of prologue—is that, before meeting Mr. Western, Cecilia was briefly engaged to a loose-living and tyrannical baronet, Sir Francis Geraldine. She knew little of his reputation, but when her pride rebelled at his treatment, she broke off the engagement. Later she meets and marries Mr. Western, but does not tell him about Geraldine.

Her reasons are trivial, but the triviality is believable. She meets Western in Italy, where she has gone to get over her broken engagement. He is there for the same reason. Cecilia has broken off an engagement with Sir Francis Geraldine; Mr. Western's fiancée has jilted him to marry a Captain Geraldine, Sir Francis's cousin. When Mr. Western tells his story, Cecilia feels the absurdity of repeating back an almost identical story, even to the names, and cannot bring herself to do it. "It seemed at first so odd that my story should be the same, and then it looked almost as though I were mocking you,"[45] she explains at the end of the book. Trollope is almost caricaturing his own analogical method. In this novel an analogy between two stories is both a structural device and an explicit part of the plot, the central problem facing the characters. Cecilia keeps her secret even after she marries Mr. Western, and lives in guilty fear that he will find out.

The harmless fact of the prior engagement is compounded by concealing it, and the secret becomes a threat to the marriage. Miss Altifiorla, a feminist who disapproves of marriage, and Sir Francis both guess that Western is still in the dark about the prior engagement, and Sir Francis sends him the news. Western is angry and immediately assumes that Cecilia had some shameful reason for keeping her secret. His jealous imagination creates an intrigue with Sir Francis, and he leaves her. His jealousy and her anger set up an unbreakable barrier between them. Meanwhile a shared

45. *Kept in the Dark* (London: Chatto and Windus, 1882), 2 volumes, 2:24:231.

hatred of Cecilia throws Miss Altifiorla and Sir Francis together. They become engaged, but she publishes the fact too soon. Ironically, she does not keep her engagement in the dark long enough, and the baronet jilts her.[46]

Trollope's basic device is to exploit almost identical stories, people, and mistakes. The pattern is a variation of what E. M. Forster calls the "hour-glass,"[47] in which two antithetical characters move toward one another, confront one another, and then change places and characteristics to become antithetical again. Trollope's variation brings two similar characters together and exploits their similarity. The book is less hour-glass than looking-glass, for Cecilia and Mr. Western act in the same way, each duplicating the other's actions. Cecilia conceals a secret for the first half of the book. Once that secret is out, Mr. Western duplicates her action by concealing another secret—his suspicions about Cecilia's prior conduct—during the second part. Trollope's pattern is even adapted to the two-volume novel, with Mr. Western's behavior in the second volume mirroring Cecilia's behavior in the first.

The relationship of the characters to one another is neatly reversed, and this story of similarities turns adroitly on itself. Cecilia no longer feels guilt and fear, only resentment. She realizes that she has been foolishly secretive, but she also knows that she has committed no crime. Unaware of Western's myth about her guilt, which he has constructed, she considers him cruel. She refuses to beg his pardon or to explain her actions. When she replaces the secret of her prior engagement with the equally well-kept secret of her innocence, the original impasse gives rise to others. Western and Cecilia exile themselves from each other and from soci-

46. Trollope seems to be imitating *Is He Popenjoy?* in which the Marquis of Brotherton makes friends with the feminist Baroness Banmann because both oppose the Germain marriage. Brotherton is pseudo-Byronic; the Geraldine name and the relationship between Cecilia and Miss Altifiorla may be Trollope's recollection of Coleridge's "Christabel."

47. E. M. Forster, *Aspects of the Novel* (New York: Harcourt, Brace, and World, 1955), p. 214.

ety, nursing their resentments. Locked in their pride, they take no steps to explain themselves. Finally Lady Grant, Western's sister, appoints herself an ambassador and her common sense brings about a reunion. Western finally agrees to return to Cecilia and say nothing about the quarrel, but at the moment of meeting she apologizes and begs his forgiveness. The book ends in mutual self-accusations and mutual assurances that these are unjustified.

But the book is something more than a neat pattern. Its concern with secrets and jealousy relates it to Trollope's other studies of obsession and guilty concealment. The first twelve chapters study the growth of guilt, for Cecilia, like Cousin Henry, thinks continually about her secret and continually fears that it will be revealed. She begins to regard it as a sin, "a heavy, grievous sin, and one that weighed terribly on her conscience. . . . Her mind entertained an exaggerated feeling of it, a feeling which she felt to be exaggerated but which she could not restrain."[48] Ironically, truth itself becomes an instrument of mischief, for the virtuous Cecilia is now in the power of the vicious Sir Francis. He can take an apparently strong moral position, declaring "I like the truth to be told. It may become my duty to take care that poor Mr. Western shall know all about it."[49] Cecilia is so obsessed by her secret that she hopes for isolation, "some minimum of intercourse with the world,"[50] even as Cousin Henry does.

The neatness of Trollope's pattern could be mere slickness, but he uses it to show us that both Cecilia and Western have a morbid streak which is at first kept in the dark. Cecilia's pride leads her to break with Sir Francis. The very pride that has caused her to break the engagement prevents her from speaking about it. Pride's corollary, an excessive sense of shame and guilt, prevents her from telling Western about her past because she is afraid that he may suspect her motives. She is convinced of her own correct behavior, but unwilling to submit it to anyone else's judgment. Because of

48. 1:6:111.   49. 1:6:127.   50. 1:7:135.

her pride, her shame is all the greater when she finds herself in a false position, and this leads to extravagant self-accusations of sin and unworthiness.

As for Western, we slowly become aware that there is something morbid in his reaction to his earlier broken engagement. Although he is convinced that the girl is worthless, the affair has aged him and driven him into exile. "In Rome it seemed to Cecilia that Mr. Western, when alone with her, had no other subject for conversation than the ill-treatment he had received from Mary Tremenhere. His eagerness in coming back to the subject quite surprised her. She herself was fascinated by it, but yet felt it would be better were she to put a stop to it."[51] After he and Cecilia have been married, Lady Grant sheds some light on his character when she tells Cecilia, "how true he is, how affectionate, how honest; but yet how jealous! . . . it is hard for him to forgive that which he considers to be an offence against his self-love. . . . Of such a man it is impossible to say what he suspects. . . . He is the noblest man on earth, and the most generous—till he be offended. But then he is the most bitter."[52] Western's pride, jealousy, and over-suspicious nature lead him to confuse Cecilia's secret with Sir Francis's bad reputation and then to believe the worst about both of them. "You were to have been to me the joy of my life,—" he upbraids her, "my great treasure kept at home, open to no eyes but my own. . . ."[53] Western's selfishness combines dangerously with his too-active imagination. His secret, which is morbid jealousy, is discovered by Cecilia and the reader at the same moment. From then on we watch it fester even as her secret has festered and made her unhappy.

To underline the morbidity of the two main characters, Trollope has presented us with a pair of villains whose mor-

51. 1:4:74.
52. 1:8:168-169. Cockshut, *Anthony Trollope*, describes the book as "a study in an abnormal state of mind" (p. 227) and notes "the mixed likeness and contrast" (p. 226) of Western and Sir Francis.
53. 1:11:228-229.

bid traits are satirically exaggerated. Sir Francis and Miss Altifiorla are both selfishly afraid of marriage. He sees it as potentially interfering with his pleasures, and spends his money on male companions instead; she believes that all men are brutes, and that marriage brings only evil to women. At the end of the book he flees to the United States to escape her, and she plans to visit the same country on a feminist lecture tour. They both devote themselves to the destruction of the Western marriage because they are incapable of marriage themselves.

One or two of Trollope's old targets come in for attention through Miss Altifiorla. Her feminist ideas are ridiculed as were those of the Baroness Banmann in *Is He Popenjoy?* though Miss Altifiorla is a different kind of feminist. As her name suggests, her feminism is romantic and sentimental, counseling a retreat from the world rather than aggressive participation in it. Her little circle has aesthetic pretensions; Cecilia "was great among French and German poets,"[54] and dreams of a romantic husband "who should sit with her during the long mornings and read Dante to her."[55]

Cecilia's romantic feminism is an important element in her character. Her habitual mode of thought as the novel opens is an odd combination of a feminist distrust—even fear—of marriage and a yearning for a romantic lover. She wishes at once to be adored, courted, attended to, and to refuse to yield or share anything of herself, the trait that eventually brings her marriage to the brink of disaster.

Trollope emphasizes her traits in the first three chapters of *Kept in the Dark*, and in this book which continually duplicates itself the Geraldine "episode" is more than just a preamble to the story of the Westerns. Cecilia's relationship with Sir Francis founders because of her own pride. She does not reject the baronet because he is a rascal, for his rascality is one more secret that is successfully kept in the dark until late in the story. She rejects him because he is not attentive enough. She resents the fact that he is sure of her

54. 1:1:2.   55. 1:4:84.

love, and that he refuses to dance attendance on her. In fact, their brief engagement is a silent battle for mastery. Sir Francis "had . . . felt it necessary that he should dominate her spirit. . . . She had not dared to ask him questions . . . or to demand from him services to which she was entitled . . . His Cecilia was becoming tame in his hands, as was necessary."[56] Cecilia, on the other hand, is too proudly reticent to tell him what she expects, and instead silently resents his lack of fervor. The two do not understand one another at all.

The broken engagement prepares us for the broken marriage. The two episodes are even similar in detail. Disappointed that Sir Francis, twenty years her senior, is not a very demonstrative lover, Cecilia marries Western. He, too, is about twenty years her senior, and he is not a romantic hero either. During the stormy scene in which they break their engagement, Sir Francis accuses Cecilia of having another lover. She is too proud to defend herself against this baseless charge, just as she will not deign to defend herself against the same charge later, when it comes from Western. Nor is she willing to correct public opinion, which believes that it was Sir Francis who broke off the engagement, just as later she is not able to communicate the truth about herself to Mr. Western.

As for Western, he turns out to be the antithesis of Sir Francis, more foolishly romantic than Cecilia herself. He flees from his marriage when he finds that he is married to a rather ordinary woman capable of silliness, and not to an ideal. Since neither Cecilia nor Western will look at each other objectively, the truth about each is a final secret that they keep in the dark from each other. Western had not bothered to know his first fiancée as she really was, nor had Cecilia bothered to know the real Sir Francis. Given a second chance, both make the same blind mistake again. It is only with their third chance, when they have been brought together by Lady Grant, that they begin to communicate.

56. 1:2:39-40.

Their life begins finally to become a shared one, symbolized by their coming child.

Within the small compass of *Kept in the Dark*, Trollope has managed a double and complementary study of morbid reticence and self-delusion. The novel's preoccupations are those of *Cousin Henry* and *Dr. Wortle's School*: secrecy, guilt, and the isolation that these engender. While the title *Kept in the Dark* could serve equally well for either of the other two novels, Trollope uses the title phrase here with noticeable persistence. Its constant recurrence is surpassed only by the constant recurrence of secrets, suggested secrets, and reticences.

✳ IX ✳

ISOLATION IN AGE

The Fixed Period, Mr. Scarborough's Family,
An Old Man's Love, The Landleaguers

What is the good of a man and he
Alone and alone, with a speckled shin?
—Yeats, *The Pot of Broth*

COUSIN HENRY, *Dr. Wortle's School*, and *Kept in the Dark* all explore the same problem, the insidious social and psychological effects of a festering secret. Trollope continued treating different aspects of a single issue in several successive novels when he wrote the last four novels of his career between December of 1880 and his death in December 1882. *The Fixed Period, Mr. Scarborough's Family*, and *An Old Man's Love* are about old men and their need to assert themselves, to insist that they are still alive and able to play some part in the world's affairs; with *The Landleaguers*, Trollope himself attempted to play some part in a controversy of the day. In *The Fixed Period*, an old man fights against an inhuman law that will take his property from him, and then his life. Mr. Scarborough is a dying invalid, who spends his scanty energy trying to control the lives of others. The protagonist of *An Old Man's Love* plans to marry a young girl who is under obligations to him. And Trollope's effort, in *The Landleaguers*, to write a novel opposing Gladstone's Irish policy, probably hastened his own death.

Trollope found his subject close to hand, for as he wrote these three novels, he himself was finding it difficult to remain an active participant in the world. In July 1880 he gave up his London house and moved to the country for his health. He had always loved the society and bustle of the capital; now he was depressed at leaving, but at the same time unable to enjoy London. "In one week more we start from here," he wrote his son. "It makes me melancholy;—though I believe I shall be happier there than I am here. I dislike dinner parties and all going out."[1] In December 1880, three days after beginning *The Fixed Period*, he wrote nostalgically about his hunting days and added, "Nothing really frightens me but the idea of enforced idleness"[2]—the worst consequence of the law in *The Fixed Period*. A year later he complains that "the time runs heavy. But alas it has come to that, that all times run more or less heavy with me, unless when I am asleep,"[3] and in January 1882 he remarks of his older brother Tom, with some irritation, "He writes as though a life indefinitely prolonged had allurements."[4] The very existence of these last novels, written by an ailing man in his mid-sixties, expresses Trollope's determination to remain a part of life.

I. *The Fixed Period*

> SIMONIDES. Is the law firm, sir?
> FIRST LAWYER. The law! what more firm, sir,
>   More powerful, forcible, or more permanent? . . .
> CLEANTHES. I think, then, 'tis the best to be a bad one.
> FIRST LAWYER. Why, sir, the very letter and the sense both do overthrow you in this statute, which speaks, that every man living to fourscore years, and women to threescore, shall then be cut off as fruitless to the republic, and law shall finish what nature linger'd at.
>
> —Philip Massinger, Thomas Middleton, and William Rowley, *The Old Law* (1656) 1:1

1. *Letters* (Trollope to Henry Merivale Trollope, 27 June 1880), p. 441.
2. *Letters* (Trollope to Henry Merivale Trollope, 21 December 1880), p. 446.
3. *Letters* (Trollope to Henry Merivale Trollope, 15 November 1881), p. 463.
4. *Letters* (Trollope to Alfred Austin, 23 January 1882), p. 469.

Trollope wrote *The Fixed Period* between December 1880 and February 1881; it was published in two volumes (February 1882) after appearing in *Blackwood's Magazine* (October 1881 to March 1882). The novel is unique in several ways. It is the only novel Trollope wrote in the first person; it is his sole attempt at prophetic science fiction or sociological fantasy; and it is the only one of his books whose debt to an old play has been generally recognized. As long ago as 1905, Gamaliel Bradford pointed out its probable source: *The Old Law,* by Massinger, Middleton, and Rowley.[5] The title of this play refers to the law of Evander, Duke of Epirus, which dooms to execution all men of eighty and women of sixty on the grounds that they are no longer useful. As in Trollope's novel, a good deal of the action revolves around interested heirs who attempt to speed up the working of the law, or dutiful heirs who try to impede it. Like Trollope, the authors of the play are not very interested in the law itself (it turns out to be Duke Evander's ruse for discovering virtuous young men), but rather in the manifestations of good or bad conduct it causes. It is simply a device that brings pity and greed into the open.

The Fixed Period is supposedly written by ex-President Neverbend of Britannula as he is carried to England under polite but effective restraint in the year 1980. Britannula, a British colony and later a republic, is somewhere in the vicinity of New Zealand, presumably not far from Erewhon (described in 1872). As the story opens, the colony has been reclaimed by England with the aid of the warship *John Bright* and its "250-ton steam-swiveller," which could easily demolish the capital city, Gladstonopolis, with a single shot.[6] Trollope must have enjoyed the double irony of nam-

<hr />

5. *The Nation* 80 (8 June 1905): 458. See Booth, *Anthony Trollope,* p. 129. *Doctor Thorne* and *The Fixed Period* are the only two instances of Trollope using a plot he had not devised himself; and in *The Fixed Period* he adopts only the initial situation from his source, and develops it quite differently. See *Autobiography* 6:115-116.

6. Trollope was in some confusion about this gun. He intended the weight for the shot rather than for the gun itself. See *Letters* (Trollope to William Blackwood, 28 January 1882), p. 470. J. H. Davidson, in "An-

ing this warship, an instrument of brute force, after a great Victorian pacifist who opposed naval expenditures, and then blandly remarking that the vessel was named "from a gallant officer, who, in the beginning of the [twentieth] century, had seated himself on a barrel of gunpowder, and had, single-handed, quelled a mutiny."[7] England is ruled by a queen in 1980 and the prime minister is Sir William Gladstone, a descendant of Victoria's Liberal premier, while the Colonial Secretary, the Duke of Hatfield, can look back to his Conservative ancestor, Lord Salisbury. Despite these touches, *The Fixed Period* is not a satire on Victorian England. It is instead—as the President's name suggests—a satire on the narrow-mindedness and the lack of human sympathy that characterize abstract reformers.

Neverbend is an enthusiast who has introduced the law of the Fixed Period in Britannula, and is very proud of this grand new social reform. The old, he insists, are useless to society. They do not produce; they only consume, and they weaken the state by retaining land and money in their own incompetent hands. He has persuaded the Britannulans to pass a law ordering the execution of everyone who reaches the age of sixty-eight. The law has not yet gone into effect, for Britannula is a young country, but Neverbend's best friend, Mr. Crasweller, is about to celebrate his sixty-seventh birthday (Trollope was nearly sixty-six when he finished the novel) and must be "deposited" in the Britannulan "college" for a year of retirement from affairs before he is actually put to death. Crasweller is unhappy at his coming fate and depressed at the pitying gloom with which

---

thony Trollope and the Colonies," *Victorian Studies* 12 (1969): 305-330, suggests that the annexation of Britannula by Great Britain owes something to the annexation of the Transvaal in 1877, brought to Trollope's attention when the Transvaal Boers rebelled to regain their independence; their rebellion broke out on 16 December 1880, the day before Trollope began work on the novel. See also David Skilton, "*The Fixed Period:* Anthony Trollope's Novel of 1980," *Studies in the Literary Imagination* 6 (1973): 39-50; Skilton describes the narrator as unreliable and fanatic.

7. *The Fixed Period* (Edinburgh and London: William Blackwood and Sons, 1882), 2 volumes, 2:8:54-55.

everyone regards him. He persists in seeing himself as a victim of a cruel law, despite Neverbend's assurances that he will be a pioneer and a Britannulan hero.

The story is complicated by two suitors for the hand of Eva Crasweller, the victim's daughter and heiress. One suitor, Abraham Grundle, is a fanatic advocate of the Fixed Period in his eagerness to gain the estate. The other suitor is Jack Neverbend, the President's son, whose pity for Crasweller and love for Eva lead him to oppose his father's project. A neat Trollopian conflict between principles and affection is set up. The President realizes that his supporter, Grundle, is motivated only by greed. Grundle's success will prevent Jack from gaining the girl and the estate. At the same time, the President is aware that his zeal in hurrying old Crasweller to death can be misconstrued as an attempt to gain an estate for his son. As for Jack Neverbend, he becomes the leader of popular opposition against his father and the Fixed Period law, not out of principle but in order to win Eva's love.

Trollope presents no final solution to the moral question. He simply sets it aside. The *John Bright* appears, at the invitation of some of the Britannulans, and the steam-swiveller is aimed at their capital just as President Neverbend is escorting Crasweller to be deposited. England refuses to allow the ceremony to continue, and a British official lands to assume the government. Neverbend is sent to England aboard the warship, lest he attempt to regain power. He writes his narrative and his defense of the law on board the *John Bright* during the journey to England.

Although the novel is supposed to be taking place in the year 1980, late twentieth-century Britannula is not very different from late nineteenth-century England. Apart from the bizarre complications caused by the Fixed Period law, people behave as they do in any other Trollope novel. There is the same interest in marrying well, the same greed for an inheritance, the same interest in real estate, the same battles between father and son and between abstract principles and private affections. Except for a few minor details—steam-tricycles and sixteen-man cricket teams—nothing has really changed very much despite a century of material progress. Trollope implies that all the agitation for reform in his own day has left the world pretty much the same. He emphasizes this by showing us England of 1980 ruled by men with the names and characteristics of those who ruled in 1880, and still equipped with a Royal Family, a navy, and a House of Lords—all institutions the reformers of his day considered to be heading for rapid oblivion. Human nature is not really capable of much improvement. Reforms, no matter how earnestly undertaken, do not really lead to any essential changes.

This thesis is essential to the theme and organization of *The Fixed Period*, for it is a long monologue from a fanatic reformer, a man blinded by doctrine, unable to admit the irrationality of human behavior and the power of human affection. He is sure that Crasweller's death, and the death of all others who reach the age of sixty-eight, will be socially beneficial. Infatuated by his doctrine, he looks forward enthusiastically to his own ultimate deposition in the college. He is surprised when Crasweller fails to show the same enthusiasm, pained when his old friend resorts to fibs about his exact age and then attempts bribery, and troubled when the man at last agrees to undergo death not on abstract grounds of principle and social utility but on irrational and emotional grounds of personal friendship and loyalty. Neverbend is too much the doctrinaire to understand the role that basic impulses like family affection, love of life, and fear of death can play in human affairs.

The apologia form of the book and the use of the first person narrator allow Trollope to present a type he distrusted. The portrait is not completely hostile. Neverbend is sincere, honest, hard-working, and genuinely dedicated to the welfare of his people. He is a man of principle whose principles have not been refuted, or even opposed: the law of the Fixed Period has been passed and several times en-

dorsed by the Britannulan Assembly. Crasweller himself
has voted for it in the past. Neverbend is not defeated by
arguments or ideas but by armed force. Trollope presents
the man as favorably as possible, and lets him justify himself, avoiding condemnation or any direct refutation of his
great idea. But Neverbend indicts himself, for he reveals his
lack of basic humanity, his inability to feel. Even when he is
deposed he cannot produce much honest indignation. He
can only argue logically. On his departure for England he
deliberately chooses to go alone, leaving Mrs. Neverbend
behind. It is only at the end of the book that he begins to
feel loneliness, and to realize the horror of a life without
friends, activities, or meaning—exactly the life to which he
had condemned those who were to pass their probationary
year in the college before death. The realization comes only
as he is about to be "deposited" in London. Trollope uses
this word at the very end of the book[8] to stress the appropriateness of Neverbend's fate, and to hint that the ex-
President himself is coming to some awareness of the pecu-
liar horror to which he had condemned others.

The possibility of this awareness is suggested earlier.
Though Neverbend is devoted to his principle and cannot
understand or admit the power of emotion, he is human
enough to feel uncomfortable at times. He is unhappy at the
hostility his reform causes in England and pained to find his
family and friends opposed. "Do have done with your Fixed
Period and nonsense," says Mrs. Neverbend sharply. "It's
all very well for the Assembly; but when you come to kill-
ing poor Mr. Crasweller in real life, it is quite out of the
question." This realistic and personal view of an abstract

8. 2:12:201-202. " 'It has not occurred to you to think,' said I, 'where he
will deposit me? Why should it do so? But to me the question is one of
some moment. No one there will want me; nobody knows me. They to
whom I must be the cause of some little trouble will simply wish me out of
the way. . . .' " Neverbend is talking about the "guard of honour" who
will accompany him to London and then leave him. Cockshut notes that
the narrator is "talkative" and "untrollopian," but does not discuss the
implications of this. He complains that the book evades the issues it raises.
See his *Anthony Trollope*, pp. 91-92.

issue makes him uncomfortable, and he is more uncomfortable when he thinks of "the much more frightful agony I should be called upon to endure when the time had actually come for the departure of old Crasweller."[9] He even begins to doubt whether his doctrine should prevail over the dictates of his heart:

> I began to doubt whether my mind would hold its proper bent under the strain . . . and to ask myself whether I was in all respects sane in entertaining the ideas which filled my mind. Galileo and Columbus,—Galileo and Columbus! I endeavoured to comfort myself with these names,—but in a vain delusive manner; and though I used them constantly, I was beginning absolutely to hate them. Why could I not return to my wool-shed, and be contented among my bales . . . as I was of yore, before this theory took total possession of me? . . . If a man be doing his duty, let him not think too much of that condition of mind which he calls happiness. Let him despise happiness and do his duty, and he will in one sense be happy. But if there creep upon him a doubt as to his duty, if he once begin to feel that he may perhaps be wrong, then farewell all peace of mind,—then will come that condition in which a man is tempted to ask himself whether he be in truth of sane mind.[10]

But this state of doubt is rare. Neverbend is usually determined, and when some visiting Englishmen criticize the law he is angry, feeling "that they were my enemies, as I was sure that they were about to oppose the cherished conviction of my very heart and soul. Crasweller had sat there perfectly silent," he remembers indignantly. "And yet Crasweller was a declared Fixed-Periodist."[11] Ironically, as Neverbend's sense of duty begins to weaken when he doubts his doctrine, Crasweller agrees to die—not because he accepts the doctrine, but because he long ago assented to the law, as well as out of his long friendship with Neverbend.

9. 1:4:106-107.   10. 2:7:1-3.   11. 2:7:10.

When we realize that Trollope's purpose is neither to advocate nor attack euthanasia, but rather to portray an enthusiastic reformer as he refuses to abandon his theories or accept life as it is, the apparent flaws of the novel are revealed as essential to this portrait. In a letter to Arthur Helps some years earlier, Trollope had criticized his brother, Thomas Trollope, for being "too didactic, too anxious to teach, to write a good novel."[12] Had Trollope set out to advocate or attack the "Fixed Period Law," the same criticism could be leveled against this book. It is Neverbend, not Trollope, who is too didactic, and who gradually reveals his obsessive nature. Trollope is not interested in the doctrine as such, only in its advocate and his reactions to the social and emotional problems his zeal creates.

Neverbend is cut off from humanity by his own fanaticism. He is further isolated by the growing opposition to his plan. When the invasion suddenly takes place, the British landing-party and the crowd of Britannulans remove the horses from his carriage, and lead Mr. Crasweller away in triumph, leaving the President stranded, completely alone. At the end of the book he goes into exile, still hoping that he will be able to communicate to some audience his theories and his enthusiasm for them, but he suspects that this will never happen. In England he will be solitary, and no one will be willing to listen to him.

Throughout the book Neverbend gradually becomes aware of this growing isolation—and, as Crasweller remarks, the isolation from normal life during the "probationary" year in the college is one of the cruelest features of the Fixed Period. At the end he is full of self-pity and loneliness. The book written on shipboard, which began as an attempt to justify and promulgate his theories, ends merely as an attempt at some kind of communication. In *his* book, Trollope has not contradicted the theory but instead allowed Neverbend to begin with confidence in it, then be-

12. *Letters* (Trollope to Arthur Helps, 26 January 1869), p. 236.

come gradually less confident as he begins to live through a situation analogous to that deposition he had endorsed. The social theory is refuted, not by argument but by showing that it destroys all relation to society. Trollope makes his book depend on an increasing tension rather than on a contradiction. As in the other novels of this period, the issue accepted as central by the characters—Popenjoy's legitimacy, the lost will in *Cousin Henry*, the illicit marriage in *Dr. Wortle's School*, the secret in *Kept in the Dark*—is less important than its effects. These novels concern themselves with the inevitable isolation that follows from an inability to obey society's laws. Obsession, either with a guilty secret or, as here, with a theory, leads to this isolation.

Trollope's distrust of reformers appears as far back as *La Vendée* (1850), his novel about the French Revolution, where Robespierre is rigidly and inhumanly doctrinaire. John Bold, in *The Warden*, is a reformer who cannot sustain his role. Because he is susceptible to human ties, he tries to abandon his crusade. *The Fixed Period* can be read as a return to some of the concerns of *The Warden*, an oblique approach to the same basic issue. Like John Bold, Neverbend is out to put an end to a social evil. And like Bold, he has a misfortune: the particular example of the social evil he brings forward turns out to have virtues which, while they do not negate the theory, render it difficult to operate in this particular instance, for they enlist popular opinion against the reform. Mr. Harding, the warden of a hospital, living on an undeservedly large income, turns out to be benevolent and honorable rather than rapacious. Mr. Crasweller, a man arrived at the age when, according to theory, physical and mental debility are supposed to start, turns out to be in excellent health and strongly attached to life. Neverbend remarks blandly that he "had fewer of the symptoms of age than any old man I had before known. He was tall, robust, and broad, and there was no beginning even of a stoop about him. . . . And then the difficulty was somewhat increased by the care and precision with which he attended to

his own business."[13] The principle is theoretically correct in
both cases, but its truth would be more plainly apparent if
Mr. Harding were a rapacious tyrant, or if Mr. Crasweller
were ill and weary of life. But theory and rigid principles
are a poor guide when dealing with people of flesh and
blood, as John Bold and President Neverbend discover.
Both men are given the chance to abandon their principles
because of affection. Bold loves Mr. Harding and wishes to
marry his daughter, Neverbend loves Crasweller and hopes
that their children will unite the two families. But both men
see these human ties as temptations and fight against them.
Neverbend is embarrassed when he remembers his own
instinctive reluctance to "deposit" Crasweller, and his relief
when the *John Bright* appeared:

> A certain sense of relief came upon my mind just then,
> because I felt sure that she had come to interfere with the
> work which I had in hand; but how base must be my
> condition when I could take delight in thinking that it
> had been interrupted![14]

Trollope suggests the confusion in Neverbend's mind between his half-acknowledged doubts about his cherished
reform and his instinctive emotional repudiation of doctrines he has arrived at logically. As the story ends, he has
not yet learned that his weakness was really his strength,
that his better emotional self had been right in rejecting the
cruelty implicit in his abstract doctrine.

As for Trollope, he is not really interested in refuting a
theory. He simply suggests, as in *The American Senator*, that
general theories often do not fit individual situations. In
such cases, theory must give way. An attempt to make the
world better can bring about present sorrow while promising vague benefits in some distant future. Sentiment must
take precedence over logic.

13. 1:2:37-38. See apRoberts's comparison of Bold and Neverbend, *The
Moral Trollope*, pp. 46-48; she argues that Trollope is showing the limitations of a purely rational approach to human problems.
14. 2:8:50.

II. *Mr. Scarborough's Family*

"I believe, you know, that you've done a monstrous
    injustice to everybody concerned."
"I rather like doing what you call injustices."
"You have set the law at defiance."
"Well; yes; I think I have done that."
       —*Mr. Scarborough's Family*, 41

Mr. Scarborough's Family, written between March and October 1881, was appearing in *All the Year Round* (May 1882 to June 1883) at the time of Trollope's death. Length and intricacy make this novel seem at first a return to the multiple structure of *The Way We Live Now* and *The American Senator*. But *Mr. Scarborough's Family* is concentrated rather than expanded. It is an ingenious variation on the narrowly focused studies of obsession which begin with *Cousin Henry*, rather than a generalization about society confirmed by a crowd of analogous characters and situations. Parallel plots, characters, and situations are present in the book, to be sure, but ultimately they all depend on one man, Mr. Scarborough, and his activities. In a sense he is a kind of self-portrait. He manipulates and parallels plots and situations as easily as his creator does, and can direct as large a cast of characters.

Mr. Scarborough's Family deals with three families interrelated by circumstances. In each family there is an elderly man, unmarried (two widowers, one bachelor), and eager to continue playing a controlling part in life. Mr. Scarborough owns Tretton Park; his goal in life is to manipulate facts and events so that he can disregard the entail which regulates the succession to his estate. He has two sons, Mountjoy and Augustus. The estate must go to his elder son, but he has found an ingenious way to circumvent this, and to decide which of his sons shall inherit. He has simply taken care to marry his wife *twice*, one ceremony occurring before the birth of his elder son, and one after it. As a result, he can play with the entail and the law of primogeniture. He can offer the record of one ceremony or the other to prove that

Mountjoy was born before or after his parents' marriage, and is illegitimate or legitimate, a bastard or the legal heir. Mr. Scarborough has turned marriage, a basic legal and familial relationship, into a trick he can use to manipulate his own sons and the law.

The other two families are headed by Mr. Grey and Mr. Prosper, and both become involved in Mr. Scarborough's plots. Mr. Grey is Mr. Scarborough's lawyer; he has a daughter, Dolly Grey. Grey is also Mr. Prosper's lawyer; Prosper, a bachelor, owns Buston Hall, an estate he has entailed on his sister's son, Harry Annesley. Harry loves Mr. Scarborough's niece, Florence Mountjoy. Mr. Scarborough's plots have the side-effect of discrediting Harry in Mr. Prosper's estimation, and Prosper begins to tamper with the succession to his own estate. The complexity of the plot is determined by Mr. Scarborough's own plotting, and reflects his manipulative and convoluted mind, housed in a tortured body—throughout the story, Mr. Scarborough is dying, in great pain, and his active mind contrasts with his helpless and bedridden state.

In addition to these basic family relationships, Trollope analyzes hatred and rivalry between brothers in Mountjoy and Augustus Scarborough; stress between cousins, when the fastidious Dolly Grey confronts the raffish Carroll sisters; Florence Mountjoy's difficulties with an uncle and aunt who take a hand in her marriage plans; and finally, the tension between the proud, shy, rather foolish Mr. Prosper and his undiplomatic nephew, which leads Prosper to plan his own marriage in the hope that he can father a son and disinherit Harry. The book's families resemble each other, and Trollope emphasizes their resemblances and interconnections by parallels, contrasts, and analogues.

Family matters spin the plot, and each of the characters has his or her place in the story because of a familial relationship. The question, which begins the book and occasions all the action, is that of defining the exact relationship between Mr. Scarborough, his dead wife, and their two sons. Like the question "Is he Popenjoy?" it is a question of legitimate family membership. *Mr. Scarborough's Family* is constructed like a genealogical chart. It explores the farthest branches of the Scarborough-Mountjoy line, along with the Greys and the Carrolls, and the Prosper-Annesley connection, tracing in each of these families the excitement Mr. Scarborough causes when he announces that Mountjoy is illegitimate, and makes Augustus his "elder" son and heir. When everyone in the three families becomes involved, Mr. Scarborough's plot has spawned further plots, counterplots, and complications, until the genealogy of the plots is as involved as the genealogies of the families. The title is ironic. Mr. Scarborough's real progeny is the family of plots he conceived at the time he was fathering his sons. Now these plots come to maturity. Mountjoy and Augustus disappoint their sire, but the plots never do. They are his acknowledged children, in his own convoluted image.

Almost every event in the book originates in Mr. Scarborough's attempt to evade the laws that govern the succession to landed property. For most of his life, he apparently intended that Mountjoy should inherit. When Mountjoy gambled and incurred heavy debts, his father realized that creditors would claim the estate. He decides to save it by producing a certificate showing that he had married Mountjoy's mother after Mountjoy's birth, but well before the birth of their second son, Augustus. Augustus has no debts, and is declared legal heir. Mountjoy's creditors find that they have no claim on an estate to which he has no legal claim.

Because of his father's plots, Augustus also takes up plotting. Now that he is heir, he decides to marry Florence Mountjoy, and to do this he spreads rumors about Harry Annesley. Harry is generally ostracized because of these rumors, Florence's mother begins to hate him, and Mr. Prosper is convinced that Harry is not worthy to inherit Buston.

An extensive progeny of further plots result from these

manipulations. Though they are remote from Mr. Scarborough's initial scheme, they are connected because of Augustus's manipulations. When Florence's mother takes her away from Harry, to Brussels, there are elaborate schemes to marry her to a British diplomat, and later to a Belgian. These suitors also begin to calculate, as does the woman Mr. Prosper approaches in his search for a wife.

Meanwhile, Augustus is busy on other fronts. To protect himself against possible lawsuits, he decides to settle his brother's debts cheaply, by paying back only the actual cash Mountjoy borrowed, without interest. This produces further schemes among the creditors.

And then, suddenly, Augustus becomes the victim of a plot, and Mr. Scarborough destroys his second son's schemes. Augustus has neglected him, has told him it is time for him to die, and has shown his father that he no longer considers him a living force in the world. But after Augustus has spent his own money to relieve Mountjoy of debt, the elder brother's creditors have no claim on the estate. Mountjoy will be able to retain whatever he inherits. Mr. Scarborough decides to revenge himself on Augustus by leaving everything "except the bare acres"[15] to Mountjoy. And then, as his final trick, Scarborough produces his first certificate of marriage, proving that Mountjoy has been legitimate all along. The land must also go to him. Augustus is ruined. All his plans are overthrown. Mr. Scarborough even writes to Mr. Prosper to justify Harry Annesley; Harry is restored to favor, and Prosper abandons his idea of marriage.

To dismiss Mr. Scarborough as an implausibly manipulative rascal is to misunderstand the character. He is not simply malevolent, and he cannot be precisely described as evil. The characters in the book who try to form a moral judgment about his conduct are baffled, and cannot find any category in which to place him. The lawyers, who try to categorize him legally, are equally baffled, for he has done

15. *Mr. Scarborough's Family,* 53:509.

nothing illegal. He simply confesses to his lawyer and to the world that he had intended to defraud Augustus by advancing the apparently illegitimate Mountjoy as heir. Then he withdraws that confession. He is not legally responsible for any of the consequences of the confession, though, as we have seen, all its results are directly attributable to his action. The lawyers in the book often remind us that a frankly acknowledged but abandoned intention to commit a fraud is not a fraud. "One cannot make an apology for him without being ready to throw all truth and all morality to the dogs," writes his doctor, who loved him, on the day after his death. "But if you can imagine for yourself a state of things in which neither truth nor morality shall be thought essential, then old Mr. Scarborough would be your hero."[16]

To the reader he is not a hero, though Trollope concedes to him intelligence, wit, bravery, and even a good deal of justification for his last plots, triggered as they are by Augustus's desire for his father's death. His sons are his pawns, and they are also his victims. Their natures have been created by his contempt for convention. He has spoiled Mountjoy "by every means in his power," he has never

---

16. 58:567-568. Trollope's partially sympathetic portrait of Mr. Scarborough, coupled with his disapproval of Scarborough's actions, has caused different critics to understand the novel in different ways. Sadleir, in *Trollope: A Commentary*, calls it "cynical, and, for its period, daring," and says that it shows Trollope's "power of sustained and dexterous raillery" (p. 397); he classifies it as a social satire (p. 420), but I cannot see what he considers Trollope's target to be. Cockshut agrees that the novel is satire, and suggests that, in portraying Scarborough's cool amorality, Trollope's aim was to call all Victorian moral and social assumptions into question (*Anthony Trollope*, pp. 231-232), but Cockshut also concedes that Scarborough is portrayed as a maniac (p. 234). Polhemus sees a theme of moral relativism and a recognition that society needs both Scarborough's ideal of "absolute personal freedom" and Mr. Grey's belief in "the absolutely just society"(*The Changing World of Anthony Trollope*, pp. 236, 241). apRoberts, in *The Moral Trollope*, also sees Trollope as "insisting on moral relativism" in this novel (p. 157). Roger L. Slakey, in "Trollope's Case for Moral Imperative," argues that Scarborough's moral confusion is portrayed in order to demonstrate the need for fixed moral imperatives. None of these discussions seem to me to deal adequately with Trollope's portrayal of a man who is in an extreme physical and mental state, and who does great harm.

loved Augustus,[17] and to neither son has he given any moral direction. "Most men have got some little bit of pet tyranny in their hearts," he tells Harry Annesley. "I have had none. . . . I let my two boys do as they pleased, only wishing that they should lead happy lives. I never made them listen to sermons, or even to lectures. Probably I was wrong."[18] His two sons are his pale reflections, each with an inherited trait that is a weaker version of something strongly present in the father: Mountjoy's gambling is a minor version of Mr. Scarborough's continual gamble with his own ability to survive and scheme, Augustus's plotting is ingenious but does not come up to the parental standard.

Trollope makes it easy for us to admire Mr. Scarborough for cleverness and vitality and for the utter discomfiture in which he leaves all his opponents and critics. At the end the worldly view is expressed by Mr. Barry, Mr. Grey's less scrupulous partner, who calls Mr. Scarborough "the best lawyer he ever knew. . . ."[19] "In my mind he has been so clever that he ought to be forgiven all his rascality," declares Barry, suggesting that the world will not make a moral judgment, but "will simply be amused." "Everyone concerned in the matter seemed to admire Mr. Scarborough; except Mr. Grey, whose anger, either with himself or his client, became the stronger, the louder grew the admiration of the world."[20]

But the judgment of Mr. Barry is not to be trusted. He is not a gentleman and he stands for a tricky morality which Mr. Grey cannot accept. There is no doubt about Mr. Scarborough's cleverness, which is the subject of the book, nor any doubt that it is a cleverness unrelated to any sense of morality. "I do not care two straws about doing my duty," he tells Augustus at their last interview. "Or rather, in seeking my duty, I look beyond the conventionalities of the world."[21] Trollope has emphasized this aspect of his character, commenting that Scarborough's pleasure lay "in thus

17. 21:191-192.   18. 40:390.   19. 62:599.
20. 58:562-564.   21. 56:544-545.

showing himself to be superior to the conventionalities of the world."[22] "I have my own ideas about marriage and that kind of thing, which are, perhaps, at variance with yours," he tells his half-admiring, half-horrified doctor. "I wished you to understand that though a man may break the law, he need not therefore be accounted bad."[23] Later the doctor discusses him with Mountjoy:

> . . . I think that he has within him a capacity for love, and an unselfishness, which almost atones for his dishonesty. And there is about him a strange dislike to conventionality and to law which is so interesting as to make up the balance. I have always regarded your father as a most excellent man; but thoroughly dishonest. He would rob anyone,—but always to eke out his own gifts to other people. He has therefore to my eyes been most romantic.[24]

Romantic is a key word here, in view of Trollope's distrust of the romantic hero and his socially disruptive self-indulgence. The confused moral attitudes of this speech, and the fact that it is put in the mouth of a naive country doctor, suggest that the reader should judge Mr. Scarborough more harshly, and not yield to the temptation of admiring his courage and ingenuity. Mr. Scarborough is essentially lawless. "To run counter to the law! That had ever been the chief object of the squire's ambition. To arrange everything so that it should be seen that he had set all laws at defiance! That had been his great pride."[25] Trollope has drawn one more portrait of a romantic temperament,

22. 21:193.   23. 21:201-202.
24. 53:514. Donald D. Stone, in "Trollope, Byron, and the Conventionalities," describes Trollope's treatment of Mr. Scarborough as the novelist seizing the chance to allow "his romantic sensibilities full rein at last. . . . Mr. Scarborough enables Anthony Trollope to exhibit his fascination with Byronic romance and, in so doing, to assert his own artistic power; and the novel allowed him, within sight of his own death, to dare the conventionalities" (p. 203). Stone also compares Scarborough to "a romantic plot maker" who "creates alternate versions of the truth in order to mystify and fool the world" (p. 202).
25. 38:366.

forced into moral isolation by living entirely according to individual will. There are Nietzschean overtones to Mr. Scarborough, and he represents an advance over Trollope's previous attempt at such a character, the Marquis of Brotherton in *Is He Popenjoy?* The Marquis is Byronic and unconventional, but his is a negative rebellion. Mr. Scarborough goes further, and repudiates the whole concept of law. He does not feel guilt, or emptiness, or unhappiness; he believes that laws are created for the weak, and he has successfully defied their spirit while contemptuously remaining inside their letter. He has devoted thirty years to arranging things so that he can leave the estate to the heir of his choice, simply so that he can feel that he has not been bound by law. As Dolly Grey remarks, he has sinned for "a fixed purpose, and not from passion."[26] We are told that he

> would speak of an honest man with admiration, meaning something altogether different from the honesty of which men ordinarily spoke. The usual honesty of the world was with him all pretence, or, if not, assumed for the sake of the character it would achieve. . . . All virtue and all vice were comprised by him in the words "good-nature" and "ill-nature." . . . That one set of words should be deemed more wicked than another, as in regard to swearing, was to him a sign either of hypocrisy, of idolatry, or of feminine weakness of intellect . . . when a woman rose to a way of thinking akin to his own, she was no longer a woman to his senses. . . . And law was hardly less absurd to him than religion. It consisted of a perplexed entanglement of rules got together so that the few might live in comfort at the expense of the many . . . taxation was robbery, rent was robbery . . .[27]

Such an outlook, carried into practice, disrupts society. Scarborough's romantic disregard of morality and convention has ruined his sons and set them at odds. Mountjoy's early life of indulgence has made him a gambler and a fool. Augustus has grown into a suspicious schemer, and his brief

26. 54:517.   27. 21:193-194.

period as heir has taken him from his profession and ended a promising legal career.

In the final pages of the book we see that all Mr. Scarborough's triumphs are only self-indulgence, with few lasting results. He has the pleasure of amazing everyone by his cleverness and by his endurance and vitality: "The squire took a pride in making the worst of his case, so that the people to whom he talked should marvel the more at his vitality."[28] He is delighted to have outwitted Mountjoy's creditors—Jewish moneylenders, proverbial for sharpness and trickery (the portraits of the moneylenders seem hostile racial stereotypes, but these men are portrayed as sharp to emphasize Mr. Scarborough's greater sharpness). Mr. Scarborough is pleased that he has even consistently tricked his own lawyer. But at the end of the book Mountjoy has again become a hopeless gambler, and Tretton Park will soon be lost for good. Scarborough's cleverness has only served to disrupt the lives of a few people for a time, to cheat a few moneylenders, and to drive Mr. Grey into premature retirement.

Mr. Grey emerges as Mr. Scarborough's real victim, and the reader must judge Mr. Scarborough with this in mind. Grey stands for the law, which is his whole life. Because he embodies the detachment and honesty of the law he is most affected when Scarborough sets it at naught. Scarborough has perhaps unconsciously chosen him as his target all along. He knows Grey to be honest, but "he fancied that Mr. Grey had adopted this absurd mode of living with the view of cheating his neighbours by appearing to be better than others. . . . Thinking Mr. Grey to be in some respects idiotic, he respected him, and almost loved him. He thoroughly believed Mr. Grey, thinking him to be an ass for telling so much truth unnecessarily."[29] As for Grey, "he did not regard" Mr. Scarborough "as an honest man regards a rascal, and was angry with himself in consequence. He knew that there remained with him even some spark of love

28. 40:388-389.   29. 21:194-195.

for Mr. Scarborough, which to himself was inexplicable."[30] Throughout the book these two are the great opponents, and yet are bound to one another. It is morality versus amorality, law versus anarchy, society and its norms versus unbridled romantic individualism.

But law and morality alike are routed. At the end, Mr. Grey embodies the law's—and society's—inability to deal with one who does not accept their premises. Mr. Scarborough does not hesitate to use Grey by callously manipulating him, and when Grey realizes he has been used, his life is ruined. He abandons his practice, for Mr. Scarborough has rendered the law—his life—meaningless. "He must have scoffed and scorned at me merely because I had faith in his word," says Mr. Grey sadly, as the full complexity of the plotting comes home to him. He realizes that he has been used "simply as a machine," that he has been fooled, and that he has lost his reputation for honesty—by assisting Mr. Scarborough's plots, he will seem to have conspired with him. "The light that has guided me through my professional life has been a love of the law," he tells Dolly, in a passage that clarifies the book's basic pattern.

> As far as my small powers have gone I have wished to preserve it intact. I am sure that the law and justice may be made to run on all-fours. I have been so proud of my country as to make that the rule of my life. The chance has brought me into the position of having for a client a man the passion of whose life has been the very reverse.[31]

Mr. Grey's relinquishment of his place in the world and his sense of betrayal determine our final attitude toward Mr. Scarborough. The novelist has constructed a trap for the reader's moral judgment. He gives us the satisfaction of seeing the unattractive Augustus get his deserts. But after we have watched two plotters trying to outsmart each other, both paying attention to legalities but neither regarding right and wrong, he suddenly shows us the innocent victim.

30. 39:373.   31. 55:530-531.

Because Mr. Grey takes morality and society seriously, a whole new dimension is added to the book. The story of Mr. Scarborough belongs in the world of Jacobean comedy, where ingenuity is of more importance than morality. But his plots have a more serious consequence than those in the plays of Jonson and Marston. By adding a believable innocent victim, Trollope denies Mr. Scarborough that approbation which his cleverness claims for him, and reveals him as irresponsible and dangerous.

Bradford Booth has suggested[32] that there may be a source for Mr. Scarborough and his commitment to intrigue in Elizabethan and Jacobean drama. I would go further, and find in these plays a possible pattern for the book's structure. Booth remarks that the figure of the scheming old man is found in *Volpone*, in Massinger's *A New Way to Pay Old Debts*, in Middleton's *A Trick to Catch the Old One*, and in Beaumont and Fletcher's *The Elder Brother*, but he does not examine these plays for other resemblances to Trollope's novel. The situation of ingenious schemes giving rise to yet other ingenious schemes is frequent in plays of this period, especially *Volpone* and *The Alchemist*. Middleton's *A Trick to Catch the Old One* has a number of situations repeated in Trollope's novel. An old uncle, Lucre, has disinherited his wasteful nephew, Witgood, and foreclosed on his property. Witgood evolves an elaborate scheme to get it back, his greedy creditors form supplementary elaborate schemes, and old Hoard prepares an elaborate counter-scheme:

> I'll mar your phrase, o'erturn your flatteries,
> Undo your windings, policies, and plots,
> Fall like a secret and despatchful plague
> On your secured comforts.[33]

The remark would be appropriate to a number of characters in *Mr. Scarborough's Family*, especially Mr. Scarborough himself. Middleton's characters and Trollope's move in the

32. Bradford A. Booth, *Anthony Trollope*, pp. 130-131.
33. Thomas Middleton, *A Trick to Catch the Old One*, 2:1.

same atmosphere of intrigue, and there are similarities of plot. In Middleton the old schemer, and not the young one, is the final victim, though Pecunius Lucre, like Mr. Prosper, is manipulated easily, and eventually pardons his nephew ("He shall be my heir; / I have no son; / I'll bind myself to that condition"[34]). Old Hoard is tricked into settling Witgood's debts and marrying his favorite prostitute; earlier he has spread rumors about Witgood, hoping to ruin him, but he is caught in his own plots and ends by outsmarting himself, as Augustus Scarborough does. As for minor details, the prostitute is named Florence, and there is a sudden violent encounter between two men in love with the same girl, in which one unfairly strikes the other, as Mountjoy Scarborough strikes Harry Annesley over Florence Mountjoy. As in the novel, one plot gives rise to another, and the last line of the play, spoken by Hoard, might have served Trollope as epigraph for his novel: "Who seem most crafty prove ofttimes most fools."

The title of Massinger's *A New Way to Pay Old Debts* is appropriate to the situation in the novel, where Mr. Scarborough and Augustus prepare a new way indeed to discharge Mountjoy's debts, but the situation is less strikingly similar than that in Middleton's play. Again there is a ruined prodigal and a schemer, the famous Sir Giles Overreach, who is finally out-plotted. Thomas May's *The Heir* suggests another of Augustus Scarborough's plots, when Polymetes spreads a rumor that his heir is dead, in order to advance his own fortune by winning a rich and greedy suitor for his daughter; May's character of Matho, the honest lawyer, resembles Trollope's Mr. Grey.

There are also affinities between *Mr. Scarborough's Family* and Beaumont and Fletcher's *The Elder Brother*, with its two brothers of opposing temperament, one a courtier and the other a scholar. Mountjoy Scarborough, the spendthrift officer in the Coldstream Guards, and Augustus, the crafty

34. 4:1.

barrister, transpose these earlier types into Victorian social categories. In *The Elder Brother*, the father, Brisac, plans to set his elder son and heir aside and commit the crime of breaking an entail. Finally, Trollope may have taken the names of his characters, and one or two other hints, from George Wilkins's *The Miseries of Enforced Marriage* (1607); some of the Scarborows in that play morally resemble Trollope's characters. There is an out-schemed schemer, Sir Francis Ilford ("Gulled, by this hand! An old coney-catcher and beguiled!"), and a money-lender who lives "by the fall of young heirs."[35]

Mr. Scarborough's Family is an almost Jacobean exercise in ingenious plotting, in which Mr. Scarborough's schemes are surpassed only by the ingenuity of his creator. This cleverness is at the service of a more serious theme: the consequences arising from the actions of an amoral and ingenious man loose in society, isolated from any conventional moral sense, any fear of punishment, without respect for public opinion or the normal decencies.

One or two themes which are almost as important are emphasized throughout the book. Perhaps the chief of these is the theme of age versus youth which we have seen as one of Trollope's concerns during this period. The book opens with a trio of old men securely in possession of considerable power. Mr. Scarborough is dying, to be sure, but until he dies he is master of Tretton, and he has managed to take its disposal into his own hands, contrary to law. Mr. Prosper is a comic parody of Mr. Scarborough; he "cannot tell wrong from right,"[36] while Scarborough is not interested in the distinction. Prosper also asserts his right to change the fixed order of things and to control young lives. As for Mr. Grey, he has tried to obey the law in everything and to live according to tradition and reason, but he too is forced into retirement. He has no defense against the pushing new man, Mr.

35. 5 ("I am gull'd . . . "); 3 ("by the fall of young heirs").
36. 25:239.

Barry, who climbs into his seat. For good or ill, the old are forced to give way to the young. The clever man, the honest man, and the fool are alike unseated.

A more interesting theme is that of isolation, which recurs in a variety of forms, as in all Trollope's novels of the period. Mr. Scarborough is isolated in his self-created moral system, and this alienation sets the book's tone. He is literally isolated as well. Augustus pays little attention to him, and even refuses to attend his funeral. Mountjoy flees into exile for a time to escape disgrace after he has suddenly been socially isolated, robbed of name, position, and prospects by his father's schemes. Mountjoy's isolation is poignantly revealed in a scene at Tretton, when he wanders alone through the great house and wonders what he is to do with himself. He is to inherit the library, and so he sits among the books and tries to read, only to realize that he can make nothing of either poetry or prose. He looks into a mirror and understands that a life lived alone will be meaningless.

Other examples of isolation or exile are common. Florence is taken to Brussels to keep her away from Harry Annesley, and at the end of the book one of her rejected suitors is preparing to depart for Kamschatka. Mr. Prosper is in a comic isolation throughout the book, his ridiculous alienation from life and society acting as an ironic counterpoint to those characters more tragically isolated, as his imaginary invalidism parodies Mr. Scarborough's deathbed. As for Harry, he is barred from seeing Florence for long periods, and finds that none of his neighbors will speak to him after Augustus's libels.

Dolly Grey's isolation is more serious. Her father's honesty isolates him from the world to some extent, but she adds a fastidiousness that makes her almost unable to live. When she considers marriage with her only suitor, Mr. Barry, her father's partner, "there was present to her a high, black, stone wall, at one side of which stood she herself while Mr. Barry was on the other. That there should be any clambering over that wall by either of them she felt to be quite impossible." When she considers how he fails as a gentleman by her exacting standards, "the wall became higher and more black than ever. And there was no coming of that miracle by which it was to be removed."[37] She rejects him, choosing instead to remain with her father; she tells him that since she cannot marry him, she will not marry anyone. In various bedroom scenes, in which Dolly and Mr. Grey come together in their night-clothes for long talks, the atmosphere is that of a marriage rather than of a father-daughter relationship. Were she to marry Mr. Barry and he to kiss her, she tells her father, "I—should plunge a knife into him,"[38] and then she puts her arms around her father.

Three minor episodes, apparently unrelated to the book's main concerns, indicate the care with which Trollope has articulated his major themes and underlined them at every opportunity. Visiting at Buston, Harry Annesley goes out with the Puckeridge Hunt. By a rare accident they find themselves joined by a rival hunt, the Hitchin, in common pursuit of the same fox—a violation of hunting etiquette. The Puckeridge master, Mr. Harkaway, is, like Mr. Grey, a man of law, and the "rules of the game . . . had to Mr. Harkaway the force of a religion. . . . To break them was to him treason."[39] The rival master, Mr. Fairlawn, only pretends to obey the rules, and is devious in his attempts to evade their spirit. The major pattern of the book is reproduced in this small episode.

A similar confrontation of types and themes occurs when Mountjoy Scarborough is enticed into a card game by a professional gambler, and loses a great deal of money. He visits Mr. Grey, and Grey warns him against those who do not cheat or break the rules, but live by coolly calculating on the weaknesses, lack of skill, or innocence of their opponents. He does not realize it, but he is describing Mr. Scarborough exactly.

37. 52:501-502.   38. 33:317-319.   39. 28:264.

Trollope's most striking achievement in this book is the scheming and unprincipled figure of Mr. Scarborough, who dominates in a way that no Trollope character since Melmotte had done. Melmotte had been insubstantial, created by society's eagerness to believe in him. Mr. Scarborough creates and sustains his own importance, and there is a human being—a deceptively and dangerously attractive human being—behind the manipulations. Trollope fully analyzes him, and though his victims are mystified, the man's motives and attitudes are clarified for the reader. Even so, when the last veil is drawn Trollope refrains from a final condemnation. The destruction of Mr. Grey is clearly an evil deed, but the novelist shows us his schemer dying serenely, confident that his God will judge him favorably (a little later, Dolly Grey comforts her father with a similar promise), and from any lesser tribunal an absolute judgment is impossible. Mr. Scarborough

> . . . died with his left hand on his son's neck, and Merton and his sister by his side. It was a death-bed not without its lesson, not without a certain charm in the eyes of some fancied beholder. Those who were there seemed to love him well, and should do so.
>
> He had contrived in spite of his great faults to create a respect in the minds of those around him which is itself a great element of love. But there was something in his manner which told of love for others. He was one who could hate to distraction, and on whom no bonds of blood would operate to mitigate his hatred. He would persevere to injury with a terrible persistency. But yet in every phase of his life he had been actuated by love for others. He had never been selfish, thinking always of others rather than of himself. Supremely indifferent he had been to the opinion of the world around him, but he had never run counter to his own conscience. For the conventionalities of the law he entertained a supreme contempt, but he did wish so to arrange matters with which he was himself concerned as to do what justice demanded. Whether he succeeded in the last year of his life the reader may judge. But certainly the three persons

who were assembled around his death-bed did respect him, and had been made to love him by what he had done.[40]

In 1856, when Longman's reader objected to the impropriety of the Signora Neroni, Trollope replied that she was "Of course . . . intended to [appear?] as indifferent to all moralities and decent behaviour—but such a character may I think be drawn without offence if her vice be made not attractive."[41] In *Mr. Scarborough's Family* he returns to this literary and moral problem in a more sophisticated way. Mr. Scarborough is "indifferent to all moralities," but Trollope attempts to understand the man and his motivation. He is willing to show such a man as attractive, and to confront a villain's attractiveness with understanding rather than dismay. He does not argue against Mr. Scarborough's behavior, nor condemn those who love the man. He simply shows the results when an attractive and intelligent but morally indifferent person disregards law and convention. And at the same time he understands a dying man's overwhelming drive to continue playing an active role in life, even if the activity itself is criminal.

III. *An Old Man's Love*

Et vicina seni non habilis Lyco.
—Horace, *Carmina* 3:19:24

An Old Man's Love, Trollope's last completed novel, was written between February and May, 1882, and published posthumously in 1884. Like its two predecessors, it is an old man's book, in which Trollope considers once again the rights and duties of the old in a world that is passing them by. Self-assertion is the central problem for the aging hero, Mr. Whittlestaff. Crossed in love long ago, Whittlestaff now sees a chance to grasp happiness by marrying his young ward, Mary Lawrie.

40. 58:567. First edition reads ". . . and took Merton and his. . . ."
41. *Letters* (Trollope to William Longman, 20 December 1856), p. 25.

Structurally the book is extremely simple, a short idyll of placid country life. There is not much plot, and of the four principal characters, two are very slight: Trollope is not really interested in Mary Lawrie, nor in John Gordon, her younger suitor. But he has developed a moral issue of considerable interest.

This moral issue stems from the opposing claims of duty and self-assertion, and three of the book's four main characters are attempting to understand and reconcile these claims. Mr. Whittlestaff must hold Mary to the promise she has given, and force her to marry him, or he must relinquish her to Gordon. He knows that she loves Gordon, and that she agreed to marriage only because she believed that Gordon had forgotten her. But he also knows that Gordon's formal proposal came later than his. He feels that he must be a man and assert his rights, though his own sensibility, reinforced by the poems of Horace, urges him to magnanimity and self-sacrifice. As for Mary, she has given her word and will hold to it, although she is sure that her only chance of happiness lies in marriage to Gordon. While Mary and Mr. Whittlestaff attempt to decide this conflict between duty to self and duty to another, their dilemma is exacerbated by Whittlestaff's housekeeper, Mrs. Baggett. She urges her master to assert himself and marry the girl; she reminds Mary that her "dooty" is to Mr. Whittlestaff. But Mrs. Baggett is also in a state of conflict. Her duty to Whittlestaff demands that she promote the marriage, but she flatly refuses to consider remaining at Croker's Hall if it takes place. For Mary to come as mistress will render her position meaningless. Her endorsement of the marriage threatens everything that gives her a role in life.

Even in this slight novel, Trollope finds room for contrast and analogy. There is another love story, that of a nearby curate, Montagu Blake, who is planning a profitable marriage. The curate is enthusiastic, talkative, and stupid— even his bride-to-be calls him "fool" and "ass." His loud and self-satisfied professions of love contrast with the more intense and private love that Mr. Whittlestaff has for Mary, while Blake's awareness of his fiancée's income and social position contrasts with Mr. Whittlestaff's generous indifference to such considerations. Whittlestaff has already given Mary all that she has in the way of income, comfort, and position. He seeks only to confer his love without calculation, while Blake is positively proud of his calculations. The death of an old rector, whose place he will fill, gives him a final satisfaction.

Trollope uses Mrs. Baggett as a double analogue for both Mr. Whittlestaff and Mary. Old, herself the victim of an unfortunate marriage, she specifically identifies with both of them, and this adds a new dimension to their relationship. Mrs. Baggett is devoted to what she considers to be Whittlestaff's interests, and the Whittlestaff family represent to her all possible earthly splendor. Because of this, any hesitation about the marriage on Mary's part becomes to Mrs. Baggett a reflection on her own values. She has devoted her life to Mr. Whittlestaff. Now Mary has been offered the same great privilege, and must not decline it.

The old housekeeper becomes a kind of advocate or representative for Whittlestaff, reminding Mary that an idealized duty demands the marriage. Mr. Whittlestaff is a kind of god and Mary must take over Mrs. Baggett's function as priestess: "Mary did feel that Mr. Whittlestaff ought to be made a god, as long as another woman was willing to share in the worship with such absolute self-sacrifice."[42] This elevation of Mr. Whittlestaff into an object of worship is, incidentally, parodied in the Reverend Mr. Blake's worship of his fiancée. Though a clergyman, he thinks and talks only of her, sings her praises and ministers to her. The parsonage must be adequately prepared for her coming, and the cathedral of Winchester and its functionaries exist only so that she may be married with appropriate ceremony.

The sacrifice of self to duty, which to both Mary and

42. *An Old Man's Love*, 4:34.

Mrs. Baggett consists in Mary's marriage to Mr. Whittle-staff, is the chief lesson that Mrs. Baggett preaches. But while both women acknowledge the importance of duty, both find themselves torn between two duties, equally strong and mutually exclusive. Mrs. Baggett has her duty to Mr. Whittlestaff, but she also recognizes a duty to her use-less husband, Sergeant Baggett, who suddenly turns up at Croker's Hall, red-nosed, wooden-legged, drunken and dis-reputable. Mary acknowledges her duty to Mr. Whittle-staff, who has supported her since her mother's death. But she loves John Gordon. He arrives with a fortune made in South Africa, turning up as suddenly and unexpectedly as the Sergeant, on the same day, and for the same purpose— to claim a wife. Mary also believes in her duty to Gordon. Three years before, they were in love but too poor to marry; now he is rich, and has come to claim her—on the day she has agreed to marry Mr. Whittlestaff. Had he arrived a day earlier, she could have acknowledged his prior rights.

At first glance, this arrival seems too coincidental, but this coincidence is the point of the problem that engages the characters, for it throws the legalistic aspects of the situation into sharper relief. Mary's honor and duty forbid her to change her mind and reject Whittlestaff for Gordon. She has, after all, agreed to marry the older man, and had only a vague understanding with his rival. Yet, as Gordon reminds her, her contract with Whittlestaff is a very recent one. It is Gordon's awareness of its newness that makes him feel he is still entitled to Mary.

The three major characters find themselves confronted by antagonistic duties and theories of duty. Mary and Mr. Whittlestaff are too reserved to state these antagonisms in their crudest and simplest forms. Mrs. Baggett performs this function, providing at the same time a theory of duty and sacrifice that the others must ponder, and either accept or reject. "Don't give up to none of 'em," she advises Mr. Whittlestaff. "You've got her word, and keep her to it.

What's the good o' your fine feelings if you're to break your heart. . . . It's in your own hands now, sir, and don't you be thinking of being too good-natured; there ain't no good comes from it. A man may maunder away his mind in softnesses till he ain't worth nothing. . . . Love! Rot it!"[43] Whittlestaff reiterates these arguments to himself, but his own gentler nature rebels. "After all," he asks himself,

> was not Mrs. Baggett's teaching a damnable philosophy? Let the man be the master, and let him get everything he can for himself, and enjoy to the best of his ability all that he can get. That was the lesson as taught by her. But as he sat alone there beneath the trees, he told himself that no teaching was more damnable. Of course it was the teaching by which the world was kept going in its present course; but when divested of its plumage was it not absolutely the philosphy of selfishness?[44]

Mary, too, advocates the Baggett theory. "You are entitled to have,—whatever it is that you may want, though it is but such a trifle," she tells Whittlestaff, when she senses that he is about to give in and relinquish her to Gordon. "A woman has a little gleam of prettiness about her,—though here it is but of a common order . . . it matters nothing. It is something soft, which will soon pass away. . . . It is contemptible." "You are just Mrs. Baggett over again," he remarks acutely, at the end of this conversation, and she replies, "Very well; I am quite satisfied. . . . By God's help I will not neglect [my duties]."[45]

Mary and Mrs. Baggett agree that Mary's duty is to give herself to Mr. Whittlestaff. They acknowledge their duty to him even as they struggle with their other, unacknowledged duties toward the rougher men who come to claim them. But Mr. Whittlestaff has a harder struggle, between his duty to himself as explicated by Mrs. Baggett and his duty to Mary—and, since he genuinely loves Mary, this too becomes a duty to himself. His pride is endangered if he does not hold the girl to her promise, for his servants and friends

43. 11:115-116.   44. 16:178.   45. 19:208-209.

will know of his failure. But his sense of personal honor is endangered if he does hold her. "What depth of self-indulgence," he asks himself, "amounted to a wickedness which a man could not permit himself to enjoy without absolutely hating himself?" He feels himself loving and wanting her more and more, but as his love grows so does his feeling that he is bound to give her up to the man he is sure she really loves. He is tempted by "ordinary selfishness" and by Mary's sense of duty toward him, for he knows that, once married, she will be a completely faithful wife, and perhaps in time will even come to love him. "It was not that he feared her for himself, but that he feared himself for her sake. God had filled his heart with love of the girl,—and, if it was love, could it be that he would destroy her future for the gratification of his own feelings?"[46] He realizes that he loves Mary enough to give her up, and by doing this he performs a deed that Trollope shows as more heroic than all John Gordon's exploits in Africa.

Trollope does not shirk his own duty as an author here. He does not fall into either of the two obvious traps, that of making Mr. Whittlestaff unrealistically benevolent—for then his sacrifice would be too easy, and seem meaningless—or that of making him an impossibly romantic example of abnegation, giving up all to ensure his lady's happiness. Whittlestaff makes his great sacrifice, but he cannot be gracious about it. The little scene in which he tells Gordon what he plans to do is a fine moment of exasperation and tetchiness. He is angry at the weather and furious when a stranger sits on the park bench he is walking toward. He snipes at Gordon throughout the interview, accusing him of dishonesty, conceit, and even suggests that Gordon will beat Mary, talks "himself into such a passion,"[47] suddenly tells Gordon he is free to marry the girl, refuses his friendship, then "hurried himself off to his hotel, and shut himself up in his own bedroom,—and when there, he sobbed, alas!

46. 19:209-210.   47. 21:231.

like a child,"[48] only to reappear soon after at Gordon's club, where he proposes to buy up Gordon's shares in the diamond mines and go off to Africa himself. His desperate attempt at a gracious act is ungraciously performed, in a thoroughly believable way.

Trollope avoids romanticizing his hero by letting him indulge in dreams of a romantic act, but not letting him attempt one. He has "a grand idea, but one very painful in its beauty . . . to do the best he could for her happiness. He loved her so well that he thought that, for her sake, he could abolish himself." Whittlestaff thinks of presenting to Mary and her lover "his money, his house, and his horses,"[49] and conceives "the romantic idea of making this girl supremely happy."[50] After comparing himself to the great lovers of literature, he decides that Horace was frivolous and Petrarch selfish; his own peers must be Arthur in his love for Guinevere, and Imogen in her love for Posthumus. He has long contemplated these great lovers, and is now "supported by the ecstasy of his thoughts"[51] as he contemplates his own sacrifice. But Trollope shows us the petty resentment mingled with these dreams of renunciation, and the would-be hero's bleak awareness that he is giving up a woman he could not really ever hope to possess. He hates Gordon because he must acknowledge that Mary loves the younger man. Whittlestaff senses that "it would not be becoming . . . to attempt to rise to the romance of tragedy" as he confronts "that hero of romance."[52] Trollope brings the old man to his senses and avoids any scene of romantic excess.

Trollope keeps so tight a rein on the romantic content of his novel that he introduces a note of irony into the great renunciation. When the sacrifice has been made, Gordon does not understand or realize Whittlestaff's generosity and "fine feelings." He simply accepts Mary as his due, reminding the older man of his prior claim.[53] Only Mary can

48. 22:237.　　49. 11:119.　　　50. 14:153.　　　51. 20:223.
52. 20:225, 21:226.　　　53. 21:231.

317

understand what has happened. But when she tries to celebrate Whittlestaff's noble action, Gordon is not really interested, and insists on talking about their future life. This
failure of understanding is a pattern throughout the book.
Earlier Whittlestaff has misunderstood Mary's self-sacrifice
for a real desire to marry him. For a long time Gordon is not
sure that she loves him, while Mary sees only Whittlestaff's
apparent determination to hold her to her promise, and fails
to see his vacillations.

Trollope devotes most of his book to exploring these vacillations and temptations. Gordon, who has no initiative in
the central question and so no real choice, is not analyzed at
all. Mary is something of a prig, cold and unyielding. She
suffers, to be sure, but she never seriously contemplates
rebellion. She learns Mrs. Baggett's lesson of female duty
too well, and thinks of herself as Whittlestaff's "slave; she
felt herself in very truth to be a poor creature whose only
duty it was in the world to obey his volition."[54] Mary begins to hate Whittlestaff, and because of this to hate herself,
but she never outwardly wavers from submission and is
determined to marry him. In fact, there is not much in
Mary to analyze. Trollope's own identification with Mr.
Whittlestaff seems to have made him uninterested in exploring the young girl's mind. This may also be the reason why
Gordon is not analyzed. Gordon has no doubts; from the
beginning of the book he is sure where love and duty lie.
But he is aware that he has no power to compel Mr.
Whittlestaff or Mary, and that Mary's sense of duty and
obligation make her unable to reject the old man, or injure
him in any way. Even when he appeals to Mr. Whittlestaff
to release Mary from her promise, he is not very deeply
stirred. The appeal is to Whittlestaff's sense of fair play
rather than his heart. Gordon's main argument is a legalistic
quibble. He argues that he knew Mary first, rather than
insisting that he loves her more fervently or more appropriately.

54. 16:170.

Mr. Whittlestaff can insist on his rights or abandon them, Mary can obey her sense of duty or her love. Mrs. Baggett is torn between more complex alternatives. She bitterly resents Mary, and sees her as a usurper. She senses her master's interest in marriage long before he proposes to Mary, and urges the girl to "sit close up to him" and show him that he need not fear to speak. But when Mary accepts Mr. Whittlestaff, the housekeeper is furious:

> He's got his plaything. That's all he cares about. I've been with him and his family almost from a baby, and have grown old a-serving him, and it don't matter to him whether I goes into the hedges and ditches, or where I goes. They say that service is no heritance, and they says true. I'm to go to—But don't mind me. He won't, and why should you? Do you think you'll ever do half as much for him as I've done? He's got his troubles before him now;—that's the worst of it.[55]

She refuses to consider remaining on after the marriage, though she has no place else to go, for she will not serve as housekeeper under Mary. At the same time, her rebellion is mingled with self-pity: "She ain't to be my mistress. I won't have no mistress. When her time is come, I shall be in the poorhouse at Portsmouth."[56] If Mary was "one of them namby-pambys"[57] who would let her continue to have her own way in the house, it would be possible to stay, but Mary will insist on running the house—a trait Mrs. Baggett demands, though she is sure she cannot live with it.

Mrs. Baggett's resentment, vehemence, duty, loyalty, and self-pity combine into a grotesque but believable character. Trollope endows this uneducated woman with as rich a set of conflicts and vacillations as her sensitive master, for both master and servant, grown old together, feel that their roles in the world are threatened. Nowhere else in his

55. 5:48.

56. 11:114-115. Cockshut remarks on Mrs. Baggett's carefully drawn perversity (*Anthony Trollope*, p. 32).

57. 11:116.

work does Trollope explore a servant's psychology so fully. There is no attempt to raise Mrs. Baggett to tragic status. She remains absurd, but at the same time pitiful and completely human.

The relationship of mutual dependence and domination between Mr. Whittlestaff and Mrs. Baggett precedes the events of the novel, and at the end outlasts them. Her strong character encourages his more delicate one. The cruel Mr. Whittlestaff who appears occasionally is in part created by her, in part the creature of his own earlier failures and disappointments (he once missed getting a fellowship, and was once jilted). Trollope adds a dimension to Mr. Whittlestaff by suggesting that his finer self, which shrinks from cruelty, is partially created by literature. The old man is particularly dependent on Horace as an antidote to Mrs. Baggett, "the poet's pretences" opposed to the housekeeper's "invitations to manly strength."[58] By introducing phrases from Horace, Trollope is able to suggest the universality of the experience he is portraying, and allows the classic world to comment on a modern incident. "Intermissa, Venus, diu rursus bella moves? Parce, precor, precor. . . . Non sum qualis eram," Mr. Whittlestaff reads.[59] "Would you have me try again the long-suspended contests of love, O Venus? Give over, I pray, give over. I am no longer such a one as I once was." He finds it uncomfortably appropriate to his own case, and devoid of consolation.

Trollope utilizes his own visit to the Kimberley diamond mines in 1877 to round out the picture of Gordon as different from the quiet stay-at-homes. Gordon thinks contemptuously of Montagu Blake as a fool who would not survive long at Kimberley, but he envies the curate's self-satisfaction and his tranquil world. At the same time a more typical diamond hunter, the disreputable Tookey, is introduced as a sample of the disintegration that the rootless life

58. 18:191.
59. 17:181. The quoted passage is from *Carmina*, 4:1:1-3; I have translated it.

of Kimberley can bring about. "If there be a place on God's earth in which a man can thoroughly make or mar himself . . . it is the town of Kimberley," Trollope remarks. "I know no spot more odious in every way to a man who has learned to love the ordinary modes of English life. It is foul with dust and flies; . . . it has not a tree near it. . . . The white man . . . is insolent, ill-dressed, and ugly. The weather is very hot. . . ."[60] Alresford's green fields and beech trees and placid inhabitants are celebrated as a contrast.

At Alresford, Gordon is in a world exactly opposite to that in which he has spent the last two years, and in which he has succeeded. Not surprisingly, he is both attracted and repelled by this gentler world, while some of its inhabitants cannot accept him as a man who belongs in ordinary society—Mr. Whittlestaff, aided by Mrs. Baggett, argues to himself that such a man is too rough, and his fortune too much of a gamble to make him a fit husband. Trollope has deliberately introduced an adventurer into a bland and idyllic landscape to make the contrast between Mary's two lovers extreme.

There is never a moment's doubt as to which man attracts her, and Trollope is characteristically not very interested in the outcome. His interest lies in portraying a placid little backwater, then disturbing it, in portraying a placid old man and then disturbing his life, first with an unexpected passion and then with a difficult moral decision. The growth of such a man's love and its conversion into sacrifice is carefully and convincingly charted. "A very common sort of an individual," Mr. Whittlestaff says of himself when looking in a glass. "But then a man ought to be common. A man who is uncommon is either a dandy or a buffoon."[61] The novel succeeds primarily as a portrait of an unspectacu-

---

60. 6:68. Trollope is restating some of his comments about Kimberley in *South Africa*, 2:9. See J. H. Davidson, "Anthony Trollope and the Colonies," p. 310.
61. 2:21-22.

larly good man who avoids extreme courses and comes with difficulty to the right but unspectacular decision. He recognizes the limitations his temperament and years place on him; he accepts these limitations at last, recognizing, as Mr. Scarborough could not, that a function of old men is to relinquish.

IV. *The Landleaguers*

> I am half reconciled to Gladstone; but nothing can reconcile me to a man who has behaved so badly about Ireland.
> —Trollope to Rose Trollope, 14 August 1882

"I observe when people of my age are spoken of, they are described as effete and moribund, just burning down the last half inch of the candle in the socket," Trollope wrote to Alfred Austin some time in 1876. "I feel as though I should still like to make a 'flare up' with my half inch."[62] In *The Fixed Period*, *Mr. Scarborough's Family*, and *An Old Man's Love*, he had portrayed old men eager to remain involved with life. His own insistence on continuing work suggests that Trollope shared this eagerness to go on playing some part in the world's affairs. When he died (6 December 1882), he was well into *The Landleaguers*, hoping to influence contemporary political events by a novel about Irish affairs, which had reached a crisis. The repeal of the Corn Laws (1846) had made agriculture less profitable for Irish landlords than the raising of sheep and cattle. Consequently, they were eager to evict tenants, and evictions were a con-

---

62. *Letters* (Trollope to Alfred Austin, c. 1876), p. 495. L. P. and R. P. Stebbins comment on the relevance of *The Fixed Period* to Trollope's own age and situation. They describe *An Old Man's Love* as "an answer to the question propounded in *The Fixed Period*" ("what is an old man to do with his life?"); with *The Landleaguers*, "it seemed that he had found an answer to that tormenting question of an old man's destiny—that there was one old man who might both serve his country and do something for the harassed land where he had learned to respect himself" (*The Trollopes*, pp. 328, 323, 330).

spicuous feature of rural Irish life until 1881, even though the Great Famine had grimly eliminated about half the tenant population through death or emigration. Gladstone's Second Land Act (1881) had ended most evictions, and promised tenants fair rent, fixity of tenure, and the free sale of land, establishing machinery to assist tenants in becoming landowners on a small scale themselves.[63] But these reforms had come too late. Parnell and his followers were already agitating for Home Rule, and Michael Davitt's Land League (1879) threatened landlords with boycott and the nonpayment of rent unless they agreed to sell land to their tenants. When the government arrested Parnell and suppressed the Land League (October 1881), the "Land War" broke out in the west of Ireland. Landlords and their agents were assassinated or boycotted, and their property was destroyed, even after Parnell was released (May 1882) in the hope of preventing further anarchy. By the summer of 1882, the Phoenix Park murders[64] had infuriated public opinion in England, and the government was pursuing a confusing policy of simultaneous conciliation and coercion. The Irish countryside had become a battleground between police and Land Leaguers, and Trollope set out to depict this situation. He believed that Gladstone had caused the crisis by treating the Irish too generously, but he also blamed Parnell and the Irish-American agitators who were supposedly supplying the Leaguers with arms, money, and advice. "My own idea is that we ought to see the Parnell set put down," he told his wife in May. "We should try it out with them and see whether we cannot conquer them. I do

63. Trollope described the government plan to secure "to the tenants fair rents, fixity of tenure, and freedom of sale" as "romantic, and therefore unjust." See *The Landleaguers* (London: Chatto and Windus 1883), 3 volumes, 3:41:162-163.

64. Lord Frederick Cavendish, the newly appointed Chief Secretary for Ireland, and the permanent secretary, Thomas Henry Burke, were assassinated in Phoenix Park, Dublin, on 6 May 1882, four days after Parnell's release from prison. Parnell denounced the assassinations as "cowardly and unprovoked" and later won an action for libel when *The Times* accused him of approving them.

not doubt but that we could, them and the American host at their back."[65]

In May 1882, Trollope visited Ireland to interview officials and landlords. In June he began to write, despite constant ill-health. He returned to Ireland for further research in August, and stayed there for a month (11 August to 11 September), this time visiting Wicklow and Dublin rather than the disturbed areas. Back in England, he worked on his book until his fatal stroke on 3 November 1882; he died nearly five weeks later, after lingering in a semiconscious state. Abandoning his life-long practice, he had allowed *The Landleaguers* to begin serial publication before he had completed it, although he had criticized Dickens, Thackeray, and Mrs. Gaskell in *An Autobiography* for dying "with unfinished novels, of which portions had been already published."[66] A three-volume edition of the completed forty-nine chapters appeared in October 1883.

Trollope incorporates into *The Landleaguers* events that were actually taking place in the spring and summer of 1882. Like Tolstoy in *War and Peace*, he was trying to show the impact of public policy and public events on private lives, but his material is more immediate than Tolstoy's. In *The Landleaguers*, current events are assimilated into fiction with remarkable speed, for Trollope is close behind the detective and the journalist, examining and interpreting events, relating those events to the fortunes of his fictional characters, and fitting them into the structure of his novel. When he stopped work forever at the beginning of November, he had involved his characters in actual events which had happened less than three months earlier.

Most of the action takes place at a small estate belonging to the Jones family, Anglo-Irish landowners living in County Galway. The Joneses are among the first victims of

---

65. *Letters* (Trollope to Rose Trollope, 23 May 1882), p. 481.
66. *An Autobiography*, 8:139. *The Landleaguers* began in *Life: A Weekly Journal of Society, Literature, the Fine Arts and Finance*, on 16 November 1882 (and therefore after Trollope's stroke) and ran until 4 October 1883.

the Land League. Some of their fields are deliberately flooded and ruined, and then the family is boycotted and terrorized. The League's supposed dependence on American agitators explains the presence of the Irish-American Gerald O'Mahony and his daughter, Rachel. Rachel and young Frank Jones, the heir to the estate, fall in love, but because the agitation has reduced the Jones family fortune they cannot marry, and Rachel goes off to seek her fortune as a singer. The love affair is inextricably mixed with public events. The adventures of Florian Jones, a child of ten, are also related to these events: converted to Catholicism, he becomes involved with the League and is set against his family, repents, and is eventually shot lest he testify against those who have destroyed his father's property. The threats against Florian, and the League's reign of terror, bring Captain Yorke Clayton of the police to the Jones estate to fall in love with Edith Jones. In London, Rachel O'Mahony's success earns enough to send her father into Parliament as one of Parnell's supporters, creating a neat circle of cause and effect: he agitates to start the troubles that prevent her marriage and send her to be a singer, her success sends him to Parliament where he will agitate further, his agitation will increase the troubles in Galway and impoverish the Jones family still further, to delay the marriage of Rachel and Frank and perhaps prevent it entirely, even though O'Mahony approves of the marriage. At every turn, public events intervene in these private lives, until the novel breaks off, eleven chapters short. A note by Henry Trollope indicates that all was to end happily, with a hanging and two weddings, but it is not clear how the somber mood was to be lightened so quickly, and how the characters were to be freed from events that were, as Trollope well knew, increasing rather than decreasing in violence. The only clue is a slight rise in spirits, and a hint that the troubles may be coming to an end, in Chapters 48 and 49, the last that Trollope wrote. But the general tone suggests that Trollope was finding a happy ending difficult, for the problems of

Ireland made such a solution almost impossible—a truth he had realized almost forty years earlier in *The Macdermots of Ballycloran*.

Trollope's knowledge of the complexities of Irish affairs, and his affection for the people and the country, made it impossible for him to write anti-Irish propaganda or to solve the political and the artistic problems he had set himself in *The Landleaguers*. In the abstract, his position was close to that of the historian W. E. H. Lecky, who was writing the Irish sections of his vast *History of England in the Eighteenth Century* (1878-90) at the beginning of the eighteen-eighties, and commenting obliquely on some of the same events.[67] Lecky was an Irish nationalist, but he opposed democratic tendencies and believed that Ireland's natural leaders were the landowning class, Anglo-Irish rather than Celtic, and Protestant in religion; and he was committed to preserving the Union between Ireland and Great Britain. Trollope shared these ideas. Had he lived long enough to see the introduction of Gladstone's first Home Rule Bill (1886), he would have become a Liberal Unionist, and Chapter 41 of *The Landleaguers*, entitled "The State of Ireland," is really a premature manifesto for that group of Liberal defectors.[68] Trollope defends the landlords and attacks their opponents. But when he attempts to portray an Anglo-Irish landlord, his honesty as a novelist makes him show us a fatal separation—religious, economic, racial, and even temperamental—between Philip Jones and his tenants.

67. Lecky published the first two volumes (of eight) in 1878. In 1892 he separated the portions dealing with Ireland from the rest and published them as *A History of Ireland in the Eighteenth Century*.

68. Bradford Booth (*Anthony Trollope*, pp. 110-111) suggests that this chapter was intended as a preface rather than as part of the novel, and that Henry Trollope misplaced it in arranging his father's manuscript. But Trollope specifically tells us that "This chapter should have been introductory and initiative; but the facts as stated will suit better to the telling of my story if they be told here." See *The Landleaguers*, 3:41:142. Liberal Unionists were members of the Liberal party who disagreed with Gladstone's policy of Home Rule for Ireland, and instead wished to maintain the Union of the British and Irish legislatures, in effect since 1800.

There is nothing of that system of mutual respect and mutual obligations which he had idealized in portraying Roger Carbury in *The Way We Live Now*. Though he is trying to justify English rule by making his Anglo-Irish landowner's just rule of his estate stand for England's just rule of Ireland, Trollope describes Mr. Jones as isolated and morose, as well as fundamentally decent and kind. "It was certainly the case with Philip Jones that he was most anxious to rob no one. He was, perhaps, a little too anxious that no one should rob him."[69] There is a more dynamic representative of English rule in Captain Clayton, but Trollope is not comfortable with Clayton's drastic methods. "It would be the grandest sight to see,—ten of them hanging in a row," exclaims Clayton, speaking of some rural assassins. When Frank Jones replies, "The saddest sight the world could show," the Captain scorns such soft-heartedness, and reminds Frank of what the Joneses have suffered from such people:

> If that could be prevented and atoned for, and set right by the hanging in one row of ten such miscreants . . . would it not be a noble deed done? . . . to those who desire to have their country once more human, once more fit for an honest man to live in, these ten men hanging in a row will be a goodly sight.[70]

Trollope perhaps intended that the marriage of Frank Jones and Rachel O'Mahony would reconcile Anglo-Irish and Celt, Protestant and Catholic, Unionist and Nationalist, tenants' rights and landowners' rights, and he died trying to create such a reconciliation. That he realized the true state of affairs is evident in the character and fate of Florian Jones, who is caught in a dual allegiance—to his Catholic co-religionists and his Protestant landowning family—which epitomizes the conflict in Irish affairs. Florian represents an attempted synthesis of these two opposing

69. 1:1:6.   70. 3:47:259-260.

forces, and he dies because they cannot exist together harmoniously.

There is poignancy in this last unfinished work, as Trollope, like the protagonists of his last few novels, tries to show that he still has some business to perform in the world by offering an opinion on the Irish crisis, reminding his readers that he is still thinking and writing, in spite of age, illness, and approaching death. The novelist who had celebrated society's ability to integrate or exclude, and who had depicted the unenviable fate of the outsider, now struggled against the most drastic exclusion of all. Old age is coming, he tells us in *An Autobiography*, when "The things around cease to interest us, and we cannot exercise our minds upon them." Things never did cease to interest Trollope. He quoted with apparent approval Horace's advice to the aging artist:

> Solve senescentem mature sanus equum, ne
> Peccet ad extremum ridendus.
> Be wise in time; turn out the old horse, lest
> His broken wind and gait make watchers jest.[71]

But it was advice Trollope was not willing to take. *The Landleaguers* did not help Gladstone or the Irish very much, but its very existence is a final determined statement of Trollope's central doctrine, his insistence on participation in life.

71. *An Autobiography*, 12:231-232. The passage from Horace is from *Epistles*, 1:1:8-9. The second line, in full, reads "Peccet ad extremum ridendus et ilia ducat"; I have translated the passage as if Trollope had quoted the entire line.

EPILOGUE

"I have shorn my fiction of all romance."
—Trollope to George Eliot, 18 October 1863

"The Poet must begin with an Idea of the world in order not to be prevailed over by the world's multitudinousness."
—Arnold to Clough, late 1848-49

WHEN WE LOOK BACK over the novels of Trollope's artistic maturity, it is clear that he was able to invent for them a form that would most appropriately convey his own attitudes toward the world and toward human behavior. These attitudes are at once skeptical and idealistic. He does not expect that ordinary men and women will rise to moral greatness, but sometimes he shows them doing so. He imagines men and women who fulfill his gentlemanly ideal, but he knows that such people will be hard to love, and even harder to like. "There was no heroism and no villainy,"[1] he says, speaking of *Framley Parsonage*, and the phrase really sums up the world of his novels. "Evil is unspectacular and always human," W. H. Auden tells us,

> And shares our bed and eats at our own table,
> And we are introduced to Goodness every day,
> Even in drawing-rooms among a crowd of faults.[2]

Auden's lines are about Melville, who discovered this "new knowledge" late in his career, but Trollope always knew it. His development as a writer was in learning how to demonstrate it, until this moral realism determined both his content and his form.

During his South African visit, in 1877, Trollope declined

1. *An Autobiography*, 8:143.
2. W.H. Auden, "Herman Melville," lines 17-20.

329

to visit the Royal Observatory, and when the Astronomer asked, "Do you care for the stars?" he replied, "In truth I do not care for the stars. I care, I think, only for men and women, and so I told him."[3] Trollope's novels are primarily about people and their social and moral interaction. His chief aim, and his chief accomplishment, is the creation of believable human beings, and his tolerance for them after he has created them. He knows them well enough to know and to pardon their limitations—to challenge readers to judge them as we judge our acquaintances rather than in the exaggerated but detached way we judge fictional heroes and villains. "What youth in his imagination cannot be as brave, and as loving, though as hopeless in his love, as Harry Esmond?" Trollope asks, in "the writer's apology for his very indifferent hero, Ralph the Heir" at the end of that novel:

> Should we not be taught to see the men and women among whom we really live,—men and women such as we are ourselves,—in order that we should know what are the exact failings which oppress ourselves, and thus learn to hate, and if possible to avoid in life the faults of character which in life are hardly visible. . . .
> Ralph Newton did nothing, gentle reader, which would have caused thee greatly to grieve for him, nothing certainly which would have caused thee to repudiate him, had he been thy brother . . . had he come to thee as thy lover, with sufficient protest of love, and with all his history written in his hand, would that have caused thee to reject his suit? Had he been thy neighbour, thou well-do-do reader, . . . would he not have been welcome to thy table? Wouldst thou have avoided him at his club, thou reader from the West End? . . . Nevertheless, the faults of a Ralph Newton, and not the vices of a Varney or a Barry Lyndon are the evils against which men should in these days be taught to guard themselves;— which women also should be made to hate.[4]

3. *South Africa*, 1:5:78.
4. *Ralph the Heir*, 2:56:338-339.

The novelist makes his characters and events realistic in order to influence behavior in the real world. Trollope's moral purpose in his realism is no longer fashionable, but the essential literary principle here is the underlying commitment to knowing and portraying people as they really are. In his *Autobiography*, Trollope makes this knowledge the first duty of the novelist:

> I am not sure that the construction of a perfected plot has been at any period within my power. But the novelist has other aims than the elucidation of his plot. He desires to make his readers so intimately acquainted with his characters that the creations of his brain should be to them speaking, moving, living, human creatures. This he can never do unless he knows those fictitious personages himself, and he can never know them well unless he can live with them in the full reality of established intimacy. They must be with him as he lies down to sleep, and as he wakes from his dreams. He must learn to hate them and to love them. He must argue with them, quarrel with them, forgive them, and even submit to them. He must know of them whether they be cold-blooded or passionate, whether true or false, and how far true, and how far false. . . . It is so that I have lived with my characters, and thence has come whatever success I have attained. There is a gallery of them, and of all in that gallery I may say that I know the tone of the voice, and the colour of the hair, every flame of the eye, and the very clothes they wear. Of each man I could assert whether he would have said these or the other words; of every woman, whether she would then have smiled or so have frowned. When I shall feel that this intimacy ceases, then I shall know that the old horse should be turned out to grass.[5]

5. *An Autobiography*, 12:232-234. In his preface to *The Portrait of a Lady*, Henry James recalled a conversation with Turgenev in which the Russian novelist made essentially the same points about the minor role of plot and the importance of knowing one's characters: " . . . I'm often accused of not having 'story' enough. I seem to myself to have as much as I need—to show my people, to exhibit their relations with each other; for that is all my measure. If I watch them long enough I see them come together, I see them *placed*, I see them engaged in this or that act and in this or that difficulty.

This kind of total commitment to his created characters, incidentally, runs somewhat counter to that account of novel-writing as a matter of regular hours, and the counting of words and pages, which most readers of *An Autobiography* find to be its most striking remarks on the subject.

Trollope tells us that as a child, barred from the society of his schoolfellows, he created and sustained elaborate stories in his imagination:

> For weeks, for months, . . . from year to year, I would carry on the same tale, binding myself down to certain laws, to certain proportions, and proprieties, and unities. Nothing impossible was ever introduced,—nor even anything which . . . would seem to be violently improbable. I myself was of course my own hero. . . . But I never became a king, or a duke . . . or six feet high. I never was a learned man, nor even a philosopher. But I was a very clever person, and beautiful young women used to be fond of me. And I strove to be kind of heart, and open of hand, and noble in thought, despising mean things. . . . I learned in this way to maintain an interest in a fictitious story, to dwell on a work created by my own imagination, and to live in a world altogether outside the world of my own material life.[6]

It is a pleasing irony that this ability, which the lonely schoolboy developed as a substitute for society, became in his maturity the means of obtaining for him an entrance to society, and became also a means toward articulating and controlling those complex multiple plots he used in so many of his novels to depict society's complex variety. "In our

---

How they look and move and speak and behave, always in the setting I have found for them, is my account of them—of which I dare say, alas, *que cela manque souvent d'architecture.* But I would rather, I think, have too little architecture than too much—when there's danger of its interfering with my measure of the truth . . . " (see *The Novels and Tales of Henry James*, "The New York Edition," 3, *The Portrait of a Lady* [New York: Charles Scribner's Sons, 1908], 1:vii-viii).

6. *An Autobiography*, 3:42-43. See Hugh Sykes Davies, *Trollope*, British Council "Writers and Their Work" No. 118 (London: Longmans, Green, 1960), pp. 11-12.

lives we are always weaving novels," he observes, "and we manage to keep the different tales distinct."[7]

Trollope's gift was a gift for dreaming truth. His imaginary world could exist parallel to the real world, and the two—contrary to geometric laws—could sometimes intersect: Disraeli introduced Melmotte to the Speaker of the House, Ralph Newton comments on a painting by Grant, Palliser visits Queen Victoria, the arrival of the Prince of Wales abridges the quarrel between Phineas Finn and Mr. Bonteen, Mr. Harding compares his own case with that of the Master of St. Cross Hospital at Winchester. Both worlds are governed by the same social and moral laws, and both are crowded with individuals who make up society.

That society exists. It is shown with its prejudices and habits. It is often dull, always complex, sometimes unattractive or absurd. But primarily, it is there, and its standards, imperfect though they may be, offer a defense against chaos. Trollope decided that it was his business to understand society and to describe it. To do this, it was necessary to work out a method of handling several stories at once, for Trollope knew that social life is crowded and varied. The story of a man or woman living in society cannot be isolated from the stories of other men and women. Even a love story has its social dimension. It is not the story of a man and a woman; it is also the story of the effect their love will have on their relatives and associates, and their probable future has to be considered. When Lord Silverbridge asks Mr. Boncassen for his daughter, the American insists first on assurances that society will accept the marriage, that Isabel will not be "excluded from the community of Countesses and Duchesses."[8]

Few writers have so consistently presented moral issues as essentially social. Dickens, Trollope reports scornfully, was "marvellously ignorant"[9] of politics, and Thackeray

7. *An Autobiography*, 9:155.
8. *The Duke's Children*, 70:556.
9. *An Autobiography*, 13:250.

never studied the subject. But Trollope's novels are all about social and political relationships—in the marriage, the family, the village, the small town, the cathedral close, the county, the nation itself. In the techniques of the single plot—for social isolation—and the multiple plot—for society's complexity—he found forms that reinforced his sense of the paramount importance of social attitudes.

Describing the genesis of *The Warden* in his *Autobiography*, Trollope attributes the story to two different stimuli. One was a real place: ". . . Salisbury . . . whilst wandering there on a midsummer evening round the purlieus of the cathedral. . . . I had stood for an hour on the little bridge . . . and made out to my own satisfaction the spot on which Hiram's hospital should stand."[10] *The Macdermots of Ballycloran* grew from a visit to a ruined house in County Leitrim; and in many later novels, Trollope starts with the social topography of a locale, anatomizing Barset in *Doctor Thorne*, or Dillsborough in *The American Senator*. But the other stimulus for *The Warden* was a moral issue. "Struck," he tells us,

> by two opposite evils . . . I thought that I might be able to expose them, or rather to describe them, both in one and the same tale. The first evil was the possession by the Church of certain funds . . . for charitable purposes . . . which had been allowed to become incomes for idle Church dignitaries. . . . Though I had been much struck by the injustice above described, I had also often been angered by the undeserved severity of the newspapers towards the recipients of such incomes, who could hardly be considered to be the chief sinners. . . .[11]

Trollope modestly suggests that his failure to take sides, his failure to draw Mr. Harding either as a "red-nosed clerical cormorant" or as a completely innocent victim of "the venomous assassin of the journals,"[12] made *The Warden* a failure. But he knew better, and in his subsequent novels he was

10. *An Autobiography*, 5:92-96.
11. *An Autobiography*, 5:93-94.
12. *An Autobiography*, 5:95.

equally unwilling to take sides, and equally honest. He
knew that both sides were generally in the right, more or
less, and that issues can rarely be seen in black and white
terms—as the unjustly criticized parodies of Dickens and
Carlyle in *The Warden* demonstrate. His practice was the
simultaneous presentation of two opposite points of view,
and a refusal to make any absolute and binding moral judgment about either one. This balance is Trollope's moral and
artistic signature.[13] It is linked with his own simultaneous
sense of himself as insider and outsider. (That £70,000,
earned by Trollope with so much effort, so easily lost by
Lord Silverbridge, comes to mind.)

Trollope prefers uncertainty to dogmatic assurance. "I am
not one of those who suppose that a mans (sic) mind should
be subject to no hesitation,—to no vacillating influences,"
he wrote George Henry Lewes. "Men who are strong
enough never to be so subject are distasteful to me."[14] He
commends Cicero because he lacked

> the fixed purpose of Caesar, . . . the unflinching princi-
> ple of Cato. . . . They suffered from none of those in-
> ward flutterings of the heart, doubtful aspirations,
> human longings, sharp sympathies, dreams of something
> better than this world, fears of something worse, which
> make Cicero so like a well-bred polished gentleman of the
> present day. It is because he was so little like a Roman
> that he is of all the Romans the most attractive.[15]

The doctrinaire and the dogmatist do not appear advanta-
geously in his novels, and he does not himself fall into the
trap of making rigid *a priori* judgments about his characters
and their conduct. In *Dr. Wortle's School*, he tells us that Mr.
and Mrs. Peacocke should have separated once they realized

13. See apRoberts's sustained argument about Trollope's moral relativism in *The Moral Trollope*.

14. *Letters* (Trollope to George Henry Lewes, 24 December 1864),
p. 160.

15. *The Life of Cicero*, 1:1:20. See apRoberts's frequent citing of Trollope's
Life of Cicero as a major statement of his moral relativism (*The Moral Trollope*), and also William A. West, "Trollope's Cicero," *Mosaic* 4 (1971): 143-
152.

their marriage was not valid—and then warmly defends them for not doing so. There are always two sides to an issue, and this moral realism is more striking even than that accuracy about customs and attitudes which has often been commended. Trollope the artist does not have a divided mind. He has a mind comprehensive enough, and realistic enough, to recognize the mixed motives and effects at work when real men and women act.

"I am realistic,"[16] he announced in the *Autobiography*, and went on to reject the conventional antithesis between realistic and sensational novels by insisting that, "A good novel should be both, and both in the highest degree. If a novel fail in either, there is a failure in Art." But for him the term "sensational" does not mean "a string of horrible incidents" or startling events. It seems rather to mean a moment when an ordinary human being, someone we have come to know in the way we know a fictional character, suddenly rises to some emotional or moral moment in a way that surprises us and at the same time seems to us exactly right, exactly the way that character would behave—as when Plantagenet Palliser, sitting alone after dinner with his son in the Beargarden library, "looked round the room furtively, and seeing that the door was shut, and that they were assuredly alone, . . . put out his hand and gently stroked the young man's hair. It was almost a caress,—as though he would have said to himself, 'Were he my daughter, I would kiss him.' "[17] The sensational, in this sense, occasionally happens in real life, and so Trollope must admit it to his realistic chronicles.

Above all, he was committed to psychological and social reality. Throughout his long career, his problem as a writer was to find ways of presenting that reality that were both convincing and artistic—and this, indeed, was one of the major problems for all the nineteenth-century social novelists. Dickens's solution was to exaggerate characters and

16. *An Autobiography*, 12:227.
17. *The Duke's Children*, 26:208.

situations; Thackeray liked to treat his with sardonic detachment; George Eliot provided minute analyses. Trollope lived
with his characters, and made the reader see their inconsis-
tencies and pettiness. He shows them to us in social contexts
and judges them by their ability to conform to social
decorum—as we would judge them if we met them in real
life; he was able to present in a controlled way the varied life
of a social class that was both large and homogenous. His age
was one of constant change, but he was able to draw on older
social codes to develop a coherent notion of how men and
women ought to behave toward one another. And he worked
out a method of shaping and patterning his material so that
the shape and pattern remained unobtrusive, and the reader
felt a kind of reality.

Trollope's art was the art that conceals art.[18] His shaping
of his material was concealed, just as society in his novels
does not control its members by rigidly codified laws. His
form and his content are one: the celebration of ordinary life
in a manner that declines to call attention to itself.

There is no explicitly stated philosophical system in Trollope, as Bradford Booth complains;[19] but Trollope's
philosophy was essentially a distrust of systems. To many
readers, the characters in Trollope's novels seem unexciting,
untouched by romance. For Trollope, life is ordinary rather
than romantic. He accepts this bleak truth and quietly dem-
onstrates it to his readers with relentless determination.
This is not something all readers of novels wish to learn—
but the reader of Trollope does not have much to unlearn.
Trollope had the courage and the art to convey the muted
sadness of people who cherish few illusions, who accept life.
"The romance of her life is gone," he says of Lady Glencora, after the Byronic Fitzgerald has vanished from her
life, "but there remains a rich reality of which she is fully
able to taste the flavour."[20] That "rich reality," with all its
imperfections, is the measure of Trollope's artistic success.

---

18. apRoberts, *The Moral Trollope*, p. 73.
19. Bradford A. Booth, *Anthony Trollope*, p. 232.
20. *An Autobiography*, 10:183.

BIBLIOGRAPHY

I. A Chronological List of Trollope's Works

Volumes marked with an asterisk have been reprinted
in the Oxford University Press World's Classics Series

The Macdermots of Ballycloran. 3 volumes. 1847.
The Kellys and the O'Kellys. 3 volumes. 1848.
La Vendée: An Historical Romance. 3 volumes. 1850.
The Warden. 1 volume. 1855.
Barchester Towers. 3 volumes. 1857.
The Three Clerks. 3 volumes. 1858.
Doctor Thorne. 3 volumes. 1858.
The Bertrams. 3 volumes. 1859.
The West Indies and the Spanish Main. 1 volume. 1859.
Castle Richmond. 3 volumes. 1860.
Framley Parsonage. 3 volumes. 1861.
Tales of All Countries. 1 volume. 1861.
Orley Farm. 2 volumes. 1862.
North America. 2 volumes. 1862.
Tales of All Countries: Second Series. 1 volume. 1863.
Rachel Ray. 2 volumes. 1863.
The Small House at Allington. 2 volumes. 1864.
Can You Forgive Her? 2 volumes. 1864 and 1865.
Miss Mackenzie. 2 volumes. 1865.
Hunting Sketches. 1 volume. 1865.
The Belton Estate. 3 volumes. 1866.
Travelling Sketches. 1 volume. 1866.
Clergymen of the Church of England. 1 volume. 1866.
Nina Balatka. 2 volumes. 1867.
The Last Chronicle of Barset. 2 volumes. 1867.
The Claverings. 2 volumes. 1867.
Lotta Schmidt: and Other Stories. 1 volume. 1867.
Linda Tressel. 2 volumes. 1868.
Phineas Finn, The Irish Member. 2 volumes. 1869.
He Knew He Was Right. 2 volumes. 1869.
The Vicar of Bullhampton. 1 volume. 1870.

An Editor's Tales. 1 volume. 1870.
The Struggles of Brown, Jones, and Robinson. 1 volume. 1870. American edition 1862.
The Commentaries of Caesar. 1 volume. 1870.
Sir Harry Hotspur of Humblethwaite. 1 volume. 1871.
Ralph the Heir. 3 volumes. 1871.
The Golden Lion of Granpère. 1 volume. 1872.
The Eustace Diamonds. 3 volumes. 1873.
Australia and New Zealand. 2 volumes. 1873.
Phineas Redux. 2 volumes. 1874.
Lady Anna. 2 volumes. 1874.
Harry Heathcote of Gangoil: A Tale of Australian Bush Life. 1 volume. 1874.
The Way We Live Now. 2 volumes. 1875.
The Prime Minister. 4 volumes. 1876.
The American Senator. 3 volumes. 1877.
South Africa. 2 volumes. 1878.
Is He Popenjoy? 3 volumes. 1878.
How the "Mastiffs" Went to Iceland. 1 volume. 1878.
An Eye for an Eye. 2 volumes. 1879.
Thackeray. 1 volume. 1879.
John Caldigate. 3 volumes. 1879.
Cousin Henry. 2 volumes. 1879.
The Duke's Children. 3 volumes. 1880.
The Life of Cicero. 2 volumes. 1880.
Dr. Wortle's School. 2 volumes. 1881.
Ayala's Angel. 3 volumes. 1881.
Why Frau Frohmann Raised her Prices: And Other Stories. 1 volume. 1882.
Lord Palmerston. 1 volume. 1882.
Kept in the Dark. 2 volumes. 1882.
Marion Fay. 3 volumes. 1882.
The Fixed Period. 2 volumes. 1882.
Mr. Scarborough's Family. 3 volumes. 1883.
The Landleaguers. 3 volumes. 1883.
An Autobiography. 2 volumes. 1883.
An Old Man's Love. 2 volumes. 1884.
The Noble Jilt. 1 volume. 1923.
London Tradesmen. 1 volume. 1927.

Four Lectures. 1 volume. 1938.

The Tireless Traveler: Twenty Letters to the Liverpool Mercury by Anthony Trollope, 1875. Ed. Bradford A. Booth. 1 volume. 1941.

The Letters of Anthony Trollope. Ed. Bradford A. Booth. 1 volume. 1951.

Did He Steal It? 1 volume. 1952. Privately printed 1869.

The Two Heroines of Plumplington. 1 volume. 1953.

Australia (the Australian chapters from *Australia and New Zealand*, 1873). Ed. P. D. Edwards and R. B. Joyce. 1 volume. 1967.

The New Zealander. Ed. N. John Hall. 1 volume. 1972.

II. Modern Editions of Trollope

No definitive collected edition of Trollope's works has appeared. The Palliser series, *The Warden*, and *Barchester Towers* have been carefully edited for the "Oxford Trollope," under the general editorship of Michael Sadleir and Frederick Page; the "Oxford Trollope" also contains the *Autobiography* and Bradford A. Booth's edition of *The Letters*. This promising enterprise, which began publication in 1948, was abandoned in the fifties. Sadleir also edited the Shakespeare Head edition of the Barsetshire novels in fourteen volumes (Oxford, 1929). Alfred A. Knopf published handsome and authoritative editions of *Orley Farm*, *The Way We Live Now*, *North America*, *Rachel Ray*, *The American Senator*, and Mrs. Frances Trollope's *Domestic Manners of the Americans* in the "Borzoi Trollope" (1949-52), now out of print. Outside the "World's Classics" series, there are modern reprints of *An Eye for an Eye*, *Harry Heathcote of Gangoil*, *Hunting Sketches*, the Palliser series, *The Way We Live Now*, and most of the Barset novels.

III. Critical Works

AITKEN, DAVID. " 'A Kind of Felicity': Some Notes About Trollope's Style." *Nineteenth-Century Fiction* 20 (1966): 337-353.

apROBERTS, RUTH. *The Moral Trollope.* Athens, Ohio: Ohio University Press, 1971.

BLAKE, ROBERT. *Disraeli.* New York: St. Martin's Press, 1967.

BOOTH, BRADFORD A. *Anthony Trollope: Aspects of His Life and Art*. Bloomington: Indiana University Press, 1958.

———. "Trollope on the Novel." In *Essays Critical and Historical Dedicated to Lily B. Campbell*. Berkeley and Los Angeles: University of California Press, 1950.

———. "Trollope's *Orley Farm*: Artistry *Manqué*." In *From Jane Austen to Joseph Conrad: Essays Collected in Memory of James T. Hillhouse*. Edited by Robert C. Rathburn and Martin Steinmann, Jr. Minneapolis: University of Minnesota Press, 1958.

BRIGGS, ASA. *Victorian People*. Chicago: University of Chicago Press, 1955. Chapter IV, "Trollope, Bagehot, and the English Constitution," discusses Trollope's political views.

CADBURY, WILLIAM. "Shape and Theme: Determinants of Trollope's Forms." *PMLA* 78 (1963): 326-332.

COCKSHUT, A. O. J. *Anthony Trollope: A Critical Study*. London, 1955. Reprint, New York: New York University Press, 1968.

DAVIES, HUGH SYKES. *Trollope*. British Council, Writers and Their Work, No. 118. London: Longmans, Green, 1960.

———. "Trollope and His Style." *Review of English Literature* 1 1960): 73-84.

DUSTIN, JOHN E. "Thematic Alternation in Trollope." *PMLA* 77 (1962): 280-288.

ESCOTT, T. H. S. *Anthony Trollope: His Public Services, Private Friends, and Literary Originals*. London: John Lane, 1913. Reprint, Port Washington, N.Y.: Kennikat Press, 1967. Badly organized and anecdotal, but Escott wrote with the advantage of personally knowing Trollope and his world.

GEROULD, WINIFRED GREGORY, and JAMES THAYER GEROULD. *A Guide to Trollope*. Princeton: Princeton University Press, 1948. A dictionary of Trollope's works and characters, especially useful for noting the recurrence of certain characters from novel to novel.

HAGAN, JOHN. "The Divided Mind of Anthony Trollope." *Nineteenth-Century Fiction* 14 (1959): 1-26.

HELLING, RAFAEL. *A Century of Trollope Criticism. Commentationes humanarum litterarum*, 22, Number 2. Helsingfors: Societas Scientiarum Fennica-Finska vetenskape-societeten, 1956. Reprint, Port Washington, N.Y.: Kennikat Press, 1967.

HENNEDY, HUGH L. *Unity in Barsetshire*. De proprietatibus litterarum, Series Practica, 28. The Hague: Mouton, 1971.

BIBLIOGRAPHY

HENNESSY, JAMES POPE. *Anthony Trollope*. London: Jonathan Cape, 1971.

JAMES, HENRY. "Anthony Trollope," *Century Magazine* n.s. 4 (1883): 385-395. Reprinted in James's *Partial Portraits* (1888); in James's *The Future of the Novel*, edited by Leon Edel, New York: Vintage Books, 1956 (this volume also contains "The Art of Fiction"); and in *Trollope: The Critical Heritage*, edited by Donald Smalley.

LEVINE, GEORGE. "Can You Forgive Him?: Trollope's *Can You Forgive Her?* and the Myth of Realism." *Victorian Studies* 18 (1974): 5-30.

MIZENER, ARTHUR. *The Sense of Life in the Modern Novel*. Boston: Houghton Mifflin, 1964. Chapter II, on the Palliser novels, originally appeared in *From Jane Austen to Joseph Conrad: Essays Collected in Memory of James T. Hillhouse*, edited by Robert C. Rathburn and Martin Steinmann, Jr. Minneapolis: University of Minnesota Press, 1958.

Nineteenth-Century Fiction. This journal has published a number of important articles about Trollope's work since its founding as *The Trollopian: A Journal of Victorian Fiction*, by Professor Bradford A. Booth in 1945.

POLHEMUS, ROBERT M. *The Changing World of Anthony Trollope*. Berkeley and Los Angeles: University of California Press, 1968.

RAY, GORDON N. "Trollope at Full Length." *Huntington Library Quarterly* 31 (1968): 313-337.

SADLEIR, MICHAEL. *Trollope: A Bibliography*. London: Constable and Company, 1928.

———. *Trollope: A Commentary*. London, 1927. Revised, 1945. Reprint, London: Oxford University Press, 1961.

SKILTON, DAVID. *Anthony Trollope and His Contemporaries*. London: Longman, 1972. Primarily an account of Trollope's critical reception in his own day, and so a useful supplement to Donald Smalley's collection, below.

SLAKEY, ROGER L. "Trollope's Case for Moral Imperative." *Nineteenth-Century Fiction* 28 (1973): 305-320.

SMALLEY, DONALD, ed. *Trollope: The Critical Heritage*. London: Routledge and Kegan Paul, 1969; New York: Barnes and Noble, 1969. A collection of reviews and articles about Trollope by his contemporaries.

SNOW, C. P. *Trollope: His Life and Art*. New York: Charles

Scribner's Sons, 1975. Splendidly illustrated comments by a twentieth-century writer who shares some of Trollope's techniques and values.

STEBBINS, LUCY POATE, and RICHARD POATE STEBBINS. *The Trollopes: The Chronicle of a Writing Family*. New York: Columbia Univerity Press, 1945.

STONE, DONALD D. "Trollope, Byron, and the Conventionalities." *The Worlds of Victorian Fiction* (Harvard English Studies 6), edited by Jerome H. Buckley. Cambridge: Harvard University Press, 1975.

THALE, JEROME. "The Problem of Structure in Trollope." *Nineteenth-Century Fiction* 15 (1960): 147-157.

TILLOTSON, GEOFFREY. "Trollope's Style." In *Mid-Victorian Studies*, by Geoffrey and Kathleen Tillotson. London: The Athlone Press, 1965.

TINGAY, LANCE O. "Trollope's Library." In *Notes and Queries* 195 (1950): 476-478.

WALPOLE, HUGH. *Anthony Trollope*. London: Macmillan and Co., 1928.

INDEX

Names of characters from Trollope's novels are preceded by an asterisk and followed by the title of the novel in which they appear. The only indexed references to such fictional characters are to those occurring outside the general discussion of the novel in which each appears.

345